Manipulating D

MW00831752

Manipulation is a source of pervasive anxiety in contemporary American politics. Observers charge that manipulative practices in political advertising, media coverage, and public discourse have helped to produce an increasingly polarized political arena, an uninformed and apathetic electorate, election campaigns that exploit public fears and prejudices, a media that titillates rather than educates, and a policy process that too often focuses on the symbolic rather than substantive.

Manipulating Democracy offers the first comprehensive dialogue between empirical political scientists and normative theorists on the definition and contemporary practice of democratic manipulation. This impressive array of distinguished scholars—political scientists, philosophers, cognitive psychologists, and communications scholars—collectively draws out the connections between competing definitions of manipulation, the psychology of manipulation, and the political institutions and practices through which manipulation is seen to produce a tightly knit exploration of an issue at the heart of democratic politics.

Wayne Le Cheminant is Assistant Professor of Political Science at Loyola Marymount University. He studies contemporary political theory, political culture, identity and gender issues, and how ideas and ideology impact political institutions.

John M. Parrish is Associate Professor of Political Science at Loyola Marymount University. He is the author of *Paradoxes of Political Ethics: From Dirty Hands to the Invisible Hand.*

Manipulating Democracy
Democratic Theory, Political
Psychology, and Mass Media

Edited by

Wayne Le Cheminant
John M. Parrish

 Routledge
Taylor & Francis Group

NEW YORK AND LONDON

First published 2011
by Routledge
270 Madison Avenue, New York, NY 10016

Simultaneously published in the UK
by Routledge
2 Park Square, Milton Park, Abingdon, Oxon OX14 4RN

Routledge is an imprint of the Taylor & Francis Group, an informa business

Typeset in Galliard by EvS Communication Networx, Inc.
Printed and bound in the United States of America on acid-free paper by Walsworth Publishing Company, Marceline, MO

Library of Congress Cataloging in Publication Data
Manipulating democracy : democratic theory, political psychology, and mass media / [edited by] Wayne Le Cheminant and John Parrish.
p. cm.
Includes index.
[etc.]
1. Manipulative behavior—Political aspects. 2. Political psychology. 3. Mass media—Political aspects. 4. Democracy—Psychological aspects. I. Le Cheminant, Wayne. II. Parrish, John M.
JA74.5.M353 2010
320.01'9—dc22
2010009006

ISBN 13: 978-0-415-87804-3 (hbk)
ISBN 13: 978-0-415-87805-0 (pbk)
ISBN 13: 978-0-203-85499-0 (ebk)

For Ian, Zoe, and Greyson
and
for Robin

Contents

List of Figures and Tables

Figures

Tables

Preface and Acknowledgments

On February 9, 2008, at the height of the most fiercely fought presidential primary contest in living memory, the Institute for Leadership Studies at Loyola Marymount University hosted seven scholars of political theory, political psychology, and media studies for its 7th annual Dilemmas of Democracy Conference on the topic "Manipulating Democracy." Seven of the essays collected here were first presented at that conference: those of Terence Ball, James Fishkin, Shanto Iyengar and Kyu Hahn, Lawrence Jacobs, George Lakoff, Rose McDermott, and Andrew Sabl. Three additional essays were later commissioned to complete the volume: those by Richard Fox and Amy Gangl, Nathaniel Klemp, and Christina Tarnopolsky. Our most significant debt is therefore to these twelve individuals who so generously said yes when we invited them to be part of this endeavor.

If the present volume would not have been possible without the Dilemmas of Democracy Conference, the conference itself would not have been possible without the help and support of many of our faculty, administrative, and student colleagues at LMU. Our first thanks must go to Michael Genovese, Director of the Institute for Leadership Studies, who greenlighted the conference topic, helped assemble the list of invited guests, served as host for the conference, and offered valuable counsel throughout the process. LMU's Bellarmine College of Liberal Arts and its then-Dean Michael Engh generously provided the funding for the conference in cooperation with the Institute. Our colleagues in the political science department, specifically Evan Gerstmann, Lance Blakesley, Jodi Finkel, Richard Fox, Fernando Guerra, Janie Steckenrider, and Seth Thompson, provided invaluable help and support throughout the conference in a variety of ways. One colleague deserves special mention. Ngoc Nguyen, our department administrator, ably managed the full range of logistical issues related to the conference, bringing to the task her characteristic calm and efficiency. Vivian Valencia ably led a team of student volunteers who provided valuable assistance throughout the conference, including especially, but not necessarily limited to, Mercedes Adams, Lucy Boyadzhyan, Raquel Castellanos, Gena Gammie, and Christina McCaffrey.

Others helped substantially in the process of turning the conference essays and the additional contributed essays into the present volume. Michael Kerns at Routledge commissioned the volume and helped guide us through the process of assembling a complete manuscript. We also appreciate the efforts of Matthew Streb in encouraging Routledge to review and eventually back the project. The staff of EvS Communications undertook the copy editing and saw the manuscript through the production process. Brendan Richards assisted substantially in the editing and formatting of most of the essays. Elizabeth Chitty assembled the index. Acknowledgement of the various helpful comments and criticisms offered regarding the essays is made by their authors in the endnotes of each chapter.

We owe special debts of appreciation to our families, who in the weeks leading up to the event heard all too often about "the conference" as excuse for our occasional deficiencies in our familial duties. John Parrish has relied as always on the love and friendship of his wife Lynn, dog George, and (in recent months) daughter Sophie as a motive and reward for his work. Wayne Le Cheminant wants to thank Monique for her support and patience during a particularly trying time in her life at the time this conference took place, and he always relies on the antics and amazing spirits of his children Ian, Zoe, and Greyson to make life not just bearable, but a pleasure.

We dedicate this book with love to Wayne's children, Ian, Zoe, and Greyson Le Cheminant, and to John's sister, Robin Parrish McAlister.

List of Contributors

Terence Ball is Professor of Political Science at Arizona State University. In addition to many articles in scholarly journals and in books, he is the author of *Civil Disobedience and Civil Deviance* (Sage, 1974), *Transforming Political Discourse* (Blackwell, 1988), *Reappraising Political Theory* (Oxford University Press, 1995), and *Political Ideologies and the Democratic Ideal*, 7th ed. (with Richard Dagger, Longman, 2008). Among the books he has edited or co-edited are *Political Theory and Praxis* (University of Minnesota Press, 1977), *After Marx* (Cambridge University Press, 1984), *Political Innovation and Conceptual Change* (Cambridge University Press, 1988), *Idioms of Inquiry* (State University of New York Press, 1987), *Conceptual Change and the Constitution* (University of Kansas Press, 1988), *Environmental Encyclopedia* (Detroit: Gale Research, 1994), *The Federalist* (Cambridge University Press, 2003), and the *Cambridge History of Twentieth-Century Political Thought* (Cambridge University Press, 2003). He is also the author of a mystery novel, *Rousseau's Ghost* (State University of New York Press, 1999).

James S. Fishkin holds the Janet M. Peck Chair in International Communication at Stanford University where he is Professor of Communication and Professor of Political Science. He is also Director of Stanford's new Center for Deliberative Democracy and Chair of the Department of Communication. He is the author of a number of books including *Democracy and Deliberation: New Directions for Democratic Reform* (Yale University Press, 1991), *The Dialogue of Justice* (Yale University Press, 1992), and *The Voice of the People: Public Opinion and Democracy* (Yale University Press, 1997). He is co-author of *Deliberation Day* (with Bruce Ackerman, Yale University Press, 2004). He is best known for developing Deliberative Polling®—a practice of public consultation that employs random samples of the citizenry to explore how opinions would change if they were more informed. Professor Fishkin and his collaborators have conducted Deliberative Polls in the United States, Britain, Australia, Denmark, Bulgaria, China, Greece, and other countries.

Richard L. Fox, Associate Professor of Political Science at Loyola Marymount University, teaches and researches in the areas of U.S. Congress, elections, media and politics, and gender politics. Most recently he has completed work on a book entitled *Tabloid Justice: The Criminal Justice System in the Age of Media Frenzy*, 2nd ed. (Rienner, 2007). He is also co-author of *It Takes a Candidate: Why Women Don't Run for Office* (Cambridge University Press, 2005) and coeditor of *Gender and Elections: Change and Continuity Through 2004* (Cambridge University Press, 2006). His work has appeared in such journals as *Political Psychology, The Journal of Politics, American Journal of Political Science, Social Problems, PS*, and *Politics and Gender*. He is currently working on a project examining political ambition and why people choose to run for elective office. He has also written op-ed articles, some of which have appeared in the *New York Times* and the *Wall Street Journal*.

Amy Gangl completed her PhD from the University of Minnesota in 2001. She is currently a Visiting Assistant Professor at Edgewood College in Madison, Wisconsin. Her research interests focus on political behavior, political ideology, and political communication. She is currently working on a project that examines the relationship between ideological identification and populist appeals in elite rhetoric. Her work has appeared in such journals as the *American Journal of Political Science, Journal of Politics, Public Opinion*, and *Political Behavior*.

Kyu S. Hahn is Assistant Professor in Underwood International College at Yonsei University (Seoul, Korea) and the Department of Communication Studies at UCLA. Hahn's research addresses the role of the news media and mass communication in contemporary politics. His works have appeared in the *Journal of Politics*, the *Journal of Communication, Communication Research, Political Communication*, and other scholarly journals. Hahn holds a PhD. (Communication) from Stanford University and a BA (Sociology) from Northwestern University.

Shanto Iyengar is Harry & Norman Chandler Professor of Communication and Professor of Political Science at Stanford University, where he is also Director of the Political Communication Lab. His research has been published in such journals as *American Political Science Review, Communication Research, Journal of Personality and Social Psychology*, and *Public Opinion Quarterly*. Iyengar also contributes regularly to Washingtonpost. com. Iyengar's books include *Media Politics: A Citizen's Guide* (W.W. Norton, 2006), *Going Negative: How Political Advertisements Shrink and Polarize the Electorate* (Free Press, 1995), *Do the Media Govern* (Sage, 1997), *Explorations in Political Psychology* (Duke University Press, 1993), *The Media Game* (Macmillan, 1993), *Is Anyone Responsible: How Televi-*

sion Frames Political Issues (University of Chicago Press, 1991), and *News That Matters: Television and American Opinion* (University of Chicago Press, 1987).

Lawrence R. Jacobs is the Walter F. and Joan Mondale Chair for Political Studies and director of the Center for the Study of Politics and Governance at the Hubert H. Humphrey Institute of Public Affairs. He also is a professor in the University of Minnesota's Department of Political Science. Jacobs' most recent books are *Inequality and American Democracy* (with Theda Skocpol, Russell Sage Press, 2005), *Healthy, Wealthy, and Fair* (with James Morone, Oxford University Press, 2005), and *Politicians Don't Pander: Political Manipulation and the Loss of Democratic Responsiveness* (with Robert Y. Shapiro, University of Chicago Press, 2000), the last of which won the Goldsmith Book Prize from Harvard University's Shorenstein Center for Press and Politics, the Neustadt Book Prize from the American Political Science Association, and the Distinguished Book Prize in political sociology from the American Sociological Association. He also authored *The Health of Nations: Public Opinion and the Making of Health Policy in the U.S. and Britain* (Cornell University Press, 1993) as well as several edited volumes and numerous articles in the *American Political Science Review, World Politics, Comparative Politics, Journal of Politics, Public Opinion Quarterly, Presidential Studies Quarterly,* and other scholarly outlets.

Nathaniel Klemp is Assistant Professor of Political Science at Pepperdine University, and is currently revising his book manuscript entitled *The Morality of Spin: Rhetoric and the Christian Right.* In it, Klemp proposes a Madisonian argument for conditions of discursive equilibrium that both discourage manipulation and encourage vibrant contestation and debate, and studies political activists at Focus on the Family to illuminate these claims from a more concrete political perspective. In addition to his dissertation, Klemp has published essays in the journal *Polity* and in edited volumes.

Wayne Le Cheminant is Assistant Professor of Political Science at Loyola Marymount University. He studies political culture and how ideas and ideology impact political institutions. He also works on contemporary political theory, identity, and gender issues. He is the author of "Bending the Frames to Corrupt the Lenses: An Examination of Cognitive Science and Corruption" in *Corruption and American Politics,* "Leadership, Cognition, and the Politics of Manipulation" in *Leadership at the Crossroads,* and "Korean Politics and the Entrepreneurial Spirit" in *Korea: Politics and Entrepreneurship* (forthcoming). He is currently working on a book entitled *Human Nature and the Political Imagination.*

George Lakoff is the Richard and Rhoda Goldman Distinguished Professor of Cognitive Science and Linguistics at the University of California at Berkeley, and is also the co-founder and Senior Fellow of the Rockridge Institute. He has published a multitude of articles in major scholarly journals and edited volumes. In addition to perhaps his most influential book, *Moral Politics: How Liberals and Conservatives Think*, 2nd ed., (University of Chicago Press, 2002), he is also the author of *Women, Fire, and Dangerous Things: What Categories Reveal About The Mind* (University of Chicago Press, 1987) and co-author of *Metaphors We Live By* (with Mark Johnson, University of Chicago Press, 1980), *More Than Cool Reason* (with Mark Turner, University of Chicago Press, 1989), *Philosophy in the Flesh: The Embodied Mind and Its Challenge To The Western Tradition* (with Mark Johnson, Basic Books, 1999), and *Where Mathematics Comes From: How the Embodied Mind Brings Mathematics Into Being* (with Rafael Núñez, Basic Books, 2000). His most recent books include *Don't Think of an Elephant: Know Your Values, Frame the Debate* (Chesea Green, 2004), *Whose Freedom?* (Farrar, Straus, and Giroux, 2006), and *Thinking Points* (Farrar, Straus, and Giroux, 2006).

Rose McDermott is Professor of Political Science at Brown University. Professor McDermott's main area of research revolves around political psychology in international relations. She is the author of *Risk Taking in International Relations: Prospect Theory in American Foreign Policy* (University of Michigan Press, 1998), *Political Psychology in International Relations* (University of Michigan Press, 2004), and *Presidential Illness, Leadership and Decision Making* (Cambridge University Press, 2007). She is co-editor of *Measuring Identity: A Guide for Social Science Research* (with R. Abdelal, Y. Herrera, and A. I. Johnson, Cambridge University Press, forthcoming). She is currently working on a new book project on the impact of pandemic disease on international security issues. She has written numerous articles and book chapters on experimentation, the impact of emotion on decision making, and evolutionary and neuroscientific models of political science.

John M. Parrish is Associate Professor of Political Science at Loyola Marymount University. His teaching and research focus especially on political ethics, the history of political thought, and political rhetoric and public discourse. He has published a book, *Paradoxes of Political Ethics: From Dirty Hands to the Invisible Hand* (Cambridge University Press, 2007), as well as articles in such journals as the *Historical Journal*, *History of Political Thought*, and *International Theory*. He is also co-editor of *Damned If You Do: Moral Dilemmas in Literature and Popular Culture* (with Margaret Hrezo, Lexington Books, 2010). His next book project, co-authored with Alex Tuckness, is tentatively entitled *The Death of Mercy*.

Andrew Sabl is Associate Professor of Public Policy and Political Science at the University of California at Los Angeles. A political theorist, Sabl's research focuses on political ethics, democratic and constitutional theory, theories of toleration and political pluralism, and, most recently, the political theory of David Hume. His book, *Ruling Passions: Political Offices and Democratic Ethics* (Princeton University Press, 2002), won the Leo Strauss Award of the American Political Science Association for the best dissertation in political philosophy. His many articles include work appearing or forthcoming in *Political Theory*, the *Journal of Political Philosophy*, *Polity*, the *American Journal of Political Science*, *NOMOS*, the *Journal of Moral Philosophy*, the *Election Law Journal*, *Society*, and *Public Integrity*.

Christina Tarnopolsky is Associate Professor of Political Science at McGill University. Her research interests include classical political philosophy, contemporary social theory, aesthetics and politics, and the role of the emotions in politics. She is the author of *Prudes, Perverts, and Tyrants: Plato and the Politics of Shame* (Princeton University Press, 2010). She has also published book chapters and articles in such journals as *Political Theory* and *The Canadian Journal of Continental Philosophy*. She is now engaged in a book project provisionally entitled *Perspectives on Aesthetic Politics: Plato, Nietzsche, and Foucault*.

Introduction
Manipulating Democracy
A Reappraisal

Wayne Le Cheminant and John M. Parrish

Manipulation is a source of pervasive anxiety in American politics, and more so today than at any time in recent memory. Accusations of manipulative practices in political advertising, media coverage, and public discourse have become increasingly widespread. Many observers claim that the American public finds itself more and more vulnerable to the manipulative practices of elites, and that the effects of manipulation are becoming more and more damaging to contemporary democracy. Among the host of societal evils which these observers attribute to the rising tide of political manipulation, some of the most egregious include: an increasingly polarized and antagonistic form of partisan politics; an uninformed and apathetic electorate; a consultant-driven mode of election campaigning that frequently exploits public fears and prejudices; a media motivated by commercial values and by the desire to titillate rather than educate; and a policy process that too often seems to produce results of symbolic rather than substantive value.

*

Consider for a moment the range of contemporary political practices from the last two decades that might be characterized as fundamental manipulations of democracy:

- Political campaigns and interest groups utilize attack ads such as the "Willie Horton," "Swift Boat Veterans for Truth," and "Kerry and the Wolves" ads, to influence the outcome of two presidential elections.[1]
- High-powered lobbyists and campaign donors such as John Huang and Jack Abramoff offer millions of dollars in illegal or improper campaign contributions, and major oil and gas contributors meet privately with Vice President Dick Cheney to suggest legal language (later adopted verbatim) for the country's energy policy.[2]
- President Bill Clinton's political adversaries orchestrate two major ongoing investigations of dubious credibility—the "Whitewater"

investigation and the Paula Jones lawsuit—eventually costing hundreds of millions in public funds, and resulting in the president's impeachment. Confronted with these investigations, the president himself breaks or at least severely bends the law by concealing relevant facts, and helps to orchestrate a merciless smear campaign against at least one apparently truthful witness, Monica Lewinsky.[3]

- Politicians from presidents on down employ micro-targeted polling techniques to determine not just which public policy initiatives to promote and how to sell them, but also such matters as where the president should vacation, or what breed of presidential pet will best fit the president's desired image.[4]
- Critics advance the serious and plausible suggestion that the Bush administration "manipulated" the country into war through a variety of techniques: controlled leaks to the press, exploitation of jingoistic sentiment, cherry-picking of vital intelligence, persecution or ostracism of war critics, and a campaign of image management and stagecraft designed to reinforce the government's daily message at the expense of a full public dialogue on the question of war.[5]
- Less consequentially, but perhaps even more disturbingly, much of what we perceive as "media coverage" is itself increasingly subject to being co-opted or shaped backstage to suit political agendas. When the Bush administration seemingly licenses its own partisans to act as fake reporters asking questions in the White House press room, or creates an entirely staged press conference with administration staffers posing as reporters before the unsuspecting public, we seem to have crossed the line from mere spin control to something approaching Orwellian mind control.[6]

Although examples of political manipulation are as widespread as is concern about its effects, our scholarly understanding of what manipulation is, what is wrong with it, and what factors facilitate or inhibit its practice has not kept pace with the rising public concern it engages. Though we are very aware that manipulation occurs in contemporary democracies, scholars across a wide range of fields are only now coming to grips with some of the deep-seated cognitive, emotional, and linguistic factors that make manipulation possible, and with some of the rapidly changing institutional factors that threaten to expand dramatically its scope and significance. Cognitive science and linguistic analysis have begun to show us why manipulation may be a more intractable problem than we have yet appreciated, while the speed and scale of institutional changes that facilitate manipulation are accelerating at an alarming rate. Yet our scholarly understanding of manipulation lags behind the expanding use of manipulative techniques, and unless our understanding can begin to catch up to the scale and scope of the changes which manipulation itself is undergoing, we will be unprepared to diagnose what ails our democracy or to prescribe effective remedies for its cure.

Part of the difficulty faced by academic analyses of manipulation lies in the fact that the concept of manipulation has both descriptive and evaluative dimensions that cannot be analyzed independently of one another. This fact has led to a breakdown of communication among empirical political scientists and normative political theorists. Empirical political scientists have made significant progress in analyzing the various inputs and outputs of democratic communication, and their findings have helped to improve our understanding of what may be practicable and impracticable in democratic theory and practice. But often these empirical efforts have failed to keep in close contact with important refinements in normative theory, which might aid in evaluating and critiquing the significance of these manipulative practices for our democratic ideals. Normative political theorists, meanwhile, have developed increasingly sophisticated ideal theories of democracy, but at the expense of failing to grapple with the toughest practical problems that obtain in non-ideal conditions. This exemplifies a larger trend throughout the study of politics of a tension "between normative approaches, which are constantly in danger of losing contact with social reality, and objectivist approaches, which screen out all normative aspects."[7] Thus there is a growing gap between normative analysis and empirical discovery that badly needs to be overcome. This volume lays a foundation for bridging this gap by bringing important recent achievements in empirical political science—including studies of the psychological, linguistic, institutional, and strategic dimensions of political action—into a productive exchange with the traditional concerns and current preoccupations of normative democratic theory.

Manipulating Democracy, therefore, offers the first volume of essays aimed at promoting a public interchange of ideas between empirical political scientists and normative political theorists regarding the definition and contemporary practice of democratic manipulation. We cannot, of course, in a volume of this size hope to represent all the theoretical perspectives that might have something to contribute to the conversation— especially not in a volume aiming not only to present rival normative theories but also to juxtapose them with insightful empirical accounts of the challenges facing contemporary democratic practice. We therefore aim not to provide a fully comprehensive or definitive account of manipulation and its relation to democratic theory; instead, we aim to open up a problem of great public significance to a general and interdisciplinary audience, bringing to bear perspectives from a variety of disciplines, fields, and orientations.

Understanding and responding to manipulation in its various forms is central to the task that confronts democratic politics in the early twenty-first century. Indeed, we suggest that in a certain sense it is not possible to talk about democracy at all without also talking about manipulation, because what counts for us as democracy must, almost by definition, exclude manipulation (at least in some forms or degrees). Our aim in the present volume is to take this insight as our starting point: that by conceptualizing (and problematizing) manipulation more clearly, and by understanding more precisely the psychological and institutional factors through which it works, we will better perceive what democracy itself is, and how far we still have to travel before we attain it.

i

Our collection of essays begins with the persistent theoretical problem of how to conceptualize manipulation. We cannot in an enterprise such as this begin from a consensus about the term's meaning as a starting point; indeed, we do not expect to produce a firm definition of manipulation at all, for reasons connected to the very sort of concept it is. If, as we have suggested, manipulation is a concept whose meaning is (necessarily) both normative and empirical at the same time, then defining manipulation will also require us to develop a jointly normative and empirical conceptualization. Manipulation is therefore a quintessential example of what philosopher W.B. Gallie famously called an "essentially contested concept": that is, a term we cannot employ in description without also, simultaneously, employing it in evaluation.[8] For such "essentially contested concepts," the nature of the phenomenon named by the term is inherently subject to contestation that is in principle irresolvable in any final sense. Characterizing an action as "manipulative" invokes certain empirical criteria: not just any action can be so characterized. But once these criteria have been satisfied, the normative background conception of our democratic theory immediately kicks in to put the action—and the person who enacts it—on the moral defensive, needing an excuse or justification to account for their presumptively wrong conduct.[9] Any descriptive term with such negative connotations built into its meaning is certain to be resisted by those to whom we seek to apply it—hence its "essentially contested" character.

There are then at least two elements of any account of manipulation: first, a set of criteria that can be used to determine whether a particular case should properly be described as manipulation; and second, a background conception of democratic theory which gives an implicit account of why conduct that meets these criteria is presumptively wrong. The evaluative connotations which the term carries necessarily are closely linked to the larger questions of ethics and democratic theory within which the concept operates. On a theory of democracy which prizes deliberation, for example, practices such as "push-polling" (polling designed to change rather than discover the subject's state of mind) may well count as illegitimate, while on a rival theory of democracy more oriented toward participation and competition as the measures of democratic health, such practices might not arouse nearly as much anxiety. Characterizing a practice as "manipulative" situates it within this larger democratic theory, but at the same time it contributes to the contestation of the larger theory itself.

For this reason, we can no more offer a comprehensive definition of "manipulation" that will command broad consent than we can offer a single democratic theory that will do so. This does not imply that we cannot gain ground in clarifying our rival conceptions and their implications; indeed, the purpose of the essays collected in the first part of this volume is to seek to refine these conceptual elements of our account of manipulation. But such refinement is necessarily limited by Aristotle's admonition that in defining manipulation, as in defining any political concept, we cannot demand more precision than our subject matter naturally admits of. As such, it is unreasonable to think of consensus regarding the definition of the term as a starting point, or even as a destination for the inquiry.

We can however expect that by giving rival and contested accounts of manipulation a place to express themselves—as we see explicitly in the essays in part 1 of the volume, and implicitly in many of the others—we *can* begin to map out more systematically the implications of our definitions for the rival views of democratic theory. Our purpose in this volume therefore is not to erase the complexity of the concept of manipulation, but rather to problematize it for readers as much as to clarify it showing how a concept that is frequently invoked in public discourse in fact has competing conceptions, each of which carry important implications for our understanding of democracy itself. We therefore begin our inquiry deliberately from a somewhat primitive set of operating definitions: we conceive of democracy as (loosely) "popular self-government" and of manipulation (again loosely) as "deceptive interference with self-government" whether individually or collectively. In doing so, we aim to maximize the range of voices and views that can be included in the conversation, and offer challenging and contestatory perspectives on its parameters. We now seek to flesh out that primitive definition to note its ambiguities and evasions, in order to situate the contributions to understanding the concept made by the three essays that constitute Part I.

The most thoroughly developed definition of manipulation is probably that offered by Robert Goodin in his book *Manipulatory Politics*, the most comprehensive survey to date of the normative landscape surrounding questions of manipulation.[10] Goodin identifies two criteria that seem central to the essence of manipulation: it must be (1) deceptive and (2) contrary to the putative will of its subjects (that is, what their will would have been if the manipulative conduct had not occurred).[11] These criteria are individually necessary and collectively sufficient to produce manipulation, on Goodin's account.[12]

If Goodin is correct that deception is a necessary condition of manipulation,[13] what counts as deception? There are obvious categories that would command wide consensus, but then there are more ambiguous potential types of deception as well. Much turns on what moral factors one believes the wrongness of deception to consist in. If its wrongness consists in the negative consequences the practice tends to produce—as in Goodin's implicitly consequentialist framework—then any practice that tends to inhibit the flow of information or obstruct the discovery of truth may be considered as manipulative as direct lies. So practices of secrecy, for example, while not straightforwardly deceptive, nevertheless may count as equally manipulative on the grounds that their effects may be indistinguishable from those of outright lies.[14] Likewise, communication whose truth value is unknown or unimportant to the speaker—including both propaganda and also what philosopher Harry Frankfurt calls "bullshit"—can obstruct truth just as well as lies, and in a consequentialist framework will therefore also count as equally manipulative, even if deception is not strictly intended.[15] As several of the factors discussed in sections II and III might tend to suggest, a variety of psychological and institutional factors are tending to make these more subtle genres of variation on deception—non-deception deceptions, if you will—increasingly prevalent in contemporary social life. If so, we can expect manipulation, with all its problematic normative features, to proliferate to the same extent.

Goodin's second criterion for distinguishing manipulative conduct is that the outcomes it produces will be contrary to the "putative will" of its subjects (i.e., what they would have chosen in the absence of such interference). Of course, as Goodin recognizes, mere interference with putative will by itself is not necessarily manipulative, since even perfectly respectful and rational persuasion would have the effect of contradicting someone's putative will. But how do we know counterfactually what the will of subjects would be, apart from the evidence of their (post-manipulation) behavior?

There are many potential answers to this question, but perhaps the most influential answer presented in contemporary political theory has been that provided by theorists of deliberative democracy, who offer the concept of rational deliberation as a possible solution to this conundrum. Deliberative democracy has become perhaps the single most widespread preoccupation of political theorists over the past two decades, and indeed now almost constitutes a kind of default starting position for conversations about most aspects of democratic theory (including manipulation).[16] With respect to manipulation and the notion of "putative will" specifically, the deliberative view purports to offer a kind of Archimedian standpoint from which to step back and criticize the formation of public opinion itself. Democratic theory holds that under certain conditions (which Habermas calls an "ideal speech situation"), public opinion really does represent something like the public will, with all the normative weight that carries in democratic theory. But in other circumstances—importantly including those tainted by manipulation—what emerges from the processes of forming public opinion will not truly be the public will, but rather a form of false consciousness that has no true normative authority. Thus, the hypothetical of the "ideal speech situation" constructed from norms implicit in our standard communicative practices produces the proper ethical standard by providing a hypothetical counterfactual answer to what would have been chosen under non-manipulated conditions.[17]

James Fishkin, in the first essay in this volume, "Manipulation and Democratic Theory," employs this deliberative model in order to re-examine how we define democracy and what counts as manipulation. Fishkin divides the ways in which we broadly think about democracy into four main theoretical perspectives: competitive, elite, participatory, and deliberative conceptions of democracy. He finds that unless there is serious deliberation among the participants in a democracy, then manipulation (understood as the ability of political elites to game the system and ignore the will of the mass public) is likely to occur. Fishkin defines deliberation as a serious, informative, and civil discussion concerning the policies and politics that affect the lives the citizenry. Without serious deliberation that has some type of binding impact on the political system, Fishkin claims, political elites are likely to manipulate the political landscape—because it is in their interest to do so, because they seek to maintain power, and because they can. Fishkin sees most forms of democratic thinking as ignoring the will of the people, since most theories of democracy shortchange the actual impact that deliberative thinking and mass participation can have on the attitudes of those who participate (and, indeed, on those of the entire polity). By means of deliberation, Fishkin shows, mass publics can both change the minds of their individual members about public policy questions and can collectively make a substantial contribution to policy decision making. Fishkin argues that the way to move towards a non-manipulated democracy is to ensure that as many people as possible have a chance to make their contribution to the polity through substantive deliberation rather than continue to try to find ways in which to rein in the manipulative forces of the political elites.

The concept of deliberation has captured the imaginations of a wide range of contemporary political theorists, and for many of them it has come to offer a kind of ideal by which we can judge the achievements or deficiencies of our public sphere. Such conceptual ideals are useful for political theory, and so the increasing refinement of this particular model by deliberative democrats is all to the good, so far as it goes. But as several of the other essays in this volume attest, the deliberative ideal seems increasingly to diverge both from the pull of powerful institutional forces transforming our society and from resilient limits to our psychological and emotional capabilities the depth of which we are only just now beginning to appreciate.[18] As political scientist Larry Bartels has argued, joined by some of the essays in Part II of this volume, the fact that human beings seem to construct their choices out of transient attitudes rather than from distinct and stable preference orderings implies that, with respect to the question of our "putative wills," there may not be any "there" there.[19] Furthermore, as the articles in Part III of the volume indicate, the capacity of the media to facilitate the deception of the public threatens to attain a wider scope of influence and a deeper impact than ever before.

Given these endemic obstacles to achieving the deliberative ideal of non-manipulated public choice, perhaps the deliberative ideal itself construes manipulation in too broad and unrestricted a fashion. The next two essays in our volume address alternative conceptions of manipulation that see a democratic role for some forms of conduct that would be condemned under the more restrictive deliberative model. In his essay, "Manipulation: As Old As Democracy Itself (and Sometimes Dangerous)," Terence Ball takes issue with the assumption that manipulation is necessarily bad and antithetical to democracy and to the actions and interactions of democratic citizens. Where deliberative theorists generally maintain that deception and other forms of manipulation are categorically wrong and that only truth-telling and "the forceless force of the better argument" should determine the outcome of political debate and discussion, Ball believes this standard to be both utopian and unworkable. Manipulation, he argues, has a place in democratic governance, as can be seen by looking at the history of democracy and democratic debate and discussion. Ball shows this by means of a series of brief case studies, including the role of the theater in democratic Athens and the debate over the ratification of the U.S. Constitution. In his chapter, Ball draws and defends a distinction between democratic manipulation (the sort that does not undermine the rule of law or lead to tyranny) and un- or anti-democratic manipulation (the sort that violates the law and leads, at least potentially, to tyranny). Drawing on the work of Aristotle, Hannah Arendt, and other theorists, Ball concludes by arguing that the Bush II administration has engaged in manipulation of the latter sort, rather than the ethically permissible forms of democratic manipulation provided by the former.

Nathaniel Klemp's essay "When Rhetoric Turns Manipulative: Disentangling Persuasion and Manipulation" develops a conceptual distinction between persuasion and manipulation as a way of pursuing a middle path between Ball's and Fishkin's, seeking to retain some of the strengths of deliberative theory without capitulating to its weaknesses. Persuasive rhetoric, Klemp argues, exerts influence transparently and respects the choices of others. On Klemp's account, persuasion takes two primary forms: "deliberative persuasion" induces agreement with an orientation toward understanding, while "strategic persuasion" induces agreement with an orientation toward success. Manipulative rhetoric, by contrast, arises when an agent intentionally uses hidden or irrational force to affect the choices of another. In democratic politics, manipulation takes three primary forms: lying, concealment, and distraction. Unlike persuasion, Klemp contends, manipulation often works covertly and diminishes both individual autonomy and democratic self-rule by interfering with other citizens' capacity to choose. Two primary contextual conditions intensify the dangers of manipulative rhetoric: invisibility and asymmetrical relations of power. Given its potential dangers, Klemp therefore concludes, manipulation ought to be viewed with a presumption of immorality and subject to robust contestation, while both deliberative and strategic forms of persuasion ought to be accepted and encouraged as healthy parts of democratic life.

ii

In addition to refining our conceptualization of manipulation, we also need to understand the empirical challenges to identifying and combating manipulation. Some of these challenges, discussed in the following part, pertain to the various institutions and media through which democratic manipulation is exercised. But another set of challenges arises from our understanding of the human mind itself: how we conceive of the political actor, how individuals respond to their surroundings, and how our attributes as humans contribute to how we think about the polity. Concepts such as personality, group behavior, emotion, learned behaviors, incentive theories, social cognitions, intergroup relations, cognitive science, and evolutionary biology all play a potentially important role in our understanding of politics generally and manipulation more specifically.[20] Political theorists from Plato and Aristotle to Hobbes and Hume and down to the present maintained that knowing the nature of the human mind, and specifically of its capacity to be misled or manipulated, was indispensable to any adequate understanding of political life.[21]

To some degree, the model of citizen rationality derived from these philosophers (and from a related group of social scientific thinkers, discussed below) remains embedded in both contemporary democratic theory and the contemporary empirical study of politics.[22] Recent advances in political psychology show new ways to think about manipulation, some of which are affirmations of what political theorists have long suspected—emotions play an important role in facilitating manipulation—and some of which are new—the ways in which the brain learns and responds to stimuli.[23] Together, these recent discoveries shine a light on the micro-foundations that enable and constrain contemporary practices of manipulation.[24]

George Lakoff's essay "Changing Brains: Lessons from the Living Wage Campaign" introduces the main themes in this section of the volume. Lakoff's extensive work in cognitive psychology, along with that of his fellow pioneers in the field, helps us to fill in the picture of the brain's neural structure, the role of this structure in the process of preference formation, and, perhaps most importantly, how we should conceive of reason itself.[25] The findings of these studies offer a provocative reassessment of the nature of political thinking.[26] Lakoff attempts to shift our understanding of political actors by showing how our traditional understanding of actors as rational agents with well defined preferences is an incorrect understanding of how we make decisions.

The specific roots of this traditional model of rationality can be traced to the early behavioralist studies in modern political science, which investigated such questions as why and how voters chose one party over another, how social groups influenced political choices, and how voters developed preferences.[27] The increasingly sophisticated use of statistical techniques that accompanied the classic behavioralist studies made it desirable to find a more parsimonious and easily quantifiable model of political behavior, requiring in turn a new model of the rational behavior of actors. The new "rational actor" model adopted an instrumental and calculative account of human rationality, positing that actors possessed clear, stable preference orderings, and that they sought to maximize their happiness according to a utility function more or less transparent to the agents themselves.[28] Manipulation, on this account, consists in rational actors exploiting or even rewriting the rules of the game to achieve their own preferred outcomes at the expense of other players, primarily by means of withholding, hiding, or skewing information relevant to the choice situation at hand. On this view, the principal way to fight manipulation is to provide for greater oversight and a freer exchange of information.

This model of rational agency, Lakoff argues, provided a kind of "folk theory" of reason, one that underlies not only much of the contemporary empirical work in political science, but more broadly much of our intuitive and theoretical understanding of democracy itself.[29] George Marcus writes that the dominant view in political science is that "rationality is the mental faculty that makes us free and that gives us the capacity to establish political regimes that are democratic and just" and that this rationality is somehow free of emotion, bias, and other undue constraints.[30] According to the picture of the mind that is emerging from contemporary cognitive psychology, however, the emotions should not be understood as at best an ancillary aspect of reasoning and at worst an impediment to it: instead, this picture contends that emotions are the foundation of reasoning itself.[31] This more nuanced approach has greatly broadened how we think of how manipulation might operate simultaneously on both our reason and our emotions.[32] As Lakoff suggests, reason should not be understood as a strictly logical process but rather as something that is driven by emotional activity that finds its roots in the limbic region of our brain. Indeed, emotions seem to function in ways that not only help to shape our preferences, but also shape the worldviews that define our rationality itself.[33] These emotionally based worldviews are not the conclusions arrived at by disinterested processes of reason; rather, reason, in this account, is almost entirely shaped by our emotionally based worldviews, and is used as an instrument to support and reinforce the worldviews themselves. Contemporary cognitive science offers an understanding of how these worldviews are created, how they are reinforced by emotions, and how they filter and constrain every aspect of our individual and shared experiences.

If contemporary political psychology shows us how to reconceive the role of emotions in our public deliberations, then what is meant by manipulation and how manipulation works will also have to be reconceptualized. As we saw in the previous section, democratic theorists have tended to conceptualize manipulation as a subversion of the purely rational processes of individual choice, by means of the interference of emotion, misinformation, or similar, "non-rational" intervening variables. Manipulation, on this account, consists in rational actors exploiting or even rewriting the rules of the game to achieve their own preferred outcomes at the expense of other players. Cognitive science, on the contrary, teaches us that human beings are emotional actors as well as rational actors, and that rational thought itself requires emotion, which alters how we look at the very idea of preferences and decision making.[34]

In her essay "Emotional Manipulation of Political Identity," Rose McDermott shows how contemporary American leaders manipulate emotions for specific political effect and partisan advantage. The advances that have been made in terms of understanding how emotions affect political decision making, McDermott argues, can help us to better explain how leaders strategically instill, manipulate, and encourage specific emotional responses in voters. In the two-party context that makes up American politics, McDermott demonstrates, leaders and citizen groups alike use these insights to manipulate emotions to polarize the electorate. The most effective and commonly used emotion is fear, which McDermott argues is very useful in garnering political support. Various actors also rely on the creation and symbolic use of opposition "outrages" to signal in-group members of the need for provocation against out-group members. The result of this process, according to McDermott, is that voters lose the ability to make informed choices concerning leadership and policy because the truth and accuracy of the information can only be judged through the relationship that the voter has with the source of information.

But should the mere presence of emotion necessarily signal to us that it is being used manipulatively? In her essay "Mimesis, Persuasion, and Manipulation in Plato's *Republic*," Christina Tarnopolsky explores Plato's attempts to distinguish his notion of emotional cultivation from the emotional manipulation characteristic of the poets and sophists in democratic Athens. Tarnopolsky examines Plato's analysis of how poets and sophists manipulated their audiences through producing pleasing images and the "positive" emotions of love and compassion. Engaging with one of the central Western critiques of emotional manipulation—Plato's condemnation of the mimetic poets—as well as one of the most influential apologies for manipulation—the "noble lie" of Plato's guardians—Tarnopolsky throws a striking new interpretive light on each in turn. In his treatment of mimēsis (imitation) in the *Republic*, Tarnopolsky shows, Plato sought to identify and distinguish the psychological elements underlying both manipulation and persuasion. Rather than condemning mimēsis entirely, Plato instead tries to encourage his fellow Athenians to engage in the right kinds of mimetic practices that will cultivate rather than foreclose the deliberative skills necessary for good democratic citizenship. And "the noble lie," according to Tarnopolsky, turns out to be better understood as a kind of fiction or frame that encourages critical thinking about one's regime rather than blind obedience to it—one that exhibits Plato's teaching about the kind of mimetic education that can serve as an antidote to manipulation. Though the manipulative strategies generally seen as negative reinforcers are effective, Tarnopolsky argues that Plato shows that positive emotions such as love and compassion are equally useful in manipulation. Tarnopolsky shows that Plato believes that, in contrast to the approach of the sophists and poets, his strategy of working through *all* of the emotions plays a necessary role in democratic deliberations.

In addition to their emphasis on the centrality of emotion, cognitive psychologists such as Lakoff also argue that our brains function primarily by means of creating and applying frames and narratives. The human brain necessarily takes experience and wraps it into a narrative that appears to be seamless and make sense, often leading us, in Marc Hauser's words, to "engage in mental somersaults to justify our beliefs."[35] Without necessarily having evidence for their various beliefs, through the repetition of key narratives a neural network forms a cognitive frame through which we perceive the world.

Political manipulation relies crucially on the susceptibility of our brains to the organizing power of frames and narratives. Through the clever repetition of stories and narratives that exploit and reinforce our emotionally grounded worldviews, elites can exploit the predictable processes of our brains. Employing well-turned phrases or subtle advertising appeals, manipulators can shape and define a neural map that then acts as a frame through which we are compelled to evaluate political actions, public policies, and candidates for office. From this we generate conceptual frames to use to relate to the world. The ways in which we reason—that is to say, the ways in which we experience the world emotionally and give reasons for our actions—are largely dependent on frames that are shaped by both the cognitive structure of our brains and our experiences.

Not all uses of language to shape or reinforce a frame are necessarily manipulative, of course; as the essays in Part I agree, we must believe that the person using such language is able to get an unfair advantage (however defined) before we would be prepared to denounce their behavior as manipulation.[36] But these findings of cognitive science and political psychology do imply that manipulation can be more subtle, more powerful, and more pervasive than democratic theory is yet prepared to answer.

As Lakoff argues, ideas are usually presented to the polity as choices that can be deliberated upon in a purely rational fashion. In fact, however, we frequently make decisions concerning these important choices based on the emotional decision-making apparatus of our brain. Once these decisions are lodged and shaped by emotions, they are difficult to change or "remove" from our brains. Therefore, Lakoff argues that we must understand the complex relationship that reason, emotions, and frames share if we are to correct the negative byproducts of manipulation in contemporary politics. Any polity that hopes to be free and democratic must have a citizenry that understands how emotions and frames shape our political decision-making in order to move control of political discourse out of the hands of the political elite and into the hands of the polity at large.

iii

We have seen how the stories and narratives that people receive about themselves and others compose the worldviews and frames through which they experience the world and their political lives, and that the language through which these narratives are told creates the landscape of their political world. But there is another dimension to the contemporary problem of manipulation: namely, these psychological vulnerabilities are coming to be amplified exponentially by the increasing power and complexity of the media and related institutions. If cognitive science points to the depth of the challenge that manipulation poses for us, the rapid changes in the institutional structure of the public sphere point instead to the increasing breadth of its impact.

To the extent that democratic theory takes the existence of media and related institutions into account, they have traditionally been asked to play the role of reliable and objective sources of information about the political world. Based on the media's neutral presentation of public events, citizens can sift through information that has been presented to them and then proceed to make rational decisions concerning their preferred outcomes.[37] If power is being abused or employed unwisely, this view supposes, then the media will ferret out the truth and report the facts to the polity.[38] Given this important watchdog function of the media, the polity will be able to make informed choices as to who should stay in office, who should be voted out, and even who should be punished.[39]

This "watchdog model" of the role of the media has long been criticized as a misleading account of what the media actually do in our society. Nevertheless, without overt acknowledgement, some version of the watchdog model continues to underwrite certain of the key premises of democratic theory: in particular the notions of an informed citizenry, rational public choice, and representative accountability. Yet as the essays in this third part of our volume demonstrate, the idea that the media can inform the populace and curb manipulation is becoming increasingly untenable given the massive changes that media institutions are presently undergoing.

When these changes are discussed in public discourse, they most commonly take the form of hand-wringing about media bias, which supposedly obstructs the media from providing the necessary, objective facts for public deliberation. There is perhaps some degree of truth to this, as far as it goes. Not only do reporters exhibit individual biases, but their standard professional practices and priorities also exhibit certain distinctive biases—and the owners of their media outlets a different set.[40] But at a deeper level, the notion of facticity is itself problematic, in a variety of complex ways. To begin with, facts seem to be, by their very nature, "constructed." Murray Edelman writes that in contemporary politics, "the very concept of 'fact' becomes irrelevant because every meaningful political object and person is an interpretation that reflects and perpetuates an ideology."[41] This constructed nature of social facts is magnified by the perpetual echo chamber, which the rise of punditry in contemporary politics has helped to facilitate.[42] Repeating the same story line and the same interpretations over and over, these pundits overwhelm the critical defenses of passive media consumers, leading people to begin to believe in the existence of weapons of mass destruction or in the existence of ties between Saddam Hussein and Al Qaeda, in contradiction to the best information publicly (and freely) available. These institutional factors amplify the already potent framing effects built into our psychology, facilitating manipulation by elites of the voting public's attention and preferences.[43]

The prevailing ethos among both political practitioners and the media who cover them seems to be that political discourse from top to bottom is nothing more than mere spin. In a world where there is no consensus on a set of facts and a narrative that the polity can hold as objective and true, there is no longer any incentive for politicians, business leaders, civic leaders, or news outlets to hew closely to the truth—only to spin the "story" in ways that garner political power, control damage, and capture an audience. Thus our increasing awareness of the socially constructed character of facts has helped to undermine our reliance on "facts" as a consensus starting point for social choices. This in turn has destablilized the basic functions of social cohesion and cooperation that the more primitive notion of "facticity" had always helped to facilitate. Kathleen Hall Jamieson and Brooks Jackson, for example, have criticized the tendency of political figures to abandon traditional consensual approaches to questions of fact in favor of a radically instrumental understanding of the role of fact in public argumentation.[44] What the studies of Jamieson and Jackson as well as others show is that we have entered a new era of virtually fact-free advertising, one in which competing voices in the contemporary American public sphere, and in particular the media, have so far proven woefully ill-prepared to challenge and correct.[45]

In addition to objective, fact-based reporting, the watchdog model of media institutions also relies on the idea that media will provide the public with shared accounts of "hard news" and substantive policy discussions relevant to their democratic choices. Yet a combination of factors, including most notably the expanding competition of reporters, news organizations, and media outlets for audiences, tends to result in the watering down of the media's product into some form of entertainment.[46] News organizations, worried about a fragmented information marketplace, apathetic and passive viewers, and financial bottom lines, have come to rely more and more on sound bites, dramatic news, and a fascination with celebrity.[47] The fragmented information marketplace and the rise of "new" media has only exacerbated these effects. With the increased ability that the individual has of choosing his or her preferred mode of news supply, each consumer in this new media environment can self-select the ideological slant and even the subject matter covered. This suggests a different kind of threat for manipulation. Since consumers of media increasingly rely on specialized outlets that reinforce their worldview, media have an incentive to placate and cater to particular worldviews.

Richard Fox and Amy Gangl, in their essay "News You Can't Use: Politics and Democracy in the New Media Environment," explore the criticisms of media scholars and democratic theorists who have increasingly bemoaned the lack of substance in journalistic accounts of electoral politics since the 1980s. Reviewing various empirical examinations of election coverage from the 1980s and 1990s, Fox and Gangl show that media outlets have tended to focus primarily on polls, campaign tactics, and the personal qualities of the candidates. Absent from most of the election coverage were stories that dealt with the candidates' policy positions and how they might handle long-term problems that were facing the country. Despite the dearth of serious campaign coverage, things have gotten worse since the 1980s as the media has come to focus more on celebrity and entertainment news, as well as the growth of the partisan press and new media coupled with the decline of network news and newspapers. Even the traditional backbone of political reporting—the networks and top newspapers—have become increasingly devoid of serious policy substance, more so than at any time in the history of our country. Fox and Gangl highlight the problems that citizens have in obtaining serious information due to various institutional norms of contemporary mainstream news media. Their empirical analysis of the 2008 election coverage turns the spotlight on declining journalistic practices, market driven media priorities, and the increased importance placed on trivial aspects of the campaigns and candidates, which leads towards the greater possibility of manipulation.

Another powerful trend is the changing usage and influence of public opinion polls. Traditionally, pollsters measured public opinion primarily to find out what the polity was thinking about a particular event or idea, in order for leaders to be guided (at least in part) by the public's judgment. Now, however, instead of indicating the pre-existing desires of the polity, politicians increasingly employ public opinion data to maneuver the polity toward their desired policy goals.[48] Such polls, purportedly representing the collective will of the people, are in fact conceived and designed solely for the purpose of promoting a predetermined end.

In "The Betrayal of Democracy: The Purpose of Public Opinion Survey Research and its Misuse by Presidents," Lawrence Jacobs starts with the observation that the public's belief in the likelihood that public opinion pollsters will tell the truth is exceedingly low. Some of this distrust might arise out the press' misleading coverage and poor understanding of sampling technique. That being said, the public still has a great deal of reason to distrust the profession. Through his examination of confidential and largely unexamined records from presidential archives, Jacobs discovers a disturbing pattern in the use of survey research. Presidents since John Kennedy have used private surveys and other forms of public opinion research in attempts to influence, rather than simply discover, public attitudes. Furthermore, the use of these surveys also attempted to disrupt public evaluations of both public policy and the president's policy positions. Also, Jacobs holds that these surveys have been used to pursue narrow responsiveness to sectional interests rather than the broad representation of the nation that is expected of presidents. The evidence of private presidential misuse of surveys is drawn from historical and contemporary illustrations as well as quantitative analyses of presidential polling data. If the central motivation of survey pioneers was to create a "tool of democracy," then, Jacobs argues, presidential conduct has undermined and indeed reversed this purpose.

In "The Political Economy of Mass Media: Implications for Informed Citizenship," Shanto Iyengar and Kyu Hahn examine some of the larger background conditions that are beginning to undermine the idea that the press can serve as a protector of the democratic citizenry from the manipulative maneuvers of political elites. As their essay shows, the rapid expansion of market-based news programming and the accompanying dilution of governmental regulation over the broadcast media have called into question the media's ability to make good on this civic responsibility. Iyengar and Hahn's essay first distinguishes between demand-side versus supply-side forces in information distribution. The demand side treats information as an individual attribute acquired by the more highly motivated and socially integrated strata of society. The supply side, by contrast, treats media systems themselves as the key predictor, presuming that public service oriented media are more likely to deliver substantive content on a more frequent basis, while market-based media are more likely to shirk their civic responsibilities. Using cross-national comparisons, Iyengar and Hahn show how public service oriented systems help decrease the "knowledge gap" between more and less advantaged strata of society due to their greater (inadvertent) exposure of less educated and affluent citizens to public affairs programming. Iyengar and Hahn then argue that the rise of "new media" has two important consequences for the interplay of these supply and demand forces. First, the availability of more choice means less demand for political programming. Most voters will prefer to watch ESPN to CNN, but political junkies will increase their intake of news (driving up the knowledge gap). Second, increased choice facilitates selective exposure. Empowered consumers will increasingly turn only to sources whose content they are likely to find agreeable, thus tending to further polarize the news audience as a whole. Finally, Iyengar and Hahn consider the implications of these new trends for democratic theory, arguing that they facilitate the potential for manipulation of mass opinion by political elites, and that they increase the likelihood that voters will be unable to recognize alternative perspectives on issues, weakening the potential for public deliberation. Iyengar and Hahn make the case for substantial policy shifts that include substantial regulation of broadcast media to promote public affairs coverage.

Finally, in "Exploiting the Clueless: Heresthetic, Overload, and Rational Ignorance," Andrew Sabl explores the normative implications of the increasing complexity of processes of public discourse and political contestation. Sabl's essay aims to flesh out the link which rational choice-oriented studies have repeatedly drawn between successful political manipulation and voters' rational ignorance, and to trace some unexpected ethical and political implications of that link. His argument has two points of departure. The first is the concept of "heresthetic." Heresthetic, a term derived from William Riker's book *The Art of Political Manipulation*,[49] is the art of applying rational choice analysis to practical problems: the heresthetician knows the laws of strategic interaction and their implications, and thus can manipulate—through such mechanisms as agenda control, issue division, and strategic voting—under the very noses of its victims, and with their full cognizance of all substantively relevant information at every stage of the process. Sabl's second point of departure is the method of manipulation, which Robert Goodin in *Manipulatory Politics* describes as overload: namely, the case where elites purposely present so much true information that the public will need to rely on those same elites to provide a frame to cut through the confusion.

Sabl argues that overload may be even more powerful and ubiquitous than Goodin describes: for it will tend to be most effective when the information in question involves political *processes*, which are harder for voters to understand and analyze than the big substantive questions (e.g., the Vietnam War) on which Goodin focuses. At least two implications follow, Sabl contends. First, while Riker's *Art of Political Manipulation* might seem (despite its title) to describe ethically neutral acts, Riker's heresthetic methods of manipulating agendas and choices do, because of overload tactics, involve deception and opposition to voters' putative wills— and thus "manipulation" in the normative sense as well. For though Riker's art is not intended to be secret, only elites and political experts will have any way of figuring out when and how it is being practiced or how to fight it. Sabl employs a concrete case to illuminate this point: Republican Party tactics of procedural obfuscation as described in Jacob Hacker and Paul Pierson's book *Off-Center*.[50] Second, Sabl argues that recognizing and evaluating this crucial form of manipulation requires stressing the validity of rational ignorance theory, and we should therefore be wary of modern democratic theory's tendency to deny the relevance of rational ignorance. Calls for ever-greater deliberation, to the extent that they dismiss or downplay necessary imbalances in heresthetic opportunities and the necessary costs of political information, may make it harder than it would otherwise be for elite political actors to combat manipulation—precisely in the course of trying to make it easier.

*

Democracy has emerged as the universally acknowledged normative ideal of the contemporary world—a standard to which nearly every nation on earth has (at least in principle) committed itself unreservedly.[51] Yet practices of manipulation seem to undercut not merely the practice of democracy, but the very core of the ideal itself. If true democracy cannot exist where (certain kinds of) manipulative practices hold sway, then in many ways our deepest moral and political aspirations will depend on our devising the best approaches we can to the problem of identifying, confronting, and counteracting (at least the malign forms of) manipulation wherever it exists.

The task will be a challenging one, not least because of the many analytical and practical complexities which the essays in this volume aim to illuminate. The diverse voices assembled in this book attest to the intricacy and intractability of the problem and to the wide range of scholarly fields and methodologies that it will be necessary to draw upon in working toward practical solutions. But with democracy itself at stake in the ongoing quandaries toward which these studies point us, we need to begin again, to talk and think afresh about manipulation as an enduring problem in democratic life—and about the endangered values it persistently threatens.[52]

Notes

1. Kathleen Hall Jamieson, *Dirty Politics: Deception, Distraction, and Democracy* (Oxford: Oxford University Press, 1992); Kathleen Hall Jamieson, *Packaging the Presidency: A History and Criticism of Campaign Advertising*, 3rd ed. (Oxford: Oxford University Press, 1996).
2. Thomas Frank, *The Wrecking Crew: How Conservatives Rule* (New York: Metropolitan Books, 2008).

3. Howard Kurtz, *Spin Cycle: How the White House and the Media Manipulate the News* (New York: Touchstone, 1998); Jeffrey Toobin, *A Vast Conspiracy: The Real Story of the Sex Scandal That Nearly Brought Down a President* (New York: Touchstone, 1999).

4. For illustrations from the Clinton years, see Elizabeth Drew, *On the Edge: The Clinton Presidency* (New York: Touchstone, 1994) and *Showdown: The Struggle Between the Gingrich Congress and the Clinton White House* (New York: Touchstone, 1996).

5. Frank Rich, *The Greatest Story Ever Sold: The Decline and Fall of Truth in Bush's America* (New York: Penguin, 2007).

6. David Brock, *The Republican Noise Machine: Right-Wing Media and How It Corrupts Democracy* (New York: Three Rivers Press, 2004); Frank Rich, *The Greatest Story Ever Sold: The Decline and Fall of Truth in Bush's America* (New York: Penguin, 2007); Kathleen Hall Jamieson and Joseph N. Cappella, *Echo Chamber: Rush Limbaugh and the Conservative Media Establishment* (Oxford: Oxford University Press, 2008).

7. Jurgen Habermas, *Between Facts and Norms: Contributions to a Discourse Theory of Law and Democracy*, trans. William Rehg (Cambridge, MA: MIT Press), p. 6.

8. W.B. Gallie, "Essentially Contested Concepts," *Proceedings of the Aristotelian Society*, vol. 56 (London, 1955–1956). See also William Connolly, *The Terms of Political Discourse*, 3rd ed. (Princeton, NJ: Princeton University Press, 1993).

9. Connolly, *The Terms of Political Discourse*, ch. 1.

10. Robert Goodin, *Manipulatory Politics* (New Haven, CT: Yale University Press, 1980). For a fuller elaboration of Goodin's larger consequentialist framework than appears in *Manipulatory Politics*, see further his *Utilitarianism as a Public Philosophy* (Cambridge: Cambridge University Press, 1995). Adrian M.S. Piper, "Utility, Publicity, and Manipulation," *Ethics* 88 (1978): 189–206, offers an important treatment of the complexities involved in conceptualizing manipulation within a utilitarian framework. Another important definition of manipulation is that offered by Patricia Greenspan, "The Problem with Manipulation," *American Philosophical Quarterly* 40 (2003): 155–65. Focusing on elements that define manipulation as wrong inherently, Greenspan identifies the essence of manipulative conduct as unfairness in social exchange. Her definition is compatible both with deontological approaches to ethics (since such conduct almost by definition constitutes a denial of respect for persons in the traditional Kantian sense) as well as more teleological and communitarian varieties of ethical theory (focusing instead on the tendency of manipulation to undermine relationships of social trust).

11. Goodin, *Manipulatory Politics*, pp. 7–26.

12. Goodin, *Manipulatory Politics*, pp. 7–8 and p. 231.

13. As we will discuss below with reference to strategic forms of manipulation, there is some reason to think that perhaps it is not. For a more developed argument that deception is not a necessary condition of manipulation, see Joel Rudinow, "Manipulation," *Ethics* 88 (1978): 338–47.

14. On the ethical problems associated with secrecy, see Dennis Thompson, "Democratic Secrecy," in *Restoring Responsibility: Ethics in Government, Business, and Healthcare*, ed. Dennis Thompson (Cambridge: Cambridge University Press, 2005).

15. Harry Frankfurt, *On Bullshit* (Princeton, NJ: Princeton University Press, 2005).

16. For a helpful orientation to this vast literature, see two important collections of essays: James Bohman and William Rehg, eds., *Deliberative Democracy: Essays on Reason and Politics* (Cambridge, MA: MIT Press, 1997); and James S. Fishkin and Peter Laslett, eds., *Debating Deliberative Democracy* (Cambridge: Cambridge University Press, 2003).

17. Among numerous writings, see Habermas, "On Systematically Distorted Communication," *Inquiry* 13 (1970): 205–18, and more broadly Habermas, *The Theory of Communicative Action*, vols. 1–2 (Boston: Beacon Press, 1985).

18. On the distinction between ideal and non-ideal modes of normative theory, see Christine Korsgaard, "The Right to Lie: Kant on Dealing with Evil," in *Creating the Kingdom of Ends*, ed. Christine Korsgaard (Cambridge: Cambridge University Press, 1996).

19. Larry M. Bartels, "Democracy with Attitudes," in *Electoral Democracy*, eds. Michael B. MacKuen and George Rabinowitz (Ann Arbor: University of Michigan Press, 2003).

20. For helpful overviews of recent scholarship in these areas, see, James H. Kuklinski, ed., *Thinking About Political Psycholog.* (Cambridge: Cambridge University Press, 2002) and David O. Sears, Leonie Huddy, and Robert Jervis, eds., *Oxford Handbook of Political Psychology* (Oxford: Oxford University Press, 2003).

21. For a thoughtful survey, see Michael Neblo, "Philosophical Psychology With Political Intent," in *The Affect Effect: Dynamics of Emotion in Political Thinking and Behavior*, eds. W. Russell Neuman, George E. Marcus, Ann N. Crigler, and Michael MacKuen (Chicago: University of Chicago Press, 2007).

22. Sears, Huddy, and Jervis note that "there is no single accepted theory of human psychology. Whether we could ever develop such a theory, whether the barriers to it are potentially surmountable with greater research or are inherent in the complex and changing nature of human behavior, is as yet unanswerable."(p. 10).

23. Joseph P. Forgas and Craig A. Smith write, "Social life is imbued with affect. Every interaction with others can influence our emotional state, and affect in turn plays an important role in the way form judgments and behave in strategic social situations" (p. 161). See "Affect and Emotion," in *The Sage Handbook of Social Psychology*, eds. Michael A. Hogg and Joel Cooper (Thousand Oaks, CA: Sage Publications, 2003). See further W. Russell Newman et. al., in *The Affect Effect: Dynamics of Emotion in Political Thinking and Behavior*, eds., W. Russell Neuman, George E. Marcus, Ann N. Crigler, and Micahael MacKuen (Chicago: University of Chicago Press, 2007).

24. Among a truly vast array of studies, some outstanding contributions include Bill McGuire, *The Poly-Psy Relationship: Three Phases of a Long Affair* (Washington, DC: International Society of Political Psychology, 1990); Don Kinder, "Reason and Emotion in American political life," in *Beliefs, Reasoning, and Decision Making*, eds. Roger Schank and Ellen Langer (Mahwah, NJ: Elrbaum, 1994); George E. Marcus, W. Russell Neuman, and Michael MacKuen, *Affective Intelligence and political judgment* (Chicago: University of Chicago Press, 2000); George E. Marcus, *The Sentimental Citizen: Emotions in Democratic Politics* (University Park: Pennsylvania State University Press, 2002).

25. See Steven Pinker, *The Blank Slate* (New York: Penguin, 2003), especially ch. 1, and Paul E. Griffiths, "Emotions," in *A Companion to Cognitive*

Science, eds., William Bechtel and George Graham (Oxford: Blackwell Publishing, 1999), pp. 197–203.

26. See also Leda Cosmides and John Tooby, "Evolutionary Psychology and the Emotions" in *Handbook of Emotions*, 2nd ed., eds., M. Lewis and J. Haviland-Jones (New York: Guilford, 2000); Drew Westen, *The Political Brain* (PublicAffairs, 2007).

27. See Angus Campbell, G. Gurin, and Warren E. Miller, *The Voter Decides* (Evanston, IL: Row Peterson, 1954), Paul Lazarsfeld and William McPhee, *Voting* (Chicago: University of Chicago Press, 1959), Agnus Campbell, Philip E. Converse, Warren E. Miller, and Donald E. Stokes, *The American Voter* (New York: Wiley, 1960), Gabriel Almond and Sidney Verba, *The Civic Culture* (Princeton, NJ: Princeton University Press, 1963); Sidney Verba and Norman H. Nie, *Participation in America* (New York: Harper and Row, 1972). For an influential critique of these traditional models, see John R. Zaller, *The Nature and Origins of Mass Opinion* (New York: Cambridge University Press, 1992).

28. Rational choice is a complex theory with a long history that has yielded important results, and in critiquing specific applications of the rational actor model for normative democratic theory we do not mean to impeach the usefulness of this approach as a basis for empirical studies. Indeed, the sharp divide between rational choice and rival approaches may be overblown, as Robert Goodin and Hans-Dieter Klingemann write: "Political scientists no longer think in the either/or terms of rationality or habituation: virtually all serious rational choice modelers now appreciate the constraints under which real people take political actions, and incorporate within their own models many of the sorts of cognitive shortcuts that political psychologists have long been studying." In *A New Handbook of Political Science*, edited by Robert E. Goodin and Hans-Dieter Klingemann (Oxford: Oxford University Press, 2000), pp. 11–12. On the relationship between rational choice theory and democratic theory, see William H. Riker, *Liberalism Against Populism* (San Francisco: Freeman, 1982). For those interested in the applications of rational choice theory to political science more broadly, a powerful critique can be found in Donald P. Green and Ian Shapiro, *Pathologies of Rational Choice Theory: A Critique of Applications in Political Science* (New Haven, CT: Yale University Press, 1994), and for a wide-ranging critical dialogue, see Jeffrey Friedman, ed., *The Rational Choice Controversy: Economic Models of Politics Reconsidered* (New Haven, CT: Yale University Press, 1996). See also Richard Tuck, *Free Riding* (Cambridge, MA: Harvard University Press, 2008).

29. Interestingly, it is quite probable that most people do not feel that they can be or are being manipulated since most people believe that they have the ability to detect deception. However, studies have shown that people really are not much better at detecting deception through their purported abilities than they would by chance. See, for example, H.S. Friedman and J.S. Tucker, "Language and Deception," in *Handbook of Language and Social Psychology*, eds. Howard Giles and W. Peter Robinson (New York: Wiley, 1990). What this means is that our purported rational abilities may not be much good in the way of overcoming manipulation.

30. George E. Marcus, "The Psychology of Emotion and Politics," *The Oxford Handbook of Political Psychology*, eds., David O. Sears, Leonie Huddy, and Robert Jervis (Oxford: Oxford University Press, 2003), p. 182.

31. See Martha Nussbaum, *Upheavals of Thought*, Marc Hauser, *Moral Minds*, Steven Pinker, *The Stuff of Thought*, and George Marcus, et al., *Affective*

Intelligence. On the implications of the findings of political psychology for normative democratic theory, see the excellent discussion by Larry M. Bartels, "Democracy with Attitudes," in *Electoral Democracy*, eds. Michael B. MacKuen and George Rabinowitz (Ann Arbor: University of Michigan Press, 2003).

32. See Antoine Bechara, Hanna Damasio, Daniel Tranel, and Anotio R. Damasio, "Decideing Advantageously Before Knowing the Advantageous Strategy," *Science*, 275, no. 5304 (1997, Feb. 28), pp. 1293–295. These authors argue that absent emotion, reason alone would not be able to compel us to act.

33. For an interesting discussion on how emotions have been examined see Randolph R. Cornelius, *The Science of Emotion: Research and Tradition in the Psychology of Emotions* (Upper Saddle River, NJ: Prentice Hall, 1996).

34. See George Lakoff, *Whose Freedom? The Battle over America's Most Important Idea* (New York: Farrar, Strauss and Giroux, 2006), pp. 14–15; George Lakoff and Mark Johnson, *Philosophy in the Flesh: The Embodied Mind and Its Challenge to Western Thought* (New York: Basic Books, 1999), pp. 514, 575.

35. See Marc D. Hauser, *Moral Minds: The Nature of Right and Wrong* (New York: Harper Perennial, 2007), p. 11.

36. See George Lakoff, *Whose Freedom? The Battle over America's Most Important Idea* (New York: Farrar, Strauss and Giroux, 2006), pp. 10–14. See also George Lakoff and Mark Johnson, *Philosophy in the Flesh: The Embodied Mind and Its Challenge to Western Thought* (New York: Basic Books, 1999), George Lakoff and Mark Johnson, *Metaphors We Live By* (Chicago: University of Chicago Press, 1980), and David Martel Johnson, *How History Made the Mind: The Cultural Origins of Objective Thinking* (Chicago: Open Court, 2003), pp. 2–39.

37. On the rational and emotional aspects of the processes by which citizens process information, see Samuel L. Popkin, *The Reasoning Voter* (Chicago: University of Chicago Press, 1991); Benjamin I. Page and Robert Y. Shapiro, *The Rational Public* (Chicago: University of Chicago Press, 1992); John Zaller, *The Nature and Origin of Mass Opinion* (Cambridge: Cambridge University Press, 1992); Arthur Lupia and Matthew McCubbins, *The Democratic Dilemma: Can Citizens Learn What They Need to Know?* (Cambridge: Cambridge University Press, 1998); and Diana C. Mutz, *Impersonal Influence* (Cambridge: Cambridge University Press, 1998).

38. Sam Donaldson nicely captures the stereotype: "If you send me to cover a pie-baking contest on Mother's Day, I'm going to ask dear old Mom whether she used artificial sweetener in violation of the rules, and while she's at it, could I see the receipt for the apples to prove she didn't steal them. I maintain that if Mom has nothing to hide, no harm will have been done. But the questions should be asked." Quoted in George C. Edwards III, Martin P. Wattenberg, and Robert L. Lineberry, *Government in America: People, Politics, and Policy* (New York: Pearson Longman, 2008), p. 215.

39. On problems manipulation creates for democratic accountability, see Shanto Iyengar, *Is Anyone Responsible?: How Television Frames Political Issues.* (Chicago: University of Chicago Press, 1991).

40. For two conflicting perspectives on the media bias debate, see Bernard Goldberg, *Bias* (New York: Harper Paperbacks, 2003), and Eric Alterman, *What Liberal Media? The Truth About Bias and the News* (New York: Basic

Books, 2003), p. 1. On the biases connected to journalistic practices, see also Thomas E. Patterson, *Out of Order* (New York: Vintage, 1994).

41. Murray Edelman, *Constructing the Political Spectacle* (Chicago: University of Chicago Press, 1988), p. 10.

42. See David Brock, *The Republican Noise Machine* (New York: Three Rivers Press, 2004); John Mueller, *Overblown: How Politicians and the Terrorism Industry Inflate National Security Threats, and Why We Believe Them* (New York: Free Press, 2006); and Kathleen Hall Jamieson and Joseph N. Cappella, *Echo Chamber: Rush Limbaugh and the Conservative Media Establishment* (Oxford: Oxford University Press, 2008).

43. On framing, see especially Shanto Iyengar and Donald Kinder, *News That Matters: Television and American Opinion* (Chicago: University of Chicago Press, 1987); Joseph N. Cappella and Kathleen Hall Jamieson, *Spiral of Cynicism: The Press and the Public Good* (Oxford: Oxford University Press, 1997); and T.H. Nelson, Z.M. Oxley, and R. A. Clawson, "Towards a Psychology of Framing Effects," *Political Behavior* 19 (1997): 221–46. On issues of attention and agenda setting, see particularly M.E. McCombs and D.L. Shaw, "The Agenda-Setting Function the Media," *Public Opinion Quarterly* 36 (1972): 176–87; and Bryan D. Jones and Frank R. Baumgartner, *The Politics of Attention: How Government Prioritizes Problems* (Chicago: University of Chicago Press, 2005).

44. Brooks Jackson and Kathleen Hall Jamieson, eds., *UnSpun: Finding Facts in a World of Disinformation.* (New York: Random House, 2007). See also Kathleen Hall Jamieson and Bruce W. Hardy, "Unmasking Deception: The Function and Failures of the Press," in *The Politics of News: The News of Politics*, eds. Doris A. Graber, Denis McQuail, and Pippa Norris (Washington, DC: CQ Press, 2008). For an influential study of the motivations and incentives that drive these media failures, see Thomas E. Patterson, *Out of Order* (New York: Vintage, 1994).

45. On the manipulative potential of television advertising, see also two books by Kathleen Hall Jamieson, *Packaging the Presidency*, 3rd ed. (Oxford: Oxford University Press, 1996) and *Dirty Politics* (Oxford: Oxford University Press, 1993); as well as Stephen Ansolabehere and Shanto Iyengar, *Going Negative* (New York: Free Press, 1997); and Ted Brader, *Campaigning for Hearts and Minds* (Chicago: University of Chicago Press).

46. See Murray Edelman, *Constructing the Political Spectacle; Neil Postman, Amusing Ourselves to* Death (Penguin, 1985); and Richard Fox, Robert Van Sickel, and Thomas L. Steiger, eds., *Tabloid Justice* (Boulder, CO: Lynne Reinner, 2007).

47. See Shanto Iyengar and Donald Kinder, *News that Matters* (Chicago: University of Chicago Press, 1989); Kiku Adatto, *Picture Perfect,* (New York: Basic Books, 1993); Thomas E. Patterson, *Out of Order* (New York: Vintage, 1994); and Kathleen Hall Jamieson and Paul Waldman, *The Press Effect* (Oxford: Oxford University Press, 2004).

48. Lawrence R. Jacobs and Robert Y. Shapiro, *Politicians Don't Pander: Political Manipulation and the Loss of Democratic Responsiveness.* (Chicago: University of Chicago Press, 2000).

49. William Riker, *The Art of Political Manipulation*, (New Haven, CT: Yale University Press, 1986).

50. Jacob Hacker and Paul Pierson, *Off-Center: The Republican Revolution and the Erosion of American Democracy* (New Haven, CT: Yale University Press, 2006).

51. John Dunn, *Western Political Theory in the Face of the Future* (Cambridge: Cambridge University Press, 1977), ch. 1.

52. Thanks to Arash Abizadeh, Lance Blakesley, Jodi Finkel, Richard Fox, Michael Genovese, Evan Gerstmann, Brendan Richards, Seth Thompson, and anonymous reviewers for helpful comments on previous drafts of this introduction.

Part I

Democratic Theory

Introduction to Part I

The three essays collected in Part I focus on the normative theory of manipulation, and in particular on the difficulty of providing a satisfactory definition of the term and of distinguishing it from related phenomena such as persuasion. All three contributors to Part I employ a similar method and approach—philosophical analysis combined with careful application to real-world cases—but James Fishkin, Terence Ball, and Nathaniel Klemp each arrive at quite different conclusions about how to evaluate various instances of apparent manipulation. Unusually for current democratic theory, the exchange between these essays represents a departure from the self-cloistering of deliberative democrats on the one hand and their critics on the other, inviting conversation between these rival theoretical accounts. Fishkin is among the most prominent proponents of the deliberative democratic approach. Ball is, by contrast, straightforwardly critical of many of that approach's most fundamental assumptions. Klemp constitutes a kind of middle case: his point of departure shares much in common with the deliberative democratic perspective, but he qualifies that position sufficiently, particularly in his embrace of what he calls "strategic manipulation," as to move him quite some distance from Fishkin's and toward Ball's perspective.

Much regarding manipulation turns on the question of the term's definition, since most observers agree that whatever conduct we identify as "manipulative" would in many other contexts count as morally blamable, and that it therefore requires some additional level of justification, even if we ultimately approve it as a necessary or proper means of political action. As we noted in the introduction, all theories of manipulation necessarily rely on some background conception of what constitutes true democracy, and that is certainly true for these three essays. Fishkin's essay "Manipulation and Democratic Theory" defines manipulation specifically in opposition to the ideal of deliberative democracy. For Fishkin, persuasion (the morally permissible form of political communication) is defined as changing minds under conditions acceptable to our theory of democracy—which conditions in turn are defined as fair conditions of rational deliberation. Manipulation, by contrast, is a variation of persuasion that is morally objectionable, where what is morally objectionable about it is precisely its violation of the norms of rational deliberation. Whereas persuasion allows for changing minds under favorable conditions for democratic deliberation, in the case of manipulation undermining good conditions of deliberation is the point of the enterprise itself.

Terence Ball's essay "Manipulation: As Old As Democracy Itself (and Sometimes Dangerous)," in contrast, defines manipulation not by its form but rather by its outcome. His distinction between "democratic manipulation" and "undemocratic manipulation" depends on a background theory of democracy that defines which outcomes promote, and which outcomes hinder, the achievement of democratic ends. Ball emphasizes that there is inevitably a close connection between politics and manipulation, since manipulation is about controlling or moving things according to your will, and to some extent so (invariably) is politics—specifically, moving one another through language to action. Employing Fishkin's typology of democracy, Ball's account is probably closest to the model of "contestatory democracy," since Ball argues that a degree—even a very significant degree—of rough and tumble manipulation is acceptable, provided that it ultimately advances rather than inhibits the flourishing of democracy itself.

In Nathaniel Klemp's essay "When Rhetoric Becomes Manipulative: Disentangling Persuasion and Manipulation," we find an attempt to blend elements of both the deliberative and contestatory theories of democracy outlined by Fishkin and Ball. Like Fishkin, Klemp defines manipulation in opposition to a normative account of morally acceptable persuasion. In contrast to Fishkin's approach, however, Klemp supports Ball's position in seeking to make room for both deliberative persuasion and what Klemp calls "strategic persuasion," persuasion oriented toward contestatory victory rather than mutual understanding. Klemp's analysis introduces two new elements into our account of manipulation. First, Klemp argues for a (rebuttable) presumption of the immorality of manipulation, and offers both consequentialist and non-consequentialist grounds for this presumption (the consequentialist justifications mirror Ball's argument, while the non-consequentialist criteria reflect Fishkin's concerns). And second, Klemp introduces a distinction, similar to John Rawls's distinction between ideal and non-ideal theory, between morally justified versus morally decent forms of conduct. Deliberation that meets all Fishkin's criteria may be fully morally justified, according to Klemp, but even so, Klemp agrees with Ball that actions which fail Fishkin's criteria may nevertheless count as morally decent actions, all things considered.

We can usefully see what is distinctive in the competing approaches offered by Fishkin, Ball, and Klemp by comparing their models to the definition of manipulation surveyed in our introduction, that of Robert

Goodin. According to Goodin, the individually necessary and collectively sufficient components of manipulative action are (1) deception and (2) intentional interference with another agent's "putative will." On the issue of deception, we can see the distinction between Ball's and Fishkin's views with great clarity. For Ball, deception is, more or less straightforwardly, permissible in the pursuit of certain ends, namely the promotion of democracy and democratic citizenship. While there are features of deception that might tend to militate against these values in many circumstances, this is by no means a necessary relationship, and therefore deception is permissible in a variety of situations when it is necessary to promote rather than obstruct these values. Fishkin, by contrast, employs a definition of manipulation that largely rules out the possibility of any legitimate form of deception. At the same time, however, Fishkin's definition of manipulation stretches more broadly than Goodin's to include not just deceptive interferences with the putative wills of subjects, but all such interferences whether they are deceptive or not. As an illustration, Fishkin offers the example of political candidates seeking to keep voters away from the polls by using techniques such as negative ads which, while not deceptive, nevertheless can contribute to a significant interference with the subjects' putative wills by priming issues which would not otherwise matter most to the voters in question.

Klemp's theory mediates between these two extremes. His account defines deception quite broadly, encompassing not only lying itself but also concealment and, to some degree, distraction. Deception in this broader sense constitutes a necessary condition of manipulation, since it always includes at least one of these three elements. The key distinction Klemp stresses, however, is transparency, which in many ways aligns him most closely with Goodin's insistence on deception as the central defining characteristic of manipulation. Klemp notes that persuasive rhetoric is transparent and respects the autonomy of the various interlocutors, whereas manipulation, by his definition, makes full use of hidden and irrational forces with the intention of achieving a particular outcome. Thus at the heart of what is immoral about manipulation is the fact that it necessarily seeks to hide information and agendas and lure listeners toward a worldview that may not comport with the listeners' true preferences. Persuasion, by contrast, in both its deliberative and strategic forms, is always essentially open, distinguishing it from the hidden or irrational forces which constitute the essence of manipulation.

With respect to the question of putative wills, the three authors also take somewhat different approaches. Ball, for the most part, does not treat the question of the subjects' putative wills as particularly important. For Ball it is the outcome of the exchange, and in particular its consequence for promoting the institutions and values of democracy, that determines whether or not manipulation is morally permissible. But Fishkin and Klemp have both defined the problem of manipulation in such a way that the putative will of subjects is crucial to the question of whether we praise or blame particular conduct. Like other deliberative democrats, Fishkin is strongly inclined to define putative will in terms of deliberation. For Fishkin, a subject's putative will is the expected outcome of the process of deliberation when conducted under favorable conditions. Manipulation, on this account, is intentional interference with the putative will of those it affects (understood as the will they would have been disposed to form under good reasoning conditions). Whereas many other influential theories of democracy are inclined to take citizen preferences as given, one of the great strengths of the approach of deliberative democrats such as Fishkin is that it offers a standpoint from which to critique the process of preference formation itself. Preferences formed under good reasoning conditions, they argue, are worthy of deeper respect than those emerging from processes that are, by definition, tainted by manipulation.

Klemp problematizes manipulation further by showing that one way to look at manipulation is to see it as a way in which speakers are able to get us to change our beliefs or concepts without our consent. For Klemp, a change in a subject's putative will is definitely not by itself a sufficient condition for an accusation of manipulation. Persuasion is equally a change in a subjects' putative will, yet it is not normatively problematic. However, there are aspects of Klemp's analysis that accord considerable importance to the question of a subject's putative will. Specifically, Klemp claims that the diminishment or enhancement of autonomy (understood as roughly equivalent to the pursuit of the subject's true will) is the defining characteristic of manipulative versus non-manipulative behavior. In offering a normative ranking giving first place to deliberative, then to strategic, and lastly to manipulative forms of communication, Klemp underlines this judgment that the more autonomy-enhancing, the more legitimate; the more autonomy-diminishing, the less legitimate.

Finally, the essays differ in their treatments of the ideal of deliberation and its potential conflicts with the strategic realities of politics. Fishkin and Ball form the most striking contrast in this respect. Fishkin, speaking for the deliberative tradition, holds up deliberation's inherent commitment against manipulation as a reason for us to accept deliberative democracy as our preferred form of democratic theory. Since deliberative democracy defines deliberation specifically in opposition to manipulation, Fishkin asserts, it is the theory best suited to guard against the normative dangers which a more permissive attitude toward manipulation might entail. He asserts that through the use of deliberative practices—open discussions concerning policy preferences and interests—we might better be able to limit the manipulative practices that often skew the polity towards the interest of the few and away from the will of the public. Fishkin is aware of the strategic dimensions of politics, and in particular of the difficulties posed by attempting to transpose the results that emerge from his "deliberative microcosms" to application for the larger polity (problems which will re-emerge with a vengeance in the essays collected in part 3 of this volume). However, Fishkin does not argue directly with the idea promoted by both Ball and Klemp that non-deliberative strategic contestation might play a role in democratic exchange normatively worthy of our respect.

Ball's theory, by contrast, is very sensitive to the demands of strategic action, going to great lengths to accommodate it. In doing so, he criticizes the deliberative tradition, directly challenging Habermas and the perspective of the deliberative democrats who have followed him (implicitly including Fishkin). On Fishkin's typology, Ball's theory is one of contestatory democracy. Ball's view values the competitive dimensions of democracy and remains strongly committed to political equality and the non-domination of the political realm. Given Ball's definition of democracy, his view is also strongly committed to political participation—but it values deliberation only instrumentally as a means to these ends, for which reason it is willing to countenance versions of manipulation if they promote rather than hinder democracy's core values. Yet Ball's account seems to lack some of the specificity about what constitutes the essence of democracy that is offered by the rival deliberative account he criticizes.

Klemp's theory is grounded in the deliberative tradition, yet while he seeks to retain some of that tradition's insights, he simultaneously seeks to accommodate the importance of the strategic element of politics emphasized by Ball. Unlike Ball, Klemp is willing to grant considerable moral ground to the importance of deliberation, describing that kind of exchange as definitive of what is morally ideal in political communication. Yet in doing so Klemp co-opts a distinction drawn by Habermas himself—that between strategic action on the one hand and communicative or deliberative action on the other—in order to argue against Habermas in favor of the legitimacy of strategic persuasion. This form of persuasion shares certain factors in common with manipulation—for example, the legitimacy of emotional appeals—and Klemp is substantially more permissive of a strategic approach emphasizing such factors than the deliberative approach is generally willing to be. This is so because, for Klemp, deliberation defines the ideal, yet is not therefore the only morally permissible form of political persuasion. Such qualities as openness to revision, sincerity, and a focus on the merits of the case may be morally preferable, but are frequently not practically attainable. In such cases, Klemp follows John Rawls in distinguishing between the requirements of ideal and non-ideal theory, stressing that in non-ideal circumstances, such qualities as our willingness to revise our views, the sincerity of our arguments, and our selectivity in using facts and arguments may all have to yield to accommodate the realities on the ground.

As we can see from these three essays, not only is manipulation a contested concept, but what counts as manipulation is closely dependent on our conceptions of democracy and our normative commitments. For example, we see that, depending on one's underlying democratic theory, political manipulation can, under the right circumstances, count as a useful tool in promoting a more just democratic state, quite as much as its more reputable relative, deliberation. For at the heart of this discussion lies a deeper philosophical issue: the ethical relationship between the means and ends of any democratic state. If we define what is normatively valuable about democracy in terms of the particular ends it serves, as Ball does, then perhaps any method of achieving those ends, including manipulative ones, might be morally acceptable. By contrast, if like Fishkin (and to some extent Klemp as well) we view the means as being themselves at the core of what is morally valuable about democracy, as proceduralist conceptions of democracy such as the deliberative tradition are inclined to do, then one cannot employ manipulative means without in the process poisoning the ends of democracy. And there remains behind these issues a further and perhaps even more intractable difficulty—the fact that manipulative practices can themselves be employed in changing our ends, twisting and warping the preferences of the polity to its own purposes until the public no longer knows how to say any more which ends are truly its own. This capacity may in the end prove to be the most dangerous of manipulation's many normative challenges to democratic life.

1 Manipulation and Democratic Theory

James S. Fishkin

Consider some famous examples of political manipulation. I have chosen examples from other countries and times to give us the perspective of distance. Since manipulation is a negative and contentious term, it is worth stepping back from current partisan divisions in order to clarify the phenomenon.

In Britain, the 1924 Labour government of Ramsay Macdonald loses the election in part because of the publication of a fake letter from the Soviet head of the Comintern, Grigory Zinoviev. The Conservatives win with a red scare drum beat of fear that Labour is in league with the Soviets, who were in fact preaching continuous world revolution. In 1999, a British parliamentary inquiry opened up the historical issues, concluding that officials in the Foreign Office knew the letter was fake but were happy to see the Labour government discredited right before the election.

In the Australian election of 2001, John Howard and his government falsely claimed that a boatload of immigrants had thrown their children overboard in order to try and seek asylum in Australia. Howard used this to whip up anti-immigrant sentiment and pull ahead of Labour in the polls just before the election. A later Senate inquiry in Australia determined that the Howard government knew that the allegations were false.

In Taiwan in March 2004, President Chen Shui-bian and Vice President Annette Lu were apparently the target of an assassination attempt on the eve of the election. A sympathy vote allowed them to pull ahead by 29,000 votes. Later it seemed that the assassination might have been faked. If so, it would be another case of political manipulation.

Add to these the more familiar cases of the "Willie Horton" ads deployed against Michael Dukakis in 1988 and the "Swift Boat Veterans for Truth" ads deployed against John Kerry in 2004.

Some of the Willie Horton ads and all the Swift Boat ads reflect the fact that campaign warfare is increasingly "asymmetrical." Just as states now face non-state actors where deterrence breaks down because the attack has no clear return address (no one knows who the terrorists are or how to find them), so political campaigns face attacks from third parties that also have no clear return address. The beneficiaries can keep their hands clean, avoiding public responsibility for the attacks. And if a campaign dialogue is hijacked by a new dimension or a trivial one, the result is literally **MAD**, what I would call **mutually assured distraction.**

Consider a policy example outside the context of elections. Interest groups now launch campaign-like advertising combined with lobbying. The coal industry has repeatedly mounted campaigns on behalf of tax subsidies for so-called clean coal. The ads describe how much cleaner and how much better for the environment clean coal is, never making it clear that the tax subsidies could divert energy use away from much cleaner sources. Clean coal may be cleaner than dirty coal, but it is much dirtier than natural gas or renewable energy. Note in this case the use of strategically incomplete rather than false information.[1] One successful wave of these efforts led to the Energy Policy Act of 2005, which included large tax subsidies for clean coal which the Bush administration implemented.

We live in a society that values freedom of expression and association—as a matter of right. The system of freedom of expression presumes that many forms of advocacy take place. What is the dividing line between mere advocacy and something that is presumably objectionable (even if lawful) that might be termed manipulation? Stephen Ansolabehere and Shanto Iyengar suggest a definition in the course of their important study of negative advertising: "Manipulation involves leading voters to select politicians who ultimately do not represent the individual's interests and preferences."[2]

This definition, while suggestive, does not cover all the terrain sketched here. First, I am interested in including efforts to manipulate voters, not only about candidate choice but also about policy choice. Second, to the extent independents are intentionally caused to change their behavior by staying home or voting otherwise than they would, this definition, as interpreted in *Going Negative*, would not term the intervention manipulation. As they operationalize their definition, voters have to have a stable party preference (representing their interests and preferences) which they are led away from by the manipulation, and independents do not have such a preference. Even if they are led to change their vote by negative ads (and 6 percent did in the study), this change was not viewed as manipulation since they had no stable party preference from which they were dissuaded. Instead Ansolabehere and Iyengar simply termed such results "worrisome" but not manipulation.[3]

In my view, all the cases mentioned are manipulation, including the calculated effort to reduce turnout, a possible use of negative ads according to Ansolabehere and Iyengar. The definition I would suggest is something like:

A person has been *manipulated* by a communication when she has been exposed to a message intended to change her views in a way she would not accept if she were to think about it on the basis of good conditions—and in fact she does change her views in the manner that was intended.

So, if she is fooled by misinformation and changes her views on that basis, then she has been manipulated. If she had good information instead, then on this definition, her views would not have changed.

In the Zinoviev case, it is likely that the voters who were changed were not Labour voters, since there was widespread sympathy for the Soviet Union among Labour voters in the early years of the Soviet Union. Rather, it was most likely independent voters who were switched and Conservative voters who were mobilized who might not have voted at all otherwise.

In the Australian case where the Howard campaign claimed that the immigrants threw their children overboard in order to gain admission to the country, there was no problem of mobilization since Australia has compulsory voting. But the sensational incident primed immigration as the key issue when it had not been a top issue at all before then in the election. It changed the basis for voting. If voters had known that the sensational charges were false and known to be false, this hijacking of an election soon before the vote through priming would not have succeeded. As one press report after the Senate inquiry summarized it, the Howard government "exploited voters' fears of a wave of illegal immigrants by demonising asylum-seekers."[4]

In the case of Willie Horton, the combustible focus group tested ads primed crime and Dukakis's judgment as issues for decision, based on a misleading account of a single incident. In the case of the Swift Boats, false allegations primed Kerry's character as the issue. The Swift Boat campaign may well have swung the election given how close it was.

In the case of the clean coal ads, if citizens had the facts about the competing energy choices, they would be unlikely to support incentives for coal compared to natural gas and renewable energy. The apparent facts are strategically incomplete, laying out the advantages of so-called clean over dirty coal, but not compared to the other alternatives.

In the case of negative ads being used to intentionally demobilize voters, if I would have voted were it not for the negative ads intended to get me *not* to vote, my behavior has been changed in the direction intended. And I am assuming that if a voter deliberated, she would likely cast a vote rather than just stay home. Or at least this would be the case in many elections where negative ads succeed in getting people to stay home. For those cases, there are clear grounds for claiming manipulation on this view.

In all these cases, the definition of manipulation turns in part on the alternative of good conditions and good information we are hypothesizing as a benchmark for comparison. Those good conditions are in fact, a good part of what I mean by deliberation, a process we attempt to implement empirically in the conduct of Deliberative Polling.

By hypothesizing what people would think under good conditions as a point of comparison, we are not asserting that whenever people are not deliberating they are then being manipulated. Others must actually *intend* to manipulate opinion in a given direction for the opinions to be manipulated. And the good conditions defined by deliberation are just a benchmark for comparison—a way of clarifying what is short circuited by manipulation. Perhaps manipulators want me to think X. Perhaps I would in fact think X, if I deliberated about the issue (particularly if I considered the competing arguments and had good information about them). On the definition offered here, I have not been manipulated if that is the case and I do think X.[5]

We can think of deliberation and manipulation as poles on a continuum. At one end we have good conditions and at the other end we have severely distorted conditions intentionally created in order to influence behavior. The good conditions include balanced messages with reasonably accurate information. Balance means that arguments offered are answered in a substantive way by arguments reflecting a competing side and those arguments are answered in turn and so on. And the information employed in these messages is factual and accurate. When arguments are offered and then answered substantively in turn, strategically incomplete arguments are defused. For example, a clean coal advocate could talk about how much better clean coal is than dirty coal, but the case for adopting clean coal would have to face criticism from the advocates of other cleaner sources. At the other end of the continuum, we have unbalanced and inaccurate messages. Arguments offered are not answered. And the lack of substantive balance and the inaccuracies are intended to move opinion in a given direction.

What is the difference between manipulation and persuasion? In a society valuing free speech, we fill the airwaves with persuasion. Clearly, there will be areas on the continuum where it is hard to distinguish. But the end points make it clear. The messages in deliberation are intended to persuade, but in a dialogue or debate in which accurate information is available and in which it is expected that the other side will have its say. Hence clear misinformation or strategically incomplete arguments that would collapse if the other side were voiced would be avoided in deliberative processes. At the other pole, the knowing use of such misinformation or misleading information is the point of the message. Perhaps you have an overwhelming ad buy or perhaps you know the charges are so sensational they will receive a massive hearing, drowning out any response. Persuasion is the life blood of politics and policymaking. Manipulation is its objectionable form. But from the standpoint of democratic theory, what, if anything, is wrong with manipulation even in its supposedly objectionable form? The answer depends on your theory of democracy. On some theories, there are no grounds for objection. But that only helps to clarify the debate about what it is that we should ultimately value about democracy.

Four Democratic Theories

To distill a longer discussion down to its essentials, I want to reduce the variety of democratic theories down to four. These four theories are distinctive combinations of four basic principles—political equality, deliberation, mass participation, and non-tyranny. Elsewhere I have developed this account in detail so I will try to just quickly summarize it here.[6] I have argued that while there are, in theory, sixteen possible combinations of commitments to these four principles, the ones that have serious normative interest reduce to four: competitive democracy, elite deliberation, participatory democracy, and deliberative democracy.

The four democratic theories each make an explicit commitment to two of the principles and leave open what they say about the other two. Their position on the other two can be taken as an empirical question or as a question that they are just not concerned about. I indicate their commitment to the principles of central concern by a "+" and their agnosticism about the other principles by a "?" (see Table 1.1).

The four positions are prominent and recognizable. First consider competitive democracy. Here the idea popularized by Joseph Schumpeter and more recently championed by Richard Posner and Ian Shapiro is that democracy is about the "competitive struggle for the people's vote."[7] But like many adversary processes, the key is winning by whatever means is available within the rules. And the rules do little or nothing to prevent the public from being bamboozled, misled, or manipulated in the ways already catalogued.

I have adjusted the position slightly to commit it to political equality in the equal counting of votes. Schumpeter, unlike his successors, was notoriously unconcerned about equally counting the votes of everyone.[8] The basic idea is that we let the parties compete as teams that will peacefully settle the question of who governs, and we allow courts to protect rights to ensure against tyranny of the majority or other truly objectionable abuses. But if really intense competition produces manipulation, that is just how the rough game of politics is played. Hard political competition among competing teams of elites has greater normative appeal if the votes are counted equally. But the issues of extreme preference distortion, what

Table 1.1 Four Democratic Theories

	Competitive Democracy	Elite Deliberation	Participatory Democracy	Deliberative Democracy
Political equality	+	?	+	+
Participation	?	?	+	?
Deliberation	?	+	?	+
Non-tyranny	+	+	?	+

we have been calling manipulation, are a continuing vulnerability of the position.

A second democratic theory, by contrast, prizes deliberation—but only by elites or representatives. Deliberation requires the balanced and informed weighing of competing arguments on their merits on the basis of good information. We will say more about this below, but, clearly, the deficiencies that permit manipulation are, by and large, responded to by deliberation. Note that the elite deliberation position does not require political equality. It is deliberation by elites—as with the Madisonian picture of filtered public opinion by representatives who "refine and enlarge the public views" as Madison posited famously in Federalist 10. It is not a position that encourages mass participation. Once again, there is a concern for protecting against tyranny of the majority, but an argument that deliberation itself may better serve the public interest than would nondeliberative public opinion.

A third democratic theory prizes the combination of mass participation and political equality. One can imagine more and more decisions becoming the purview of plebiscitary democracy or mass decision. But as I argue elsewhere it is very difficult to foster serious mass public deliberation. Each individual in the large scale nation state has incentives for "rational ignorance" and, in that sense, little reason to pay attention and become informed about the details of public policy issues. Participatory democracy may signal a certain kind of mass consent, typified by a referendum, but it need not be a very thoughtful or informed sort of consent. Referendum campaigns can be as misleading and bamboozling as candidate elections, as most observers of initiative, referendum, and recall in the western U.S. states will attest.

A fourth democratic theory would embrace the combination of deliberation and political equality. The idea is that the mass public should somehow deliberate and its deliberations should be made consequential for public decisions. One clear strategy for achieving this combination of political equality and deliberation is the deliberative microcosm chosen by lot or random sampling—a form of democracy that goes back to ancient Athens. Every citizen has an equal chance of being selected and the processes themselves attempt to embody political equality. But in addition, the discussions attempt to be substantive and balanced on the basis of good information. As we have seen, the provision of substantive and balanced information, in a context where people pay attention to it, can be an antidote to manipulation.

Facilitating the Public Will

One reason to argue for one of the two deliberative theories (elite deliberation or deliberative democracy) is that without some such commitment there are no really fundamental grounds for objecting to the kind of manipulation we surveyed at the beginning, the kind that clearly undermines any claim to collective informed consent. What could consent of the governed mean if the people are simply misled? Participatory democracy and competitive democracy do not deal with the issue of preference formation; they deal with how people vote or participate with the preferences they have. Once the issue of preference formation is highlighted, then there are grounds for demanding that people get good information, have access to arguments on competing sides, and have the chance to weigh the merits of those arguments—in short, that they deliberate to some substantial degree.

If one believes that public will formation is potentially meaningful, then manipulation is objectionable, because it is intended to undermine and distort the public will for the sake of political advantage. By contrast, deliberation is to be prized on such a perspective because it facilitates public will formation. It facilitates the provision of competing reasons that are to be weighed in the process of the people making up its mind.

Yet the deliberative microcosm chosen by random sampling, brought to realization in the modern era with efforts such as Deliberative Polling, is not necessarily efficacious in undermining manipulation. A key problem is that manipulation may work with the broader public even if it encounters an antidote in the deliberations of a microcosm.

One strategy is to make the deliberations of the microcosm consequential in themselves. In that way, deliberation by the microcosm, rather than manipulation of the broader public, is consequential in its impact. In Texas, a series of Deliberative Polls were employed in "Integrated Resource Planning" to decide how electric power was to be provided in each of the state's eight regulated service territories. The deliberations were balanced and informative. The real benefits of coal, availability and price, were weighed against environmental effects. The meaning of clean coal came out in the discussion since advocates of all the competing energy sources answered questions on the same panel. While support for coal was modest in most of the eight projects, support for renewable energy and for natural gas (which is cleaner than coal) was consistently high. The eight projects led directly to massive investments in wind power, moving Texas from one of the lowest states in wind power in 1996 to the leading state by 2007.

The key in Texas was that the microcosm was empowered to the extent that the official integrated resource plans had to take account of the results of the Deliberative Poll. It is not at all clear what the results might have been if the issue had been decided simply in open meetings or by referendum. In open meetings self-selected groups of lobbyists or advocates could have distorted the process. In a referendum campaign subject to advertising techniques, manipulation of the results would certainly have been possible. But in the transparently balanced and substantive atmosphere of a microcosmic deliberation, the strategies of misinformation or strategically incomplete information can be countered among those who decide. And a microcosm of the mass public will tend to come with an open mind and be available to weigh arguments on the merits.

The basic idea of a deliberating microcosm is not, by itself, enough to avoid manipulation. Random sampling is extremely useful to prevent capture by self-selected groups that could mobilize to distort and in that sense offer a pseudo-public consultation. Norman Bradburn, former director of the National Opinion Research Center, has coined the term SLOPs for self-selected listener opinion polls, and there are many public consultations, especially those that take place online, that purport to represent the public but that actually represent efforts to capture a representation of public opinion through mobilization. SLOPs allow people to vote over and over and to offer their intense views as if they were representative of the broader mass public. Random sampling engages social science to prevent capture and create a microcosm. Of course then, the question is what are the good conditions to which the microcosm is subjected.

A second guarantee against manipulation is the avoidance of false consensus through social pressure. Public consultations that seek agreement, in the mode of jury verdicts, will expose participants to social pressure to reach agreement. It is a far better guarantee to avoid consensus-seeking processes and to gather the opinions, before and after, in confidential questionnaires or secret ballots.

A third institutional design that can help avoid manipulation is to arrange for an advisory committee for the process that includes the competing stakeholders. If policy elites have to agree on an account of the initial basis for discussion, the competing arguments that most deserve a hearing on the basis of good information, then they lose their opportunity to distort the process with misinformation or strategically incomplete information. In Deliberative Polls, an advisory group typically involves all the competing stakeholders who have to agree on a briefing document suitable for the mass public. This briefing document lays out the main policy options with arguments for and against, agreed to by the competing stakeholders and experts. They need not (and will not) agree about what should be done. But they can agree that the information in the briefing document is accurate and that the main arguments on either side have been expressed clearly and in a balanced way. The work from such an advisory group is a useful and simple institutional bulwark against manipulation of the microcosm.

A fourth institutional design is the use of moderated small group discussions that ensure balance and that prevent anyone from dominating the discussions. The key nexus for deliberation is a manageably small group discussion that allows balanced participation in an atmosphere of mutual respect. Trained moderators can do a great deal to facilitate such discussions.

But even with an appropriate institutional design that avoids manipulation of the microcosm, manipulation of the broader mass public is entirely possible through the normal investments in strategic communication through the media. Even here, deliberating microcosms can be useful, however. A Deliberative Poll, for example, can offer a road map to responsible advocacy. By responsible advocacy, I mean advocacy based on good information and balanced argumentation. In a Deliberative Poll, when conducted well, the best arguments on each side have been tested against each other in a context where the public can get its questions answered and focus on the merits. The arguments that succeed in such an environment clearly have weight with the public if given an appropriate airing. Retracing that argumentation with good information is not manipulation, because it reproduces the considerations that weigh with the public under good conditions.

For example, in the European-wide Deliberative Poll, the contentious issue of pension reform revealed surprisingly that the EU public was willing to work longer and raise the retirement age in order to keep the current "pay as you go" pension systems solvent.[9] Once they realized the demographic and fiscal challenges ahead, the changing ratios of retirees compared to workers and the resulting deficits facing the pension systems if the current retirement ages and benefits were kept in place, deliberators moved to support keeping the benefits but paying for them by working to a later age. They preferred this solution to privatizing the systems, probably because of the risks involved in individual accounts. These results suggest a strategy for successful advocacy of how to keep the pay as you go systems solvent but with a clear sacrifice (later retirement) as part of the trade-off. The demographic and fiscal information about what would happen with continuation of the status quo is a necessary backdrop to the success of the argument.

Democratic practices have largely traced a path from Madison (who conceived of adapting the public will to a Republic in the late eighteenth century) to Madison Avenue (the home of the advertising industry). But there is a crucial distinction between manipulative practices of persuasion, which we tolerate for selling consumer products, and the sort of collective public will formation that makes democracy meaningful. Some democratic theories do not aspire to collective will formation. In our typology of four theories, only two make the thinking processes of the public central. The two deliberative theories (whether the deliberations of representatives on behalf of the people or the deliberations by the people themselves) provide at least a partial antidote to manipulation. For the other two theories, there is no fundamental basis for objecting to manipulation. For those theories, the key is just that there be elections, no matter how distorted in substance, or that there be participation, no matter what the people are thinking, or not thinking. If one wishes to revise participatory or competitive democracy to take account of manipulation, one enters the realm of at least some commitment to deliberation, some commitment to the notion that the people not be misled or have their views determined on grounds other than those they would think defensible if they thought about it. Avoiding manipulation, one is led to deliberation—to at least some degree and in some institutional contexts by or on behalf of the people. The cure for Madison Avenue is a dose of Madison, or at least the value Madison emphasized but thought most suitable for representatives.

Notes

1. See Richard Conniff, "The Myth of Clean Coal," Yale 360 at http://e360. yale.edu/content/feature.msp?id=2014
2. Stephen Ansolabehere and Shanto Iyengar, *Going Negative* (New York: Free Press, 1995), p. 65.
3. Ansolabehere and Iyengar, *Going Negative*, p. 95.
4. Kim Arlington, "Hawke: Children Overboard the Most Despicable of Lies." *Melbourne Age*, August 24, 2004, http://www.theage.com.au/articles/ 2004/08/24/1093246520431.html?from=storylhs
5. Manipulation is sometimes used more broadly, but I am focusing here on its objectionable forms.
6. See my *When the People Speak: Deliberative Democracy and Public Consultation* (Oxford: Oxford University Press, 2009).
7. Joseph A. Schumpeter, *Capitalism, Socialism and Democracy* (New York: Harper and Row, 1942); Richard A. Posner, *Law, Pragmatism and Democracy* (Cambridge, MA: Harvard University Press, 2003), p. 269; and Ian Shapiro *The Moral Foundations of Politics* (New Haven, CT: Yale University Press, 2002).
8. See Robert A. Dahl, *Democracy and its Critics* (New Haven, CT: Yale University Press, 1989), pp. 121–22 for a critique of Schumpeter on the issue of inclusion.
9. See http://cdd.stanford.edu/polls/eu

2 Manipulation

As Old as Democracy Itself (and Sometimes Dangerous)*

Terence Ball

When we think of manipulation we are likely to come up with a list of nefarious examples. High on my own list would be the following. "Ideology" and "false consciousness" (Karl Marx). "The manufacture of consent" (Walter Lippmann and Noam Chomsky).[1] "Hidden persuaders" (Vance Packard). Brainwashing. And movies: *The Manchurian Candidate. The Stepford Wives. The Truman Show.* All of these, and many more besides, draw upon a deep well of anxiety about being manipulated. This is not necessarily a neurotic but an altogether healthy anxiety. To the degree that our thoughts and actions are manipulated by others, we are unfree and our autonomy is threatened. Or so it might appear. I want to suggest that such appearances may be misleading, at least in some circumstances.

Before I begin, a caveat: I am not concerned here with any and all kinds of manipulation, but only with *political* manipulation. That is, for present purposes I am not interested in the kind of manipulation used by a Lothario or Don Juan to seduce young women, nor that employed by Bernard Madoff and other crooked financiers to hoodwink investors. Instead, I want to explore selected aspects of the *public* or *political* manipulation of the beliefs, outlooks and attitudes of *citizens* by orators and others. More specifically still, my aim is to address the matter of manipulation as it relates to democracy. In so doing, I propose to take issue with what seems to me to be an unexamined assumption that underlies many inquiries into and critiques of manipulation, i.e., that manipulation is necessarily bad and that political manipulation is antithetical to democracy and to the actions and interactions of democratic citizens. This is, of course, an important and influential theoretical perspective advanced by (among others) Jürgen Habermas.

Habermas holds that deception and other forms of manipulation are categorically wrong and that only truth-telling and "the forceless force of the better argument" should hold sway in democratic discourse and determine the outcome of political debate and discussion.[2] This I believe to be both utopian and unworkable, and perhaps even, in some instances, undesirable. Manipulation of a certain sort has its proper place in democratic politics (as a dedicated small-d democrat, I do, however, have objections to certain *kinds* of manipulation).[3] Instead of making my case in the form of an abstract argument, I propose to consider a series of brief (but, I hope, illuminating) case studies. These run the gamut from the role of the theater in Athenian democracy to Lincoln's Gettysburg Address and other familiar texts, which I hope to show in a somewhat different and unconventional light.

I plan to proceed in the following way. First, I want to say something about the concept of manipulation, and particularly how its primary meaning has shifted away from one involving physical referents to more mental and political ones. The latter involves manipulating the minds of citizens by means of rhetoric or oratory, among other means. Next, I shall suggest that there is nothing necessarily un- or anti-democratic about manipulation, by drawing and subsequently defending a distinction between *democratic* and *undemocratic* manipulation. I then go on to offer a series of illustrations of democratic manipulation. These are then followed by several illustrations of undemocratic manipulation, as analyzed by Aristotle and possibly exemplified by some of the machinations of the recently retired Bush-Cheney administration.

I

Our words "manipulate" and "manipulation" derive from the Latin *manus*, meaning "hand." Manipulation originally meant moving things about by using one's hands. We sometimes still use the word with this meaning in mind. But nowadays by "manipulation" we more often mean moving people (not things) by using language (not hands). The late Swiss political theorist Bertrand de Jouvenel observed that "The elementary political process is the action of mind upon mind through speech."[4] Politics is the practice of using language to move people to think and act in ways that they might not otherwise think and act (and interact). There is a longstanding link between rhetoric or oratory—persuasive speech—and politics, as Plato and his pupil Aristotle were among the first to recognize and reflect upon in a theoretical way. Nowadays, the oft-heard dismissive remark, "Oh, that's just rhetoric," is not merely a slap at persuasive speech but also at politics itself, that is, the action of mind upon mind through speech. At a much more refined theoretical level, a similar slap is administered by some theorists of deliberative democracy and the proponents of the-truth-and-nothing-but-the-truth political discourse. I happen to have both civic and professional reasons for believing that this attitude represents a real loss, and for thinking that it is important to counter and resist this dismissive—and even, I believe, dangerous—view.

We are apt to think—or rather to assume without thinking—that "democracy" and "manipulation" are incompatible, and that manipulation means the corruption or subversion of democracy. And this is because democracy is an open and transparent form of government, while manipulation is done in the dark, behind closed doors, by devious anti-democrats bent on having their own way, even if that means subverting democracy itself. I want to suggest that this is a caricature. Now, like any good caricature, it contains a grain of truth; but this caricature can be, and often is, misleading, as I hope to show.

The first thing to note is that democracy and manipulation have been bedfellows since the origin of democracy. One of the stock weapons in the arsenal of aristocrats and other opponents of democracy is the assertion that, of all forms of government, democracy is most open to manipulation—to disinformation, appeals to prejudice, and the machinations of demagogues. Instead of rule by the wise one (monarchy) or the best few (aristocracy), democracy was rule by and on behalf of the unwise and unwashed many, the *demos*, the ordinary people, the craftsmen and artisans who were largely uneducated and unlettered and therefore amenable to manipulation by a cunning individual or cabal. This claim—and arguments against it—were rehearsed repeatedly in Athens, and nowhere more pointedly than in the theater.

II

The theater in Athens was not merely a space for the performance of plays but was itself a democratic forum in which the problems of democratic self-rule were rendered in fictional form, dramatized, and performed in the open air.[5] There is a very long list of plays, both comedies and tragedies, with democratic themes and political problems at their center: Think, for example, of such comedies as Aristophanes' *Lysistrata* and *The Congresswomen* or tragedies such as Sophocles' *Antigone* and Aeschylus' *The Persians*. I could make and illustrate my argument about the intimate relation between democracy and manipulation by focusing on any or all of these well-known plays. But for the sake of brevity, I want to focus on only one play—Euripides' *The Suppliants*, first performed in Athens in 422 B.C.E.

The subject of *The Suppliants* is justice versus revenge, and how democracy favors the former and tyranny the latter. The setting of *The Suppliants*, like that of Euripides' rival Sophocles' tragedy *Antigone*, is the immediate aftermath of the fratricidal war in Thebes, in which Oedipus' two star-crossed sons, Polynices and Eteocles, slay one another. The Thebans, under the generalship of Prince Eteocles, defeated the invading Argive forces led by his rebellious brother Polynices. Their uncle, Creon, becomes the new *tyrannos* of Thebes and, as a demonstration of his supposed strength and superiority, he refuses (in stark contravention of religious ritual) to allow the bodies of the slain Argive soldiers to be collected and buried (his traitorous nephew Polynices receives the same treatment). The suppliants who give this drama its name are the mothers of the slain soldiers who come to Athens to appeal to the Athenian leader Theseus.

Righteously angered by Theban injustice, Theseus takes the suppliants' side and, to make a long story short, he recovers the bodies of the slain soldiers after waging war against Thebes and defeating Creon's Theban army. Justice triumphs over injustice, and democracy over tyranny.

Here I want to focus on a single short scene in *The Suppliants*. Creon has sent a messenger to Athens to say that Thebes has no quarrel with Athens and that Athens should not meddle in Thebes' and Creon's internal affairs. The unnamed messenger has just arrived in Athens and is met by Theseus. My text is from *The Suppliants*, lines 394–465:

Theban messenger: Who is the tyrant who rules this land? To whom must I deliver my message from Creon, ruler of Thebes?

Theseus: Esteemed visitor, your speech proceeds from a false premise. No tyrant rules here, for this city is free. Here the people rule, without respect to wealth or poverty.

Messenger: Surely you jest. The city from which I come is ruled not by the gullible multitude but by one man only. No one there uses high-sounding words to pander to the crowd, manipulating them for his own advantage while cloaking his crimes and failures in fair-sounding phrases. So I ask you: since the common people are such poor judges of everything, how can they possibly govern the city? They have neither the time nor the talent to understand the intricacies of politics. Even if he had been educated, a poor working stiff would have no time or energy left over from his labors to learn about political affairs. Besides, wiser and better people would recoil from a system in which such a man might, through his own way with words, manipulate the people and rise from being a nobody to occupy high office.

Theseus: You yourself have a way with words and would, if you could, fool us with your kit of clever verbal tricks. But since you have chosen to play this game of words, permit me to take my turn while you listen. Nothing is worse for a city than a tyrant. Wherever he rules, the law does not. In his hands there is no law that rules over all alike. But where the laws (*nomoi*) rule, all—rich and poor, powerful and weak—are equal before them. There the poor are able to speak the same language as the strong—the language of law and justice. If his cause be just, a poor man can prevail against a wealthy adversary. The hallmark of freedom is this: Anyone having good advice to give to the city should be heard ... What greater equality (*isonomia*) can exist in a city? [Theseus goes on to give a long list of the vices of tyrants, before concluding as follows:] This thunderbolt I hurl in answer to your words.... If you weren't a messenger and therefore under the protection of the law, you would pay dearly for your outrageous remarks. It is the messenger's duty to deliver one message and to return with another. So take this reply back to Creon: Next time, send a messenger who talks less foolishly than this one.[6]

Now, what exactly is going on here? Several things, simultaneously. The first is a rehash of common criticisms of democracy (from the Theban messenger). The second is a countering of these criticisms (from Theseus). The third is a criticism of tyranny (from Theseus). And—not least—the fourth is a masterful "stroking" of the Athenian audience, the vast majority of whose members would have been democrats (this from the playwright himself).

Taken together, these constitute a kind of manipulation, albeit perhaps of a rather benign kind that is cheerful, uplifting, and self-congratulatory: "It's morning in Athens." But all this has a darker and more serious side, in that it serves to remind the audience that (1) There are criticisms—and critics—of their cherished democracy and their democratic way of life. (2) These critics do not and need not come from abroad (as the Theban messenger did), but are present within the ranks of the Athenian citizenry (as Athens' repeated cycles of democratic and aristocratic or tyrannical rule so amply attest—most notoriously the Thirty Tyrants who ruled briefly but bloodily from 404 until 403 B.C.E. until being overthrown by the resurgent democracy). (3) The audience is also reminded that under certain circumstances and conditions these criticisms of democracy can be and are *valid*—the common people sometimes actually *are* gullible and open to manipulation by demagogues (which means, literally, leaders of the *demos*). Sometimes citizens *are* ignorant, intolerant, and inattentive to matters of common concern. (4) The audience is also reminded that democratic citizenship is a protracted struggle within and among themselves to render these criticisms of democracy *in*valid—for example, by being informed, attentive, and on guard against mindlessly following demagogues and other manipulators bent on undermining or destroying their democracy. (5) And, not least, eternal vigilance against the ever-present possibility of un- or anti-democratic manipulation is the price of democratic liberty.

But—and here is my main point in a nutshell—not all manipulation is necessarily un- or anti-democratic. Euripides, Sophocles and other tragedians were masterful manipulators of people's beliefs and emotions, such that, as Aristotle noted in his *Poetics*, a *katharsis* (an intellectual and emotional purging or cleansing) would have taken place by play's end.[7] Nor, of course, was such manipulation confined to the theater.

Pericles' famous Funeral Oration is a masterpiece of manipulation, but it is a premier example of *democratic manipulation*. It belongs to a readily recognizable oratorical genre in ancient Greece, the *epitaphios logos* (epitaph speech or funeral oration), which consists of a number of standard rhetorical moves, the sum total of which is to commemorate—that is, to remember together—the lives and sacrifices of the glorious dead who have fallen in Athens' defense. They gave their lives that Athens—and Athenian democracy—might live.[8] The funeral oration was one important way in which, as Nicole Loreaux has argued persuasively, Athens was able to regularly rejuvenate or "reinvent" itself by recalling its recent and ancient history, to reinvigorate the civic spirit of the Athenians so that they might love their democracy all the more and be willing to forgo their comforts and even to lay down their lives, if need be, that it might live and remain the birthright of their children and their children's children.[9] (I'll suggest shortly that this is also what Abraham Lincoln attempted to do with the Gettysburg Address, the American funeral oration par excellence.)

So how do we distinguish between democratic and undemocratic manipulation? As a rough first cut the distinction can be described and defended as follows. Democratic manipulation serves to promote, protect, and defend democracy. It is speech that warns citizens against dangers posed by ignorance or inattentiveness or the machinations of demagogues, that educates and inspires them to be better democratic citizens, that motivates them to put into practice the principles of the democratic creed, that promotes justice and equality, and so on. Undemocratic manipulation, by contrast, undermines democracy and democratic citizenship by, among other things, withholding information that citizens and/or their representatives need in order to arrive at reasonable and informed decisions regarding legislation and public policy; telling lies about matters of mutual or common concern; spreading disinformation that deceives the public and/or their representatives; playing to (and upon) the fears and prejudices of the citizenry; and so on. These are precisely the tactics and techniques of tyrants. The classic discussion of undemocratic or tyrannical manipulation can be found in Book 5 of Aristotle's *Politics*, to which I will return in my conclusion.

III

To this point my illustrations of democratic manipulation have come from the ancient world. But Americans—many of them, anyway, including many of my students—are impatient with and unimpressed by examples drawn from a world long dead. They are impatient with the past, and their attitude rather resembles Henry Ford's: "History is bunk." But surely this widely shared attitude is a strange one for Americans, of all people, to hold. And that is because Americans live in a constitutional republic that was designed and created by men who believed that history taught lessons and that the most valuable of these lessons derived from antiquity (Dryden's translation of Plutarch's *Lives of the Noble Greeks and Romans* was a staple of every gentleman's library).

To read the records of the constitutional convention in Philadelphia, and subsequently the two sides of the ratification debate of 1787–88— *The Federalist* and assorted Antifederalist papers—is to be struck by the importance the founding generation attached to history, and especially ancient history, not for its own sake but because it teaches us about the attractions *and the dangers* of democratic government.[10] Their problem was to devise a form of government that was popular, i.e., of and by the people, but that was largely immune to the perils and dangers of democracy in its classical sense.

Before we get to the Federalist/Antifederalist debates over ratification, however, let's look again at a most familiar—perhaps, indeed, a too-familiar—document, the Declaration of Independence. In my newly adopted state of Arizona, the legislature recently decreed that high school students be required by law to memorize the first (and, frankly, most memorable) part of the Declaration. Surely, this is to some degree a good thing: nowadays too few students ever memorize anything, and this (from what little I know about cognitive science) impairs cognitive development. But when I ask my grandchildren, who have dutifully memorized the required portion of the Declaration, what this or that word or phrase or passage means, they give that all-too-familiar deer-in-the-headlights look. "That's not part of the assignment," they say. "We just have to know the words." And so, like students in some Middle Eastern *madrassa*, they memorize what they are required to memorize of our own sacred text. It's not for nothing that Pauline Maier calls the Declaration "American Scripture."[11]

If we are to recognize and appreciate the real or pre-scriptural purpose and meaning of the Declaration of Independence, we must restore it to its original setting in the context of Great Britain's American colonies in the mid-1770s. The Declaration was intended to accomplish a particular purpose—to inspire, to motivate and, yes, to manipulate public opinion not only in Britain's America colonies but in Britain itself and, no less importantly, in France. There is scarcely a word or phrase in that document that is not designed to appeal both to the emotions and the intellect. That we can still feel their power even today attests to the appeal that the Declaration had to the colonists, many of whom could not read, but who heard it read aloud in coffee houses, taverns, and on street corners all across the thirteen American colonies. Jefferson meant it to be read aloud, to motivate and to inspire, to point to a possible world that existed in imagination and aspiration only, and not (yet) in fact.[12] (In these respects the Declaration resembles the Pledge of Allegiance, to be considered shortly.) Thus the Declaration, as Lincoln later recognized, was addressed to posterity as much as to those present in 1776.[13]

That is why John C. Calhoun's pro-slavery and anti-egalitarian diatribe against the Declaration strikes us as so flat-footed, pedantic, and laughable. His critique is, in effect, that the Declaration offers a defective description of human nature and the natural order. The Declaration, on

Calhoun's telling, is a blatant exercise in manipulation that rational folk such as himself and his fellow Southern slave-holders (or sympathizers) will recognize as such, and repudiate. Here is Calhoun:

> ... [The key proposition in the Declaration of Independence] is the most false and dangerous of all political errors. The proposition to which I allude, has become an axiom in the minds of a vast majority on both sides of the Atlantic, and is repeated daily from tongue to tongue, as an established and incontrovertible truth; it is that "all men are created equal."

> ... Taking the proposition literally ... there is not a word of truth in it. It begins with "all men are born," which is utterly untrue. Men are not born. Infants are born ... [It] concludes with asserting that they are born "free and equal," which is not less false. They are not born free. While infants they are incapable of freedom ... [and] are necessarily born subject to their parents ... Nor is it less false that they are born "equal." They are not so in any sense ... and thus, as I have asserted, there is not a word of truth in the whole proposition...[14]

Calhoun's dander was up because abolitionists often quoted the Declaration, and this "proposition" in particular. In one respect, however, Calhoun was entirely correct: the Declaration of Independence is indeed an exercise in manipulation—the manipulation of emotion and intellect in almost equal measure. Calhoun's diatribe was offered as a countervailing manipulation, in favor of slavery and inequality. Both, then, were manipulatory manifestos. But there is surely no doubt as to which one was an exercise in democratic manipulation and which was not.

IV

I turn now from the Declaration to the Constitution or, more precisely, to the debate over whether to ratify the newly drafted constitution. A recurring charge on both sides of the issue was that the other side was attempting to manipulate public opinion (as though that were necessarily a bad thing to do). Antifederalist foes of the proposed constitution accused its Federalist friends of using language to deceive and manipulate the public. Here I want to consider only a single word or concept that was central to the debate. That word is "republic."

The U.S. Constitution mentions "republic" (or rather its cognate "republican") only once, and democracy not at all. "The United States shall guarantee to every state in this Union, a republican form of government" (Article IV, section 4). But what, exactly, is a republic? And how does it differ (if at all) from a democracy?

In the late eighteenth century, when the Constitution was drafted and debated and finally ratified, the only clearly agreed-upon meaning of "republic" was that it was a form of government in which a monarch did not rule and the people did, either directly or through their representatives; beyond that, definitions differed. During the ratification debate of 1787–88 one of the charges leveled repeatedly against the proposed constitution was that the government it would create was not really republican—by which was meant that it would disempower ordinary citizens and empower elites. As the pseudonymous Antifederalist author "The Federal Farmer" (probably Richard Henry Lee of Virginia) put it:

> If any names are applicable to the parties, on account of their general politics, they are those of republicans and anti-republicans. The opposers [of the proposed constitution, i.e. the Antifederalists] are generally men who support the rights of the body of the people, and are properly republicans. The advocates are generally men not very friendly to those rights, and [are] properly anti republicans.[15]

In reply, the authors of *The Federalist* (chiefly James Madison and Alexander Hamilton) worked very hard to convince their readers that the proposed constitution was fully in "conformity . . . to the true principles of republican government" (No. 1) as well as "republican in spirit" (No. 39) and "wholly and purely republican" (No. 73). Madison elicited howls of protest when he drew a novel distinction (in *Federalist* 10) between a democracy and a republic: by the former he meant a system in which the people themselves gather to draft, debate, and pass legislation; by the latter he meant a system in which citizens dispersed over a wide territory elect representatives to perform those tasks for them.[16]

Despite Madison's game attempt to reiterate and defend the distinction in Numbers 14 and 37, most Antifederalists and many of Madison's fellow Federalists, including John Adams and Thomas Jefferson, thought this distinction impossible to sustain and defend. Adams thought it a distinction without a difference: "Mr. Madison's ... distinction between a republic and a democracy cannot be justified. A democracy is really a republic, as an oak is a tree or a temple a building."[17] And Jefferson wrote:

> Indeed, it must be acknowledged that the term *republic* is of very vague application in every language ... Were I to assign to this term a precise and definite idea, I would say, purely and simply, it means a government by its citizens in mass, acting directly and personally, according to rules established by the majority; and that every government is more or less republican, in proportion as it has in its composition more or less of this ingredient of the direct action of the citizens.[18]

In other words, Jefferson's definition of republic corresponds at all points to Madison's definition of democracy. Little wonder, then, that Jefferson's friend Madison later abandoned the republic vs. democracy dichotomy. His brazen attempt at linguistic legerdemain had failed. Or had it?

In fact, the republic vs. democracy dichotomy was not dead then, and remains a staple of anti-democratic discourse even today. In the first half of the nineteenth century—the era of Jeffersonian and subsequently of Jacksonian democracy—the distinction was reinvoked by defenders of slavery to rebut the recurring Abolitionist charge that the Southern states were woefully undemocratic inasmuch as slaves could not vote or even voice their views. Citing Madison's distinction and the Constitution's guarantee that every state shall have "a Republican Form of Government" (Art. IV, sec. 4), defenders of slavery retorted that the states are semi-sovereign republics, not democracies, and besides, the great republics of antiquity—Sparta and Rome foremost among them—were slave-owning societies. A century later Strom Thurmond and other staunch segregationists defended the continuing disenfranchisement of African Americans by saying that the states are republics, not democracies in which every man has a vote.

In short, the republic vs. democracy dichotomy has a rather unsavory history as an instrument of political manipulation. Even today the dichotomy is invoked and defended by the John Birch Society, the Ku Klux Klan, and other racist and reactionary groups for purposes of undemocratic manipulation. If nothing else, the invocation throws a high-sounding but threadbare cloak of legitimacy over their anti-democratic machinations. Madison could hardly have foreseen the nefarious and anti-democratic manipulatory uses to which his well-meant distinction would later be put.[19]

V

I want next to look briefly at another familiar exercise in democratic manipulation—Lincoln's Gettysburg Address. Now it might seem strange and even disrespectful to call Lincoln's brief but powerful eulogium "manipulative." Mournful, yes; moving, yes; but manipulative? Surely not. But consider just what Lincoln does in that short address. First, he radically reinterprets the meaning of the American Founding by recasting the Founders' intentions in ways that would have astonished and perhaps even appalled all or most of them. If you do the math (four-score and seven = 87; 1863 minus 87 = 1776), Lincoln dates the American founding back to 1776 and the Declaration of Independence, and not to 1788 and the ratification of the Constitution. The Declaration says that all men are created equal, with certain unalienable rights, including the rights to life, liberty, and the pursuit of happiness; the Constitution denies what the Declaration declares and affirms, and condones the institution of slavery (which is mentioned three times in the Constitution, without actually using the words slave or slavery).[20] In so doing Lincoln signs on, implicitly, to the Abolitionist view (voiced by William Lloyd Garrison and Frederick Douglass, among others) that the Declaration, not the Constitution, is the true charter of American liberty, and the Constitution is forever freighted and stained with the blood of slaves.

But Lincoln isn't finished. He then goes on to reframe and reinterpret the reasons for which the Civil War was still being fought. As a matter of historical fact—attested to by Lincoln's pre-war speeches, along with letters and speeches early in the war—the war was waged originally to keep the Union intact, and nothing more. But as a matter of *moral meaning,* the Civil War was soon recast by Lincoln as a conflict of an altogether different sort—as a struggle to deliver on the promise of the "real" founding of 1776, which was stated in the form of a "proposition" that all men are equal. (This is, of course, the very same proposition that Calhoun was so keen to repudiate.) In one brief speech Lincoln reframes the Framing, refounds the Founding, and radically recasts the meaning of the murderous and fratricidal Civil War—no mean feat, surely.

Lincoln's was a blatant act of manipulation. In *Lincoln at Gettysburg* Garry Wills notes that in one brief address Lincoln

> performed one of the most daring acts of open-air sleight-of-hand ever witnessed by the unsuspecting. Everyone in that vast throng of thousands was having his or her intellectual pocket picked. The crowd departed with a new thing in its ideological luggage, that new constitution Lincoln had substituted for the one they brought there with them. They walked off, from those curving graves on the hillside, under a changed sky, into a different America. Lincoln had [given Americans] a new past to live with that would change their future indefinitely.

Thus "the Civil War *is,* to most Americans, what Lincoln wanted it to *mean.* Words had to complete the work of the guns."[21]

At least some of Lincoln's contemporaries noticed what he had done, and decried the deed. Editorial writers all over the country said that Lincoln had traduced the Constitution he had sworn to uphold and in so doing had dishonored his office and demeaned the dead. The Constitution, they noted, says nothing about equality *and* it condones slavery. The *Chicago Times* was typical in quoting the words of the Constitution back at Lincoln and then, continuing,

> It was to uphold this constitution, and the Union created by it, that our officers and soldiers gave their lives at Gettysburg. How dare he, then, standing on their graves, misstate the cause for which they died, and libel the statesmen who founded the government? They

were men possessing too much self-respect to declare that negroes were their equals, or were entitled to equal privileges.[22]

Factually and historically, and as concerns the "original intent" of the Founders, the *Times* editorialist was entirely correct. But, democratically and aspirationally, Lincoln was correct and on the right side of history— and of democracy.[23] His was an act of manipulation, to be sure, but also and more importantly, an act of *democratic* manipulation, inasmuch as it served to further the cause of democracy in America.

VI

Some twenty-nine years after Lincoln's little speech at Gettysburg another iconic text of American democracy was penned in Boston. I refer, of course, to the Pledge of Allegiance (1892). Its author was Francis Bellamy, a Baptist minister and a socialist (his cousin Edward, also an ardent socialist, would shortly go on to write the best-selling utopian-socialist novel *Looking Backward*). Here is the Pledge, as originally written:

I pledge allegiance to the flag of the United
States of America and to the Republic for
which it stands, one Nation, indivisible,
with liberty and justice for all.

When, as a schoolboy in the still-segregated south, I recited these words (with "under God" added in 1954), I didn't really understand them. In fact, I systematically *misunderstood* their meaning. I thought that the Pledge provided a *description* of the actual state of the union. What I didn't understand then was that, far from being descriptive, the Pledge supplied a radically aspirational vision of what America could conceivably *become* but that did not yet exist. The Pledge was meant to manipulate and redirect the thoughts, beliefs, and aspirations of those who recited and heard it, and in a more democratic direction. We pledge allegiance, then, to an *aspiration*, not an actuality.

By "one nation, indivisible" Bellamy invoked the idealistic vision of a nation united and undivided by race, class, sex, or vast disparities of wealth and life-chances. America in the late nineteenth century came nowhere near to fitting this description. Harsh segregationist Jim Crow laws kept African American males from registering and voting, and rope-wielding "night riders" of the Ku Klux Klan terrorized them into submission by beating and lynching anyone who crossed them. Women could not vote or run for public office. The mines, mills, factories, and sweat shops in which laborers, including young children, worked up to 70 hours a week were unsanitary and unsafe. Wages were low. Unions were forbidden to organize and recruit members. In the "Gilded Age" (as Mark

Twain called the 1890s) the rich "Robber Barons" were very, very wealthy and their workers very, very poor. The rich bought and paid for politicians, who in turn passed laws favorable to the interests of the wealthy and disadvantageous to the poor. (Legend has it that when someone asked the financier J.P. Morgan why he didn't run for the Senate, Morgan replied that he already had the best senators and congressmen money could buy.) "One nation, indivisible, with liberty and justice for all" was, in Bellamy's day, an aspiration, not a description of things as they actually were. (The words "under God" were not added until 1954, during the "Red scare" of the McCarthy era. By invoking the deity, the Congress meant to rebuke "godless, atheistic Communism" and thus to secure God's blessing on America—something that the Baptist minister somehow overlooked in 1892.)

The Pledge of Allegiance: manipulative, yes; democratic, yes. And Americans—some of them, anyway—are still trying to turn its words into a description of the real state of their union.

VII

I want to conclude by returning to the ancients, or rather to one in particular—Aristotle—and to do so in a way that is both personal and political.

For many years I've taught a two-semester, year-long course on The History of Political Philosophy ("From Plato to NATO," some call it). After reading and discussing the provocative and brilliantly written dialogues of Plato, we turn to his pupil Aristotle, a turn described by generations of students as a "downer." If there's one adjective my students apply to Aristotle, it's "dry."

But over the last three or four years, my students have shown a surprising shift of attitude, at least when we consider Aristotle's analyses of democracy and tyranny in the *Politics* (particularly in Bk. V). Their ears perk up when we talk about Aristotle's view of democracy (much more favorable than his teacher's) and how democracies can and often do degenerate into tyrannies. A shudder of recognition reverberates around the room as we discuss Aristotle's account of how tyrants think and act. So, begging the reader's pardon, I'd like by way of conclusion to see if you are similarly struck by the contemporary relevance and timeliness of Aristotle's account of tyranny and democracy, and the relation between the two.

Although critical of democracy for its shortcomings, Aristotle is much more appreciative of its strengths and advantages than Plato was. Democracy is the "least bad" of the three bad or perverted regime-types (the others being oligarchy and tyranny). And that is because democracy permits the participation of all citizens, allowing them "to rule and to be ruled in turn." Another of democracy's strengths is its recognition that many heads are better than one, or a few. The more points of view that are brought to the table, the wiser the resulting decision is likely to be.

Aristotle readily recognizes that human beings (or at least male citizens) are apt to be swayed by persuasive speech. It's important to remember that Aristotle, unlike his teacher, wrote a systematic treatise on rhetoric, a practice that he (again unlike Plato) dissected but did not disparage. (While disparaging rhetoric, framed as a critique of the sophists, Plato was himself a master rhetorician of the written if not of the spoken word.) Aristotle the consummate realist recognized that persuasive speech was an essential and indeed ineliminable feature of political life in general, and of democratic political life in particular.

And yet democracy is defective, Aristotle believes, because it is partial inasmuch as it promotes the interests of the common people and not the interests of everyone. Another way of putting Aristotle's point is to say that while in a democracy the *process* is good, the *outcomes* tend to be less than optimal. The process is good in that all citizens are entitled to take part in debate and deliberation about matters of common concern, but the results tend to be bad because they favor the numerically largest class. In short, democracy promotes the interests of the majority at the expense of the minority which then breeds resentment and fuels class conflict. Another disadvantage of democracy is that the views of the least educated and least knowledgeable citizens tend to carry the day. But perhaps the greatest and most dangerous disadvantage of democracy is that such citizens are alternately agitated, pandered to, flattered and fooled by demagogues who play to their hopes, their prejudices, and—most especially—their fears.

All too often democratic citizens willingly surrender their liberty to a demagogue, especially if he can through various wiles persuade them that they are in grave danger from some real or imagined enemy. That's why, for Aristotle (as for Plato), there is an intimate and immediate connection between democracy and tyranny. In fact, democracies tend to degenerate into tyrannies, thereby destroying themselves from within.

According to Aristotle, tyranny is far and away the worst of the three "perverted" regime-types. Tyranny is typically rule by one man or by a small number of men (as was the case with the Thirty Tyrants). In studying and analyzing tyrannies, Aristotle and his students at the Lyceum (sort of an Athenian Institute for Advanced Study) gathered data on tyrannies past and present, comparing them, noting characteristics that all tyrannies have in common. These common characteristics include the following features, all of which constitute veritable paradigms of what I have called *undemocratic manipulation*—that is, the sort of manipulation that undermines democracy, democratic citizenship, and the rule of law:

- Tyrannies typically come into being when a demagogue or ruler creates (or exploits an already-existing) fear of a real or imagined enemy.

- The tyrant endears himself to the people by presenting himself as their friend and their savior from this foe.
- He starts a war against this real or imagined enemy, based on bogus reasons which the gullible people accept (fear having made them even more gullible), and leaving them "always in need of a leader."
- This war serves to distract the people, preventing them from paying attention to what the tyrant is doing domestically, including his dismantling of the constitution, making his cronies and hangers-on wealthy at public expense, and expanding his power into areas that were previously constitutionally off-limits.
- The tyrant maintains and increases his power by distrusting anyone outside himself and his inner circle.
- He tells lies that the people believe.[24]
- He plants spies in their midst who undertake domestic surveillance to ferret out would-be critics and dissidents.
- He withholds information and practices censorship.
- He divides the people among themselves by "sowing dissensions" and "creating quarrels" over real or imaginary issues of little or no importance, thereby turning the people against each other so that they wrongly see their fellow citizens as enemies and don't pay attention to what the tyrant is doing.
- The tyrant implicates as many people as possible in his crimes, so that they share responsibility for them.
- He subverts the administration of justice by "altering the constitution" and putting innocent men on trial and letting guilty men go unpunished if they are willing to serve him.
- He uses the courts and other agencies of government to help his friends and harm his enemies.
- He distracts the people with spectacles and entertainments (as the Roman emperors were later to do with free bread and with circuses featuring lions, tigers, gladiators, and Christians; now we have Fox News and talk radio).
- He makes some people beholden to him by enriching them at public expense.
- And, above all, the tyrant maintains the outward *appearance* of being a good man and just ruler. He "*pretends* to be a guardian of the public treasury" even as he plunders it by spending recklessly. He will "*seem* to be a steward of the public rather than a tyrant." Finally, though not least, he will, in public, "*appear* to be particularly devout in his worship of the gods."

By these means the tyrant practices undemocratic manipulation, lulling the people into a deep civic sleep, the better his dastardly deeds to perform. If and when they wake up, it's likely to be too late to retrieve and revive their rights and liberties.

When my students ask, with apparent alarm, whether the Bush-Cheney administration is (or now, was) a tyranny, I make the usual professorial move, and ask: "I don't know. What do you think?"

But, of course, that feint was disingenuous. The Bush-Cheney administration *was* a tyranny from which we have not yet escaped entirely. Presidents—even progressive ones—do not willingly give up the illegitimately expanded powers they inherit from their predecessors.

Notes

* An earlier version of this paper was presented at the conference "Manipulating Democracy," sponsored by the Institute for Leadership Studies, Loyola Marymount University, Los Angeles, February 10–11, 2008. For comments and criticisms I am indebted to the conference organizers, professors Wayne LeCheminant and John M. Parrish, to various members of the audience, and especially to Andrew Sabl, who made several useful suggestions for improving my paper.

1. In *Manufacturing Consent* Noam Chomsky and Edward Herman leave the misleading impression that Lippmann was somehow in favor of "manufacturing consent." In fact, however, Lippmann viewed "the manufacture of consent" (his phrase) as an unfortunate but inevitable fact of modern political life against which citizens must be on their guard (he was not optimistic, however, about their chances of success). See Walter Lippmann, *Public Opinion* (New York: Macmillan, 1922) p. 153.

2. Jürgen Habermas, "Wahrheitstheorien," in *Wirklichkeit und Reflexion* (Pfullingen, Germany: Neske, 1973).

3. My thinking about manipulation and related matters has been much influenced by the work of Mary Dietz, who reminds us that politics is not a parlor game played by polite people in ideal speech situations but a much more rough-and-tumble practice. See Mary Dietz, *Turning Operations: Feminism, Arendt, and Politics* (New York: Routledge, 2002), esp. chapters 7 and 8; see, further, Bryan Garsten, *Saving Persuasion: A Defense of Rhetoric and Judgment* (Cambridge, MA: Harvard University Press, 2006).

4. Bertrand de Jouvenel, *Sovereignty: An Inquiry into the Political Good*, trans. J.F. Huntington (Chicago: University of Chicago Press, 1957), p. 304.

5. See J. Peter Euben, *The Tragedy of Political Theory* (Princeton, NJ: Princeton University Press, 1990), esp. Part II; and Euben, ed., *Greek Tragedy and Political Theory* (Los Angeles: University of California Press, 1986).

6. Euripides, *The Suppliants*, trans. Terence Ball, in Ball and Richard Dagger, eds., *Ideals and Ideologies: A Reader*, 7th ed. (New York: Longman, 2009), p. 15.

7. Aristotle, *Poetics*, ch. VI, 10. It's possible, even probable, that Aristotle's account of *katharsis* is a reply to Plato's criticism that tragedy illicitly stirs and exploits the heightened emotions of the audience. See Plato, *Republic*, Bk. X, 605.

8. Our sole source for Pericles' Funeral Oration is Thucydides, *The Peloponnesian War*, Bk. II, 34–37.

9. Nicole Loreaux, *The Invention of Athens: The Funeral Oration in the Ancient City*, trans. Alan Sheridan (Cambridge, MA: Harvard University Press, 1986).

10. See Douglass Adair, "'Experience Must be Our Only Guide': History, Democratic Theory, and the United States Constitution," in his *Fame and the*

Founding Fathers (Indianapolis, IN: Liberty Fund, 1998), chapter 5. The "experience" to which the Founders referred repeatedly was not their own but that of long-dead ancestors, and especially Greek and Roman ones.

11. Pauline Maier, *American Scripture: Making the Declaration of Independence* (New York: Knopf, 1997).

12. Jefferson's own copy of the Declaration included notations showing where to pause, which words to emphasize, etc. See Pauline Maier, *American Scripture*, pp. 131–32.

13. Abraham Lincoln, "Speech on the Dred Scott Decision," June 26, 1857, in Don E. Fehrenbacher, ed., *Abraham Lincoln: Speeches and Writings*, 2 vols. (New York: Library of America, 1989), vol. 1, pp. 398–99.

14. John C. Calhoun, "Speech on the Oregon Bill" (June 27, 1848), in Ross M. Lence, ed., *Union and Liberty: The Political Philosophy of John C. Calhoun* (New York: Liberty Fund, 1992), pp. 565–66.

15. "The Federal Farmer" (Richard Henry Lee?), Letter VI in Herbert J. Storing, ed., *The Anti-Federalist* in one volume, abr. by Murray Dry (Chicago: University of Chicago Press, 1985), pp. 67–68.

16. See Alexander Hamilton, James Madison, and John Jay, *The Federalist*, ed. Terence Ball (Cambridge University Press, 2003), No. 10 [Madison], pp. 40–46, at 43–45.

17. Quoted in Gerald Stourzh, *Alexander Hamilton and the Idea of Republican Government* (Palo Alto, CA: Stanford University Press, 1970), p. 55.

18. Thomas Jefferson to John Taylor, 28 May 1816, in Joyce Appleby and Terence Ball, eds., *Jefferson: Political Writings* (Cambridge University Press, 1999), p. 207.

19. An amusing coda: Angered by Republican legislators' eagerness to cut taxes paid by their wealthy campaign contributors while slashing spending for K–12 and higher education, mental health, public safety, and other programs, Arizona voters have in recent referendums taken matters into their own hands. In passing Proposition 301 in 2001, Arizonans voted to raise their own taxes in order to support public education at a minimally decent level. And, to ensure that their voice would not only be heard but heeded, they approved the Voter Protection Act which forbids the state legislature from undoing their handiwork. This proved to be too much democracy for the Republican leadership to take, and in 2003 they mounted a crusade against democracy—literally. House Majority Leader Eddie Farnsworth said that "democracy is the worst way to protect individual freedoms" and he drew a sharp distinction between a "democracy" and a "republic." He said he "grows tired of explaining to people that the United States is not a democracy, it's a republic" (*Arizona Republic*, March 16, 2003, p. A6).

20. United States Constitution, Art. I, sect. 2 (the three-fifths clause), Art. I, sect. 9 (that congress may not restrict or outlaw the slave trade before 1808), and Art. IV, sect. 2 (escaped slaves must by law be returned to their masters). For Madison's awkward and half-hearted defense, see *Federalist* No. 54.

21. Garry Wills, *Lincoln at Gettysburg: The Words That Remade America* (New York: Simon & Schuster, 1992), p. 38.

22. "The President at Gettysburg," *Chicago Times*, Nov. 23, 1863; quoted in Wills, *Lincoln at Gettysburg*, pp. 38–39.

23. In *This Republic of Suffering: Death and the American Civil War* (Knopf, 2008), Drew Gilpin Faust suggests that the Civil War was all senseless slaughter and carnage, and—*contra* Lincoln and others—without any larger moral meaning or purpose. But in so doing she seems to commit some-

thing like a category mistake, for meaning is not something that inheres in the phenomena—the rotting corpses on bloody battlefields—but in what Americans made and still make of that war. We *make* and *ascribe* meaning; we don't simply find it. She seems to believe that neither is an option. In opting for the first, Lincoln recognized this more acutely than any of his contemporaries, excepting, perhaps those Union soldiers who, although at first opposed to abolitionism, came increasingly to believe that the Civil War's greater purpose was the emancipation of the slaves. Drawing upon their diaries and letters Chandra Manning, *What This Cruel War was Over: Soldiers, Slavery, and the Civil War* (Random House, 2007) documents this transition in (at least some) soldiers' thinking.

24. The nonpartisan Center for Public Integrity has documented at least 935 false statements made by Bush, Cheney, and seven other high-level officials in the two years following 9/11. These were part of an orchestrated campaign to mislead, misinform, and manipulate the public regarding the "threat" posed to American security by Saddam Hussein (www.publicintegrity.org/WarCard/).

3 When Rhetoric Turns Manipulative

Disentangling Persuasion and Manipulation

Nathaniel Klemp

Rhetoric occupies a tenuous place within democratic theory. Plato describes rhetoric as "the ghost or counterfeit part of politics" because it produces "delight and gratification" without imparting any real knowledge.[1] This suspicion of rhetoric persists in a more attenuated form in many ideal theories of deliberative democracy and discourse ethics. Jurgen Habermas and Joshua Cohen, for example, do not overtly reject rhetoric as Plato once did. Yet their ideals, which exclude "all force ... except the force of the better argument," leave little room for speech that influences through eloquence and appeals to emotion.[2]

In response to these ongoing suspicions of rhetoric, many theorists call for a rehabilitation of rhetoric. In the *Rhetoric*, Aristotle redescribes rhetorical modes of persuasion as inescapable and even beneficial. To engage effectively in political debate, he insists, "You must make the audience well-disposed towards yourself and ill-disposed towards your opponent, magnify or minimize the leading facts, excite the required state of emotion in your hearers, and refresh their memories."[3] Today, a growing number of democratic theorists defend rhetoric, defined variously, along similar lines. They argue that rhetoric helps "get an issue on the agenda for deliberation,"[4] that it promotes "communication across wide differences of culture and social position,"[5] and, above all, that "a politics of persuasion ... is worth defending."[6]

Such theories have played an important role in challenging the presumption against rhetorical forms of speech implicit within many deliberative theories. Yet they also run the risk of glorifying rhetorical speech and over-stating its moral and democratic virtues. In particular, existing theories of rhetoric tend to lack a nuanced account of the distinctions between morally ideal, morally decent, and morally problematic forms of rhetoric.

In this essay, I aim to disentangle these various moral qualities of rhetorical speech. The first part of this essay argues for a conceptual distinction between manipulation and persuasion. This distinction differentiates between rhetoric that demeans and rhetoric that promotes individual autonomy and democratic self-rule. On my account of this distinction, manipulation arises when (1) agent A uses hidden or irrational force to affect agent B's choices and (2) agent A acts intentionally. Of its many varieties, I outline three primary types of manipulation: lying, concealment, and distraction. Persuasion, by contrast, respects the choices of others and takes two forms. "Deliberative persuasion" arises when rhetoric is used openly to induce agreement with an orientation toward mutual understanding, while "strategic persuasion" arises when agreement is induced openly with an orientation toward winning.

The final part of the essay examines the moral dimensions of deliberative, strategic, and manipulative rhetoric. In contrast to persuasive rhetoric, manipulation threatens both individual autonomy and democratic legitimacy. These dangers, I argue, intensify in the presence of two contextual conditions: invisibility and asymmetrical relations of power. Given these dangers, manipulation ought to be viewed with a presumption of immorality and subject to robust public contestation.

A Brief Definition of Rhetoric

Before exploring its moral dimensions, the word "rhetoric" demands at least some preliminary definition. While ancient thinkers like Plato, Aristotle, and Cicero disagree as to whether rhetoric constitutes a virtue or a vice, they all point toward a similar definition. In the *Gorgias*, Socrates defines rhetoric as "the artificer of persuasion," to which Gorgias replies, "the definition seems to me very fair, Socrates; for persuasion is the chief end of rhetoric."[7] Aristotle shares the idea that rhetoric seeks persuasion as its primary end, defining it as "the faculty of observing in any given case the available means of persuasion."[8] Finally, Cicero argues that a vital part of politics arises from "that form of artistic eloquence which is generally known as rhetoric, the function of which is that of speaking in a manner calculated to persuade, and the goal of which is that of persuading by speech."[9]

These ancient definitions highlight two primary qualities of rhetorical speech: an orientation toward persuasion which seeks to induce the agreement of listeners, and a "calculated" use of various linguistic techniques to induce persuasion through "eloquence" and other "artistic" uses of language. On these views, the end of persuasion is reached through the speaker's conscious use of linguistic techniques such as eliciting emotion, redescribing perceived virtues or vices, or appealing to the values and beliefs particular to each audience.

My own conception of rhetoric shares this two-fold definitional structure but departs from the ancients' emphasis on the end of persuasion. In contrast to these conceptions, I argue for a more expansive conceptual understanding of rhetoric's end. I presume that although political rhetoric often is "designed to persuade,"[10] it can also be designed to exert other forms of influence. As Kenneth Burke suggests, rhetoric is not inherently persuasive. Rather, it simply consists in "the use of words by human agents to form attitudes or to induce actions in other human agents."[11]

This more expansive view suggests that the practice of rhetoric is not confined to situations in which the speaker seeks to persuade listeners by inducing agreement. In some instances, rhetoric may also be used to manipulate—to reshape the actions or beliefs of listeners in ways that diminish their capacity to choose for themselves.[12]

While I call for a more expansive view of rhetoric's end, I share the second half of the ancient conception of rhetoric: the idea that rhetoric involves "eloquence" and other "artistic" uses of language as its means. Iris Marion Young's definition of rhetoric nicely highlights this quality of rhetorical speech. As she puts it, rhetoric is concerned with "the way content is conveyed as distinct from the assertive value of the content."[13] Unlike purely rational argumentation, rhetoric appeals to emotion, metaphor, eloquence, and other linguistic techniques that enhance the way content is conveyed. While rhetorical speakers often present substantive arguments, it is the additional use of such linguistic techniques that typifies this mode of speaking.

Toward a Conception of Manipulation

What is the nature of manipulative rhetoric? One response argues that persuasion offers listeners the choice as to whether or not to be influenced, whereas manipulation effectively coerces them. As Bryan Garsten puts it, "the speaker who manipulates his audience so as to bring them to a belief or action without their consent, as Kant thought orators moved men 'like machines,' has not persuaded but coerced them."[14]

Manipulation does indeed bring actors "to a belief or action without their consent." Yet this response conflates manipulation and coercion. As Nozick reminds us, the essential feature of coercion is that it operates as a known threat.[15] Coercion arises when A "threatens to do something" if B does not comply with A's desires and B knows about this threat.[16] Thus transparency and the use of explicitly communicated threats are central features of coercion. If someone jumps out of a dark alley and shouts, "give me your money or I'll kill you," and you produce the money, then you have been coerced.

Manipulation alters the beliefs, actions, and choices of others in a different way. Consider an example. Suppose that I try to manipulate you to vote Democratic. Rather than influencing you by presenting arguments, I affect your choices and actions by working behind the scenes to restructure your informational environment. Imagine that you are a newcomer to the details of party politics but a fervent opponent of abortion. If I can for a short time shield you from learning that most Democrats support abortion rights, I may be able to get you to vote Democratic at least once. Without telling you, I filter the political information you receive. I provide selected news and information, change the subject when the issue of abortion arises, and tell your colleagues and friends to do the same.[17] In this case, I have interfered with your choice of candidates using covert tactics that you do not fully understand. This is a paradigm case of manipulation.

The combination of two conditions distinguishes manipulation. The first stipulates that in manipulation, A uses hidden or irrational force to affect B's choices. This condition specifies two of manipulation's essential features. First, it stipulates that manipulation is a form of force. Unlike other forms of power, which offer other agents a choice between compliance and noncompliance, the hidden or irrational force in manipulation diminishes the capacity of others to comply. Like other forms of force, manipulation changes others' actions, beliefs, or choices, whether or not they choose to comply. In Bachrach and Baratz's words, when forced, "the intended victim is stripped of the choice between compliance and noncompliance."[18] This is what occurs in the Democratic voting example. When I get you to vote Democratic by depriving you of information, I take away your choice as to whether to comply with my wishes. Instead, it is me—the manipulator—who chooses for you. I never threaten you with sanctions or deprivations. I simply change your actions invisibly, without your knowledge, choice, or consent.

In contrast to Bachrach and Baratz, I understand the kind of force used in manipulation as a form of power. On their view, power only arises (1) when A and B have conflicting interests, (2) when B complies with A's wishes, and (3) when "B does so because he is fearful that A will deprive him of a value or values which he regards more highly than those which would have been achieved by noncompliance."[19] According to this conception, power is limited to coercion—to actions where agents use explicit threats to affect the choices of others.

Following Steven Lukes, I think of power more expansively. As Lukes puts it, the central idea of power is that "A in some way affects B ... in a non-trivial or significant manner."[20] Manipulation satisfies this broader criterion, for it arises in situations where A and B have a "latent" conflict of interest, and A uses an indirect form of force to change B's choices, beliefs, or actions. On Lukes' more expansive concept of power, manipulation is indeed a form of power that affects others using hidden or irrational force.

This first condition also stipulates a second essential feature of manipulation. It asserts that manipulation is a particular kind of force—one exercised in hidden or irrational ways. While I define manipulation as a form of force, it is important to point out that many other forms of force operate in non-manipulative ways. For instance, if I get you to vote Democratic by carrying you over my shoulder to the voting booth, selecting the Democratic candidate, wrapping your hand around the voting lever, and pulling your arm down, I have forced but not manipulated you to vote Democratic.

What makes the form of force used in manipulation distinctive is that it is either hidden or irrational. Consider first manipulation based on hidden force. *Covert manipulation* occurs when A affects B's choices using hidden forms of force. In such instances, the victim of manipulation does not fully understand the nature of the manipulator's wishes. As Alan Ware puts it, in such cases, "B either has no knowledge of, or does not understand, the ways in which A affects his choices."[21] Most forms of manipulation consist of such hidden forms of force. In fact, many theoretical accounts limit manipulation solely to such hidden or invisible actions. [22]

Now consider manipulation based on overtly irrational force. *Overt manipulation* arises when agents openly interfere with the rational capacities of others by exploiting the victim's irrational tendencies. As Gutmann and Thompson point out, "not all manipulation is deceptive. A politician can manipulate potential supporters by openly exploiting their weaknesses."[23] As I will discuss later on, not all appeals to emotion or other non-rational considerations constitute an irrational form of force. Far from exerting irrational force on the choices of others, many appeals to emotion serve as a pointer to reason. They encourage, rather than diminish, the capacity of other agents to weigh the costs and benefits involved in choosing between various options. When, however, emotional appeals overwhelm or bypass the listener's capacity to choose, they exert a manipulative form of irrational force. Such appeals overwhelm and distract others in ways that disrupt their capacity to choose freely.

To illuminate this possibility, consider a variant on the Democratic voting example. This time imagine that I use a variation on Lyndon Johnson's 1964 "daisy commercial" to induce you to vote Democratic. I show you the image of an innocent little girl counting daisies. Next, you hear the menacing voice of a military commander, counting down to a nuclear explosion. As the countdown reaches zero, you see the graphic imagery of a mushroom cloud. I then leave you Johnson's chilling voice-over: "These are the stakes," I insist: "we must either love each other or we must die. Vote for the Democrats on November 3rd. The stakes are too high for you to stay home."[24] My intent here is to use fear to overwhelm your rational capacities—to get you to vote Democratic on the basis of the irrational thought that you might die if you vote Republican. If my efforts are successful here, if my appeals to fear significantly distort your capacity to choose, I will have overtly manipulated you.

The second condition stipulates that in manipulation, A's use of hidden or irrational force is intentional. In all examples used thus far, the manipulative agent's actions were intentional. The absence of such intention changes the moral quality of actions. Returning to the first example, suppose that I keep you from knowing the Democrat's position on abortion simply because the issue makes me feel uncomfortable and, as a result, I change the subject whenever it comes up in conversation. The effects might be the same. You might still end up voting for Democrats on the basis of incomplete information. Nevertheless, under the conception I propose, we would not say I "manipulated" you. Manipulation requires intent. It demands that interference in the choices of others be intentional.[25]

In addition to these two conditions, manipulation shares with coercion and persuasion the requirement that B's actions or beliefs change to meet A's wishes. A citizen has not been *persuaded* unless the speaker convinces them to change his or her mind. Similarly, a citizen has not been *manipulated* unless the speaker's covert tactics or appeals to irrational impulses successfully override his or her rational capacity to choose. This prerequisite specifies that changing B's beliefs or actions is not enough. To persuade, coerce, or manipulate, A must induce a change in B that aligns with the change A intended to induce. In the Democratic voting example, I only manipulate you if I get you to vote Democratic. If my efforts to change your actions result in your voting for the Communist Party, I have not manipulated you.

Three Forms of Manipulation

Another task in understanding manipulation is to examine the specific forms it takes in modern politics. Of its myriad forms, I outline three varieties. *Lying* and *concealment* represent manipulation's invisible forms. *Distraction* is manipulation's most ambidextrous form; it can exercise force covertly or overtly. For each form of manipulation, I provide a political example. These examples are not meant to provide a comprehensive empirical case for manipulation but to illuminate the distinctive qualities of the three forms.

The first form of manipulation is lying. When speakers lie, they affect the choices of others by intentionally disseminating information they know to be false. Lies enable manipulators to surreptitiously reshape the beliefs, actions, and choices of others. As Sissela Bok points out, by distracting agents or affecting their assessments of certainty, lies interfere with their capacity to choose.[26] If one of your objectives is to run a marathon, and I tell you that long distance running has been found to cause cancer, I have covertly altered the nature of your choice to run the marathon.

One of the most famous recent political lies occurred in January 1998. When confronted with allegations that he had an affair with former White House intern Monica Lewinsky, President Clinton insisted, "I did not have sexual relations with Monica Lewinsky. I have never had an affair with her." Four days later, Clinton declared, "There is not a sexual relationship, an improper sexual relationship, or any other kind of improper relationship."[27]

This case illuminates the complexities in identifying lies. In Clinton's mind, he did not have "sexual relations with Monica Lewinsky" because he never had sexual intercourse with her. In this sense, Clinton's initial statement may not have been a lie, for he may have actually believed that he never had "sexual relations." Yet Clinton's later statements represent a paradigm case of lying. While Clinton may have believed he never had "sexual relations" with Lewinsky, he could not have believed this was a "proper" relationship. By claiming to have had no such "improper relationship," therefore, Clinton lied. He sought to manipulate citizens and the grand jury—to influence them by intentionally disseminating information he knew to be false.

The second form of manipulation is concealment. Concealment arises when speakers intentionally withhold relevant information from other agents.[28] When politicians intentionally withhold information that might undermine their case for going to war, for instance, we say that they "manipulated" fellow citizens. Yet the simple act of withholding information is not inherently manipulative. When voicing arguments, lawmakers and citizens often legitimately withhold information that might undermine their character or the merits of their proposal. As Bok points out, the complexity of even the most mundane human actions makes full disclosure of the truth nearly impossible.[29] No matter how complete, our descriptions are likely to omit some relevant facts or motivations.

Concealment, however, is a distinctive form of omission. While other forms of omission may be purely incidental or motivated by concerns over propriety, in concealment, speakers omit information with the intent to hide. It is this intent that makes concealments manipulative. When speakers intentionally conceal facts and information that would influence the choices of others, they exert a hidden form of force. They intentionally affect the choices of others in ways that cannot be fully understood.

Consider an example of manipulative concealment. In the early 1990s, the Christian Coalition adopted a strategy that its own leaders described as "stealth" campaigning.[30] Christian right activists sought to take control of school boards, city councils, and local-level Republican Party Committees by running political campaigns based on a two-tiered message. Within friendly churches, candidates described in detail their plans to legislate according to divine principle. In more public settings, candidates dropped references to God, pretending to be "ordinary" Republicans concerned primarily with economic issues. Christian Coalition leaders instructed activists to "hide your strength," "don't flaunt your Christianity," and "give the impression that you are there to work for the Party, not to push an ideology."[31]

The Christian Coalition's concealment of its religious convictions was manipulative. Stealth candidates hid their religious convictions to win over citizens who would ordinarily oppose their religious agenda. These tactics were also intentional. As Ralph Reed, former head of the Christian Coalition, remarked when describing these tactics, "I want to be invisible. I do guerrilla warfare. I paint my face and travel at night. You don't know it's over until you're in a body bag. You don't know until election night."[32] Reed's words illustrate that during this period, the concealments of the Christian right were not accidental. They were part of a carefully orchestrated plan to influence fellow citizens in ways these citizens could not fully understand.

The third form of manipulation is distraction. Manipulative distraction takes on two forms. The first arises from "informational distraction." This tactic covertly alters the choices of others by flooding the information space with so much information that listeners become confused and overwhelmed. As Goodin points out, "The opportunity it [this tactic] sees for manipulation lies not at the level of fudging facts but rather at the level of interpreting them. Once you have overloaded people with information, all of it both pertinent and accurate, they will be desperate for a scheme for integrating and making sense of it. Politicians can then step in with an interpretive framework which caters to their own policy preferences."[33] In this form of manipulation, politicians exploit their disproportionate power to shape and control the content of public political debate. They rig discursive conditions by flooding fellow citizens with irrelevant information to ensure that their view prevails.

A second form of distraction—"emotional distraction"—also arises in political settings. Tactics of emotional distraction have a long history in the rhetorical tradition. As Cicero puts it, "you must try to shift or impel them [listeners] so that they become ruled not by deliberation and judgment but rather by sheer impetus and perturbation of mind."[34]

Rhetorical appeals to emotion turn manipulative in two circumstances. The first arises when speakers covertly appeal to listeners' irrational tendencies. When the speaker intentionally triggers the emotional responses of others in ways that fall beneath the awareness of listeners, such appeals become manipulative. This covert form of emotional distraction arose during the 1988 Presidential Election. To undermine the credibility of his Democratic opponent Michael Dukakis, George H.W. Bush and his aides communicated an implicit racial message by invoking the case of Willie Horton. Horton was an African American man convicted of murder in Massachusetts and sentenced to life in prison. During Dukakis' term as governor of Massachusetts, Horton escaped while on furlough, assaulting a white family and raping the woman.

As Tali Mendelberg points out, throughout the campaign, neither Bush nor his aides ever made any explicit mention of Horton's race.[35] Instead, they relied on the media to communicate an implicitly racial message. Whenever the Horton story surfaced in media accounts, the visual imagery of Horton's mug shot lurked in the background, offering voters a subtle reminder that Dukakis allowed a *black* man to rape a *white* woman. Using this implicit message, the Bush campaign was able to appeal to the racial prejudices of voters without ever making these appeals explicit. It was able to prime the predispositions of voters in a silent and invisible way that interfered with their capacity to choose. There is also evidence to suggest this strategy was intentional—that the Bush campaign intentionally sought to sway the public on the basis of this implicit racial message.[36]

The second form of emotional distraction is more overt. Rather than appeal to the emotions of listeners in implicit ways beneath their awareness, it makes appeals to emotion explicit. Overt forms of emotional distraction arise when speakers intentionally seek to override the listener's rational capacity to choose through direct appeals to irrational tendencies, prejudices, or fears.

This form of manipulation arose in Lyndon Johnson's 1964 "daisy commercial." As mentioned previously, Johnson sought to portray Republican opponent Barry Goldwater as a radical extremist by appealing to deep-seated fears of American citizens. Using the graphic imagery of a nuclear explosion, his campaign sought to influence voters by eliciting emotions that overwhelmed their capacity to choose. Unlike the implicitly racial message of the Horton ads, the daisy commercial sought to alter the choices of voters by using explicit and overt appeals to emotion. It used horrific imagery and messages to affect the choices of others by inciting a sense of terror designed to compel them to vote for Johnson—the candidate who stood for love.

Emotion and Manipulation

The Willie Horton and daisy commercials illustrate the manipulative potential of distracting rhetorical appeals to emotion. Yet is all emotional rhetoric manipulative? On some accounts of deliberative democracy, this conclusion seems plausible. Such accounts define deliberation as a process of discussion based on reason alone, free from appeals to passion and emotion. For instance, as Joshua Cohen defines it, "Deliberation is *reasoned* in that parties to it are required to state their reasons for advancing proposals."[37] Habermas also insists upon the primacy of reason. "Participants in argumentation," he argues, "have to presuppose in general that the structure of their communication ... excludes all force ... except the force of the better argument."[38] Such passages do not directly argue that all emotional rhetoric is manipulative. Yet by placing reason at the center of deliberation, they imply that emotion has corrosive effects on the deliberative process, for it introduces into discussions a form of force other than "the force of the better argument."[39]

Recently, many deliberative democrats have shifted away from this implicit rejection of emotion, toward ideals that more explicitly embrace rhetorical appeals to emotion.[40] Gutmann and Thompson, for example, assert that "in the political arena passionate rhetoric can be as justifiable as logical demonstration."[41] Underlying this shift is the notion that reason and emotion are not inherently at odds. John Dryzek, for instance, tells us "emotions themselves can be subjected to rational justification, because emotions often rest on beliefs."[42] On this view, emotions are not inherently irrational.[43] While they may override reason in some cases, they may serve as an important "pointer to ethical judgment" in others.[44]

To illuminate the possibility of emotion working alongside, rather than against, reason, Dryzek points to Martin Luther King's rhetoric. During the civil rights movement, King frequently invoked rational arguments based upon the Declaration of Independence and the Constitution when speaking to white audiences. Yet, as Dryzek suggests, these arguments were not purely rational:

> [I]t was the place of the Declaration of Independence and the Constitution in the *hearts* of white Americans that King could reach. The attachment to these documents and the processes that created them is largely, though not exclusively, emotional, rather than a matter of prudent calculation ... Certainly there was rational argumentation here too, but the transmission was aided, perhaps even made possible, by the accompanying rhetoric.[45]

Such examples complicate the simple dichotomy between emotion and reason. They show that, more often than not, persuasive political arguments appeal to a mixture of reason and emotion. They also show that no necessary antagonism exists between these two human capacities.

What distinguishes emotional manipulation from fully legitimate forms of persuasion that appeal to the emotions? The two conditions of manipulation help draw this distinction. The first concerns the effect of emotional rhetoric on listeners. It stipulates that manipulation occurs when emotional rhetoric overwhelms, distracts, or bypasses listeners' rational capacities. When appeals to emotion no longer incite or aid rational reflection but, rather, interfere with the agent's capacity to reason, rhetoric turns manipulative. Such forms of rhetoric depart from legitimate forms of persuasion because, as Dryzek puts it, they create psychological conditions where emotion no longer "answer[s] to reason."[46]

The second condition concerns the speaker's intention. It asserts that in persuasion, the speaker's appeals to emotion arise with the intent to openly induce agreement. Emotion is used, not to override listeners' rational capacities, but to enhance the prospect of achieving understanding or success. In manipulation, the speaker's appeals to emotion arise with the intent to interfere with the other agent's rational capacity to choose. In such cases, emotion is not used with an intent to prompt rational reflection but to distract others or bypass rational reflection altogether.

Two Forms of Persuasion

Now consider the distinction between manipulation and persuasion. Think of persuasion as "the addressing of arguments or appeals to a person in order to induce cooperation ... or agreement."[47] This act of inducing agreement often includes more than rational arguments. In Aristotle's definition, persuasion arises from both the quality of argument and the quality of the rhetorical context. He tells us that "persuasion is a sort of demonstration."[48] It is a demonstration "furnished by the spoken word" that succeeds or fails based upon three qualities. First, the possibility of persuasion depends on the kinds of arguments used to induce agreement. In Aristotle's words, "persuasion is effected through the speech itself when we have proved a truth or an apparent truth by means of the persuasive arguments suitable to the case in question."[49] Second, it depends on the speaker's character. Character can be persuasive, Aristotle argues, because "we believe good men more fully and more readily than others."[50] Finally, it depends on the audience's emotional state. Friendly audiences are more likely to be influenced than hostile audiences. By refining these three qualities of the speech situation, Aristotle argues, speakers increase their chances of inducing listeners to cooperation or agreement.

Theorists of deliberation point to an important distinction between two primary ways agents use speech within such contexts of persuasion to induce agreement. Benjamin Barber, for instance, distinguishes between "talk" and "speech." He argues that "talk" has a reciprocal quality. It "involves receiving as well as expressing, hearing as well as speaking."[51] "Speech," on the other hand, works unilaterally. It arises when the speaker seeks to induce agreement without full consideration of the arguments and concerns expressed by others. As Barber puts it:

> "I will listen" means ... not that [1] I will scan my adversary's position for weaknesses and potential trade-offs ... It means, rather, [2] "I will put myself in his place, I will try to understand, I will strain to hear what makes us alike, I will listen for a common rhetoric evocative of a common purpose or a common good."[52]

The first statement, where the speaker scans "the adversary's position for weaknesses," reflects a strategic form of speech. The second statement reflects a different mode of democratic conversation – one in which the speaker seeks to induce agreement by understanding the views of others and searching for common ground.

Habermas draws a similar distinction between "communicative" and "strategic action." Like Barber's notion of "talk," communicative action arises when agents use speech to forge mutual understanding. Communicative action occurs when "actors seek to reach an understanding about the action situation and their plans of action in order to coordinate their actions by way of agreement."[53] Strategic action, by contrast, arises when agents orient their action not toward understanding but success. When acting strategically the agent "is oriented to his own success and behaves cooperatively only to the degree that this fits with his egocentric calculus of utility."[54]

The reflections of Barber and Habermas point to a distinction between two basic forms of persuasive rhetoric: *deliberative persuasion* and *strategic persuasion*. In both forms of persuasion, speakers seek to induce cooperation or agreement in other actors. What distinguishes them is the nature of the speaker's intent and relation to other agents.

In *deliberative persuasion*, the speaker seeks to induce agreement with an orientation toward mutual understanding.[55] Consider an example. Suppose I seek to persuade you to vote for the Democratic Party's candidates in the upcoming election. If I am engaged in deliberative persuasion, I will provide arguments and reasons that I genuinely believe. I will also *listen* to your reactions and counter-arguments. I will try to find common ground, and I will be open to the possibility that your responses might prompt me to reconsider my support for the Democrats. In this sense, my efforts at persuasion are oriented toward reaching understanding— toward arriving at a fuller appreciation of the relative advantages of the Democratic and Republican platforms.

This orientation toward understanding arises from three primary qualities of deliberative persuasion. The first is *openness to revision*. In deliberative persuasion, speakers engage in debate with a willingness to revise their preexisting beliefs and preferences. As Bernard Manin points out, the word "deliberation" itself embodies this spirit of openness. According to Hobbes' definition, for instance, "Deliberation is nothing else but a weighing, as it were in scales, the conveniences, and inconveniences of the fact we are attempting."[56] These definitions illustrate the two-tiered structure of deliberation. They remind us that deliberation occurs externally, when parties exchange reasons, and also occurs internally, when individuals balance reasons for and against their own beliefs and plans of action.

When engaged in deliberative persuasion, parties talk in a *deliberative* way. They leave open the possibility of revising their own beliefs and preferences. As Manin puts it, when deliberating

> [participants] know what they want in part: they have certain preferences and some information, but these are unsure, incomplete, often confused and opposed to one another. The process of deliberation, the confrontation of various points of view, helps to clarify information and to sharpen their own preferences. They may even modify their initial objectives, should that prove necessary.[57]

This deliberative spirit of openness does not, however, mean that speakers are no longer engaged in persuasion. It simply means that in their efforts to persuade, speakers offer arguments and information with an openness to the possibility that the agreement they originally sought to induce needs alteration or revision.

This second quality of deliberative persuasion is *sincerity*. In deliberative persuasion, speakers offer arguments and reasons they genuinely believe. If I am truly interested in understanding, I will refrain from using purely strategic reasons that I do not accept but that put my position in its best possible light. While such arguments may increase my chances of persuading you, they do so at the expense of the deliberative commitment to understanding.

The third quality is a *focus on the merits*. In deliberative persuasion, speakers refrain from strategic efforts to selectively use facts and arguments to bolster their case. Instead, deliberative speakers engage in what Joseph Bessette calls "reasoning on the merits of public policy."[58] They seriously examine and consider all relevant facts and arguments. They seek not to distract others from important considerations but to engage in the good faith exploration of the substantive issues at stake. In the above example, my persuasive efforts embody this quality. They are based on appeals to facts and arguments relevant to your choice of candidates.

In *strategic persuasion*, the speaker's efforts to induce agreement are oriented toward winning rather than understanding. Strategic speakers seek not to achieve mutual understanding but to successfully convince others to adopt *their* view or to agree with *their* proposed course of action. Consider the following variation on the Democratic voting example. Rather than presenting my best arguments in the hopes of achieving a better understanding of the relative advantages of the two parties, suppose I offer arguments crafted solely for the purpose of winning the debate. I scan your arguments and beliefs for potential vulnerabilities. I find that while you support the Republicans on most issues, you reject the party's opposition to abortion. Despite my own reservations about legalizing abortion, I build my case for voting Democratic on the abortion issue. I convince you that abortion is a crucial issue and that the Democrats are the only party that will support your convictions. Throughout our discussion, I do not hide my strategic intentions. Both you and I know I am acting strategically, with the intent to successfully induce you to vote Democratic. In this example, I use rhetoric to win—to successfully induce your agreement—not to achieve understanding.

It is important to note that strategic persuasion is not defined by the mere existence of an orientation toward winning. In all forms of persuasion, even deliberative persuasion, some orientation toward winning exists, for all forms of persuasion seek to win over the listener by successfully inducing agreement. The defining characteristic of strategic persuasion is that this intent to win trumps the intent to achieve mutual understanding. In strategic persuasion, the speakers' primary intent is to win—to induce others to adopt his or her position. In deliberative persuasion, by contrast, the speakers' primary intent is to understand. They seek to successfully induce agreement but act with a provisional commitment to their own point of view. They are open to clarifying and revising their view in light of the reactions of others.

Strategic persuasion's orientation toward winning over understanding arises from three primary qualities. The first feature of strategic persuasion is that speakers engage in discussion with an *unwillingness to revise* existing preferences and beliefs. Unlike deliberative persuasion, in strategic persuasion the agreement that speakers wish to induce remains static throughout the discussion. Strategic speakers seek not to explore the merits of issues to achieve mutual understanding but simply to win over the listener. When I seek to strategically persuade you to vote Democratic, for instance, I am not open to changing my own position based upon your reactions. Instead, I use carefully crafted arguments and rhetoric to induce you to agree with my preference for the Democrats.

The second is the potential for *insincerity*. Speakers engaged in deliberative persuasion appeal to sincere reasons and arguments, but speakers who persuade strategically need not express genuine beliefs. They might express sincere arguments when it proves expedient. Yet they will often abandon sincerity, opting for arguments crafted for the purpose of convincing the audience at hand. Strategic speech, therefore, is not inherently insincere. There may be instances when strategic speakers rely on sincere arguments and reasons. Unlike deliberative persuasion, however, in strategic persuasion speakers may appeal to insincere arguments and reasons crafted to win the debate.

The third feature of strategic persuasion is the *selective use of facts and arguments*. In the *Oxford English Dictionary*, the words "strategy" and "strategic" often refer to the direction of military campaigns. "Strategy" is defined generally as "a plan for successful action based on the rationality and interdependence of the moves of the opposing participants."[59] In the realm of political discourse, strategic action thus entails using facts and arguments selectively to anticipate the moves of the opposition and outmaneuver them. So unlike deliberative persuasion, where the actor focuses on the merits to achieve understanding, in strategic persuasion the actor uses facts and arguments selectively in attempts to win.

It is important to note that I view these two forms of persuasion and my conception of manipulation as ideal moral types. My claim in outlining the conceptual qualities of these forms of speech is not that all real-world political rhetoric fits neatly into these three conceptual boxes. Instead, it is that these categories illuminate the moral qualities of purely deliberative, purely strategic, and purely manipulative speech. In practice, political rhetoric falls somewhere along this spectrum from purely deliberative to purely manipulative speech.

Disentangling Manipulation from Persuasion

These three categories of rhetoric provide the theoretical tools for disentangling manipulation from other forms of power and influence. Consider the difference between manipulation and persuasion. If I were to persuade you to vote Democratic, instead of hiding information from you, I would use arguments, stories, or talking-points to convince you that Democrats offer a better set of policies than Republicans. Such persuasive actions differ from manipulation in three primary ways. First, unlike manipulation, persuasion is always transparent. Both deliberative and strategic persuasion change others' beliefs or actions in ways that both parties understand. In persuading B, A does not hide her wishes but communicates these wishes to B. Second, in contrast to manipulation, persuasive actions allow other actors to choose whether to comply with the persuader's demands. In my efforts to persuade you to vote Democratic, you have the ultimate choice over whether to comply with my wishes. In my efforts to manipulate you, by contrast, I take away this choice.

Finally, unlike manipulation, persuasive actions offer choice and respect the other agent's capacity to choose. As Bachrach and Baratz point out, in persuasion, agents seek compliance not by exerting force but by exerting influence. In their definition, one person has *influence* over another "to the extent that the first without resorting to either a tactic or an overt threat of severe deprivations, causes the second to change his course of action."[60] Unlike manipulation or coercion, influence affects others without resorting to threats or taking away others' choice to comply. Like other forms of influence, persuasive actions respect other agents' capacity to choose. In Kant's words, they treat others not as mere means but as ends in themselves.[61]

While not the central focus of this inquiry, it is also worth distinguishing manipulation and coercion. If I were to coerce you to vote Democratic, rather than hiding information or offering you reasons, I would threaten you. I might tell you that if you do not vote Democratic, I will light your front lawn on fire. Coercive actions differ from manipulation in two ways. First, unlike manipulation but like persuasion, coercion works transparently. It occurs only when I threaten you and you understand the nature of this threat. Second, in contrast to manipulation, coercion resembles persuasion because it allows other agents to choose whether to comply with the coercer's demands. Even if I threaten to kill you if you don't hand over your money, you still have a choice. You may choose to give up your life rather than comply with my demands, but this a decision that you have the ultimate capacity to make.

Despite these differences, manipulation and coercion share one important characteristic: both fail to respect the choices of others. Manipulation fails to respect others' choices by using hidden or irrational tactics to interfere forcefully with others' capacity to choose. Coercion does so by invoking threats and sanctions. In both cases, other agents lose their capacity for rational self-determination. They are treated not as ends but as mere means, as instruments whose capacity to choose can be worked using threats or force. Features of persuasion, coercion, and manipulation are presented in Table 3.1.

Table 3.1 Features of Persuasion, Coercion, and Manipulation

	Type of relation?	Trans-parent?	Others given a choice?	Choices of others respected?	Use of sanctions or threats?
Persuasion	Influence	Yes	Yes	Yes	No
Manipulation	Power by Force	Some-times*	No	No	No
Coercion	Power by Threat	Yes	Yes	No	Yes

This figure illustrates the distinctive features of persuasion, coercion, and manipulation.
* It is a fact that while most manipulation is covert, arising from hidden force, it can also occur overtly, arising from openly irrational force.

In addition to these general distinctions between persuasion, coercion, and manipulation, consider the more particular distinctions between our three primary speech types: deliberative persuasion, strategic persuasion, and manipulation (see Table 3.2). To illuminate the various qualities of these three forms of speech, I outline below how these three forms of rhetoric vary with respect to four primary qualities of speech: (1) the speaker's openness to revise existing beliefs, (2) the speaker's sincerity, (3) the speaker's rhetorical emphasis, and (4) the speaker's general orientation.

Manipulation shares many of the qualities of strategic speech but departs from purely strategic speech in three ways. First, manipulation always involves some level of insincerity. In fact, manipulative actions are the antithesis of sincere ones. When speakers lie, conceal relevant information, or distract listeners by appealing to irrational tendencies, they act with a lack of genuineness and with hidden ulterior motives. Such actions are in direct opposition to the "honesty," "genuineness," and "straight-forwardness" defining sincerity.[62]

Table 3.2 Features of Deliberative, Strategic, and Manipulative Speech

	Speaker's Openness to Revise Existing Beliefs	Speaker's Sincerity	Speaker's Rhetorical Emphasis	Speaker's General Orientation
Deliberative Persuasion	Openness to Revision	Sincere	Focus on the Merits	Under-standing
Strategic Persuasion	Unwillingness to Revise	Sincere or Insincere	Selective Use of Facts and Arguments	Winning
Manipulation	Unwillingness to Revise	Insincere	Use of Hidden or Irrational Force	Winning at All Costs

Second, unlike deliberative speakers who focus on the merits, and strategic speakers who selectively use facts and arguments, manipulative speakers use hidden or irrational force to influence others. In manipulation, speakers use these forms of force to achieve their ends in ways that interfere with other citizens' capacities to choose. Finally, unlike strategic speakers who act with an intent to win, manipulative speakers act with an intent to win *at all costs*. In other words, manipulative speakers are so intent on winning—on controlling others' actions and beliefs—that they are willing to resort to immoral tactics that diminish the listener's autonomy. They win by acting outside the norms of good-faith political discussion.

Figure 3.1 illuminates the three primary moral dimensions of political rhetoric. The three categories of speech mark out the contours of a moral spectrum running from morally ideal forms of deliberative persuasion to morally problematic forms of manipulation. Between these polarities lie morally decent forms of strategic persuasion. While contextual conditions often influence our moral evaluations of particular forms of speech, my task in the remainder of this essay will be one of disentangling the various moral dimensions of these three ideal types.

What makes the third dimension—the dimension of manipulation—a greater threat to individuals and democracies than the others? When it emerges in everyday life, manipulation produces a psychological loss of trust and feelings of betrayal. Yet I argue that these feelings also have a moral core. While not all manipulation is immoral, I argue that it ought to be viewed with the presumption of immorality. Put differently, it ought to be viewed prima facie as a moral wrong.[63] This means that the burden of proof ought to rest on those who manipulate. Their use of lies, concealments, or distractions should be considered immoral unless and until they provide a compelling justification.

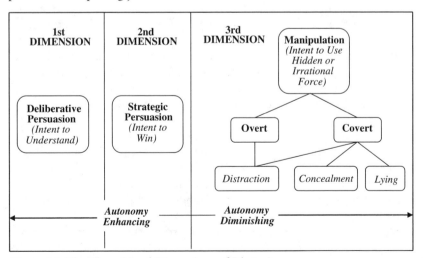

Figure 3.1 The Three Moral Dimensions of Rhetoric

This presumption of immorality rests on two primary sets of arguments. The first is non-consequentialist in nature. It contends that manipulation undermines individual autonomy. By enabling other agents to interfere with our beliefs, actions, and choices, manipulation creates conditions that diminish our capacity to choose our own ends. Kant's moral philosophy illuminates the threat manipulation poses to our capacity for rational self-determination.[64] For Kant, freedom arises from the capacity to choose one's own ends and to reason for one's self. To ensure that we respect the freedom of others in our actions, Kant asserts the "Formula of Humanity": "Act so that you treat humanity, whether in your own person or in that of another, always as an end and never as a means only."[65] Acting in accord with this formula demands that we act towards others in ways they could assent to.

As I present it, deliberative and strategic persuasion cohere with Kant's "Formula of Humanity." Even when my efforts to convince you to vote Democratic are oriented toward winning, I still treat you as a rational being. I respect your capacity to choose by being open about my efforts to induce agreement. In persuasion, listeners have the capacity to choose for themselves whether to comply with the speaker's wishes.

Manipulation, by contrast, treats listeners as a means. Although Kant never directly addresses the morality of manipulation, he does address deception, which plays an essential role in many forms of covert manipulation. Kant considers deception an immoral, even evil, practice because it undermines the Formula of Humanity. Instead of treating others in ways they could assent to, deception deprives others of the ability to assent altogether. In Korsgaard's words, "people cannot *assent* to a way of acting when they are given no chance to do so … the victim of a false promise cannot assent to it because he doesn't know it is what is being offered."[66] Manipulation more generally has similarly corrosive effects on an agent's capacity to choose freely. Intentionally depriving listeners of crucial information, telling them falsehoods, or overriding their rational capacities demeans individual autonomy. By covertly or overtly removing the individual's ability to assent to the other agent's actions, manipulation treats its victims as mere means, not as ends in themselves.

Yet the dangers of manipulation extend beyond such non-consequentialist concerns over individual autonomy. Manipulation also produces damaging consequences both at the individual and social level. It distorts informed decision making, while also undermining the legitimacy of the democratic process. Thus the danger of manipulative rhetoric is not simply that it treats others as a "means" but that it creates conditions of choice that distort sound decision-making and erode the democratic ideal of popular sovereignty.

At the individual level, manipulation erodes the conditions of choice in two primary ways. First, it undermines the accuracy and reliability of the information that citizens use in making political decisions. As Bok explains, "all our choices depend on our estimates of what is the case; these estimates must in turn often rely on information from others. Lies distort this information and therefore our situation as we perceive it, as well as our choices."[67] Bok's reflections on lying can be extended to manipulation more generally. Manipulative lying, concealment, and distraction all have similar effects on the individual: they diminish significantly the capacity to choose on the basis of sound facts and information.

Second, manipulation creates asymmetrical power relations in favor of the manipulator. As Bok puts it, "To the extent that knowledge gives power, to that extent do lies affect the distribution of power; they add to that of the liar, and diminish that of the deceived, altering his choices at different levels."[68] In the language of Philip Pettit, the asymmetries in power that arise from manipulation constitute a relationship of domination. Such conditions enable the manipulator to interfere with the choices of other agents on an arbitrary basis or, as Pettit puts it, "at their pleasure."[69] By exerting either hidden or irrational force, in other words, manipulation takes away the capacity of others to challenge or contest the influence of the manipulator.

Manipulation is even more dangerous in the social or political realm. When political actors withhold crucial information, lie about the possible costs and benefits of policies, or distract citizens from important considerations, they erode the capacity of large numbers of citizens to engage in collective decision-making. By broadening the scope of manipulation to a national scale, political manipulation poses two additional dangers. First, it erodes the epistemic quality of political debate.[70] Rather than enabling citizens to challenge relevant facts, assumptions, and arguments, manipulation silently conceals, distorts, and perverts these considerations. It obscures implicit assumptions, distracts listeners from important reasons, or disseminates outright lies. As a result, manipulation diminishes the likelihood that public deliberations will result in sound epistemic outcomes.

Second, and more fundamentally, political manipulation threatens the ideal of democracy as rule of the people. As noted earlier, the word "democracy" embodies this ideal of rule of the people; it is a fusion of two Greek roots: *demos* (the people) and *kratos* (rule). Implicit within this ideal is the notion that ultimate political authority resides with the people themselves, not with a monarch or group of elites. As Madison expresses it, "the people are the only legitimate fountain of power, and it is from them that the constitutional character, under which the several branches of government hold their power, is derived."[71]

Political manipulation undermines this democratic ideal. If the principle underlying democracy is rule of the people, the principle underlying manipulation is rule of the rhetorically devious few.[72] Lies, concealments, and distractions enable skillful manipulators to wield unchecked and often invisible force over the actions and beliefs of others. These tactics erode publicity and transparency. More important, they create danger-ously asymmetrical relationships of power. When manipulated, citizens are denied what Pettit calls the "power of challenge": the power to scru-tinize publicly the actions of other citizens and representatives to ensure that these actions represent the people's common interests.[73] The people can no longer exercise this power because when done covertly, political manipulation removes this capacity without anyone ever being the wiser.

Now consider the moral qualities of deliberative persuasion, which I deem morally ideal, and strategic persuasion, which I deem morally decent. Despite their differences, I argue that both forms of persuasion steer clear of the moral dangers of manipulation by respecting the capacity of listeners to choose. When speakers employ either mode of persuasion, their intent to induce agreement is transparent to listeners. All parties understand that the speaker's words are oriented toward convincing lis-teners to accept the agreement that the speaker hopes to induce. As a result, both forms of persuasion allow listeners to choose whether or not to be persuaded by the speaker's rhetorical appeals. Listeners have full awareness of the speaker's intent to influence them and retain ultimate choice over whether to accept or reject the speaker's appeals.

While both forms of speech respect others' choices, deliberative per-suasion is a more normatively desirable form of speech. Rather than using rhetoric simply to promote their own views and interests, deliberative speakers use rhetoric to achieve mutual understanding and solidarity. In democratic politics, the sense of respect and civility expressed by this deliberative kind of "talk" is preferable to the adversarial and confronta-tional forms of "speech" used in strategic political contests. Deliberative forms of persuasion are more likely to cultivate what John Rawls calls "civic friendship." As Rawls puts it, such relationships arise from delibera-tions where citizens

> exchange views and debate their supporting reasons concerning pub-lic political questions. They suppose that their political opinions may be revised by discussion with other citizens; and therefore these opin-ions are not simply a fixed outcome of their existing private or non-political interests.[74]

Purely strategic speakers lack this openness to revise existing beliefs and thus engage with fellow citizens in a more adversarial manner. As a result, their orientation toward winning runs a greater risk of cultivating polar-ization and intolerance between groups, parties, and individuals.

The moral preference for deliberative persuasion does not, however, mean that strategic persuasion is wholly immoral or illegitimate. On my view, strategic persuasion occupies an important middle ground between deliberative persuasion and manipulation. It is a form of speech that is often morally decent. The morally decent status of strategic persuasion means that it neither diminishes nor enhances democracy in significant ways. It plays a legitimate role in politics but is less desirable than deliberative persuasion.

Why should we regard strategic persuasion as morally decent? Consider three primary reasons. First, strategic persuasion lacks the morally ideal qualities of deliberative persuasion. As mentioned previously, strategic forms of persuasion often lack the virtues of mutual respect and civic friendship. They cultivate a more adversarial discourse—one based less on understanding than winning.

Second, strategic persuasion lacks the morally problematic qualities of manipulative rhetoric. While less desirable than deliberative persuasion, strategic persuasion shares two vital democratic virtues. Strategic persuasion embodies the virtue of transparency and the virtue of respect for the choices of others. Like more deliberative forms of persuasion, it involves the open exchange of reasons and leaves listeners free to decide for themselves whether to be persuaded. This means that in contrast to manipulative forms of speech, which distort choice, strategic forms of persuasion offer others the capacity to choose for themselves.

Third, strategic persuasion pervades modern democratic politics. To reject all forms of strategic speech would be to reject many core practices of democratic politics such as campaigning, debating, and advocacy. Within electoral competition between parties and interest groups, strategic action is inevitable. Given that democratic institutions create significant incentives to political success, rival parties and interest groups can be expected to use language to promote their own interests and out-maneuver opponents. Denying the legitimacy of all forms of strategic persuasion would deny the legitimacy of many strategic practices that play an essential role in real-world democratic politics.

Exceptions to the Immorality of Manipulation

Is manipulation always immoral? Considering the dangers that both personal and political manipulation pose it is tempting to answer "yes"—to take an absolute stance against the practice. This categorical rejection of manipulation, however, is too strong. Moral evaluations of manipulation depend on context. In most circumstances, we are likely to reject manipulation—to argue that it is an immoral and undesirable form of political speech. Yet the circumstances of politics are complex, and situations will inevitably arise where manipulation is morally permissible.

In game situations, for instance, where all players consent, manipulation is often morally permissible. In gambling and sports, the rules of the game permit manipulative and violent acts that would otherwise be morally impermissible. In football, deceiving opponents, using trick plays, concealing strategies, and engaging in other kinds of manipulative action is permitted and encouraged. Certain forms of manipulation are also permitted in poker and more informal game situations like deceptive bargaining in a bazaar.[75] In each of these instances, manipulation is permissible because agents autonomously choose to enter the game.

There are, however, important limits to the moral permissibility of manipulation in such game situations. First, the consent of players must be informed and voluntary. They must freely decide to enter the game and fully understand the manipulative practices that its rules permit.[76] Second, the game's manipulative practices must not have detrimental effects on non-players.[77] Manipulation, deception, or violence cannot be justified if they negatively affect non-players. While manipulation may be permissible in poker or football, it is not in public debates between candidates. In the latter case, manipulation may misinform and mislead non-players who do not fully understand the manipulative nature of the game.

Finally, players must not face barriers to exit.[78] If players cannot easily exit the game or if circumstances of poverty or deprivation force them to play, the game's manipulative practices lose their moral permissibility. In such instances, players no longer make an autonomous choice to play. Instead, they are forced into the game as a result of bad fortune.

In certain circumstances, manipulation may also be trivially immoral.[79] Its effect may be so insignificant that it no longer demeans autonomy and democratic legitimacy. For instance, relatively harmless forms of manipulation often arise in everyday conversation in the form of white lies or minor concealments. As anthropologist Harvey Sachs points out, the decorum of polite conversation often requires a certain degree of manipulation. When someone says "How are you?" Sachs observes, we tend not to say "Rotten!" even though that may be true. To prevent our conversational partner from having to say "Really, what happened?" and engage in the long conversation that would surely ensue, we tend to just say, "Fine, how are you?"[80] Sachs' study illuminates the inevitability of certain forms of manipulation. Yet manipulation in such contexts is a relatively harmless form of manipulation—one we might regard as trivially immoral.

Such cases illustrate that context plays a profound role in determining the moral status of specific acts of manipulation. To further illuminate the influence of context, consider two contextual conditions that magnify the potential harms of manipulative speech: *invisibility* and *asymmetries of power*. Both conditions limit the capacity of victims of manipulation to contest, challenge, or even understand the ways manipulators use force to affect their choices. Put differently, these conditions intensify the extent to which manipulative speech interferes with the capacity of other agents to choose, while also diminishing the possibilities for publicly contesting and challenging manipulation.

The first contextual condition concerns the visibility of manipulation. As manipulative acts become increasingly covert, victims of manipulation become increasingly unaware that their choices have been interfered with.

Invisibility leads to unawareness. This loss of awareness diminishes the capacity of citizens to contest and challenge manipulative actions. When manipulated covertly, agents lose their capacity to choose for themselves and also lose their capacity to expose and challenge the manipulator's tactics, for their choices are affected without their knowing the nature or existence of this manipulative form of force.

In conditions of transparency, manipulation still poses dangers to individual autonomy and democratic decision-making. Yet the openness of overt manipulation diminishes these dangers. When manipulation is visible, citizens gain the awareness that their choices have been shaped by manipulative force. While transparency may not always enable them to resist manipulation, it creates awareness and opens the possibility that citizens might contest and challenge the actions of those who manipulated them.

Second, manipulation is increasingly dangerous as power relations become more unequal and asymmetrical in favor of the manipulator. Within symmetrical power relationships, manipulation may often be relatively harmless. When a lawmaker seeks to override the rational capacities of other similarly powerful lawmakers in the course of negotiations over a bill, manipulation appears harmless, for it arises in a symmetrical context of power. Other lawmakers have roughly equal political skills, knowledge, and resources. They have equal capacities to expose and challenge these tactics or to counter them through the use of similar tactics.

As power relationships grow more asymmetrical, however, the immorality of manipulation increases. When a lawmaker seeks to emotionally manipulate members of a disadvantaged minority group, her tactics become increasingly problematic. In conditions of inequality, members of the disadvantaged group lack the political and financial resources to fight back. They may be unable to expose or counter the lawmaker's tactics of manipulation. In such instances, the same problem arises as in invisibility. By diminishing the victim's capacity to challenge and contest manipulative acts, asymmetrical power relations intensify the force of manipulation and diminish the possibilities for curtailing manipulative speech. They increase the extent to which manipulators can successfully interfere with others' capacity to choose for themselves.

Given its dangers, manipulation should also be subject to robust public scrutiny and contestation. The force exerted by manipulative speech is most often covert. Manipulation works in the shadows to reshape the choices of others. As a result, the most effective antidote to manipulation is public scrutiny and exposure. When manipulative acts are brought out from the shadows, when the "private assumptions" and "hasty calculations" of would-be manipulators are contested, the force of manipulative actions is diminished.[81] Once exposed, those who resort to manipulative speech often pay a high price. Public exposure of their manipulative actions not only reduces the force that their actions exert on the choices of others. It also results in the loss of credibility, esteem, and the trust of other citizens.

This essay has sought to explore the moral qualities of strategic and manipulative forms of rhetoric. While such forms of speech pervade contemporary democratic politics, they tend to be overlooked by the mostly ideal emphasis of deliberative theories of democracy. To enrich existing theories, I have outlined three primary moral dimensions of political rhetoric. Deliberative persuasion arises with the intent to understand; strategic persuasion with the intent to win; and manipulation with the intent to interfere using hidden or irrational force. This three-fold distinction helps disentangle morally decent forms of persuasive rhetoric from morally problematic forms of manipulation. It provides a conceptual framework for understanding when rhetoric respects the values of individual autonomy and democracy and when it diminishes these values.

Notes

1. Plato, "Gorgias," in Benjamin Jowett, trans. and ed., *Essential Dialogues of Plato* (New York: Barnes and Noble Classics, 2005), pp. 134–35.
2. Jurgen Habermas, *The Theory of Communicative Action*, trans. Thomas McCarthy (Boston: Beacon Press, 1984), p. 25. Cohen cites Habermas in his statement of the second condition of the ideal deliberative democratic procedure. See Joshua Cohen, "Deliberation and Democratic Legitimacy," in David Estlund, ed., *Democracy* (Oxford: Blackwell Publishers, 2002), p. 93. For a discussion of Habermas on rhetoric, see James Bohman, "Emancipation and Rhetoric: The Perlocutions and Illocutions of the Social Critic," *Philosophy and Rhetoric* 21, no. 3 (1988).
3. Aristotle, "Rhetoric," *The Complete Works of Aristotle*, ed. Jonathan Barnes (Princeton, NJ: Princeton University Press, 1984), 2268, Bk.3: 1419b10.
4. Iris Marion Young, *Inclusion and Democracy* (Oxford University Press, 2000), p. 66.
5. Iris Marion Young, "Communication and the Other: Beyond Deliberative Democracy," *Democracy and Difference*, ed. Seyla Benhabib (Princeton, NJ: Princeton University Press, 1996), p. 132.
6. Bryan Garsten, *Saving Persuasion* (Cambridge, MA: Harvard University Press, 2006) p. 3. For other defenses of the use of rhetoric in democratic deliberation, see Bernard Manin, "On Legitimacy and Political Deliberation," *Political Theory*, 15.3 (1987). Amy Gutmann and Dennis Thompson, *Why Deliberative Democracy?* (Princeton, NJ: Princeton University Press, 2004), pp. 50–51.
7. Plato, "Gorgias," 125, 453a.
8. Aristotle, "Rhetoric," 2155.
9. Quentin Skinner, *Reason and Rhetoric in the Philosophy of Hobbes* (Cambridge University Press, 1996), p. 2.
10. Bryan Garsten, *Saving Persuasion* (Cambridge, MA: Harvard University Press, 2009), p. 5.
11. Kenneth Burke, *A Rhetoric of Motives* (Los Angeles: University of California Press, 1969), p. 41.
12. While the ancients cite persuasion as the explicit end of rhetoric, the end of manipulation is often implicit in their accounts. In Cicero's *De Oratore*, for

instance, Antonius declares that in addressing an audience, "you must try to shift or impel them so that they become ruled not by deliberation and judgment but rather by sheer impetus and perturbation of the mind." I am grateful to Skinner for this quote: see Skinner, *Reason and Rhetoric in the Philosophy of Hobbes*, p. 121.

13. Young, *Inclusion and Democracy*, p. 65.
14. Bryan Garsten, *Saving Persuasion* (Cambridge, MA: Harvard University Press, 2006), p. 7. Bok draws a similar analogy between manipulation and coercion: see Sissela Bok, *Lying* (New York: Vintage Books, 1999). For a popular account of manipulation as a form of coercion, see Douglas Rushkoff, *Coercion: Why We Listen to What "They" Say* (New York: Riverhead Trade, 2000).
15. For more on coercion, see; Scott Anderson, "Coercion," *Stanford Encyclopedia of Philosophy* (2006).
16. Nozick, "Coercion," p. 441.
17. I am indebted to William Connolly who uses a similar set of examples to illuminate conceptions of power. See William Connolly, *The Terms of Political Discourse* (Oxford: Blackwell Publishers, 1974).
18. Peter Bachrach & Morton S. Baratz, *Power and Poverty* (Oxford University Press, 1970), p. 28.
19. Bachrach and Baratz, *Power and Poverty*, p. 24.
20. Steven Lukes, *Power: A Radical View* (New York: Palgrave Macmillan, 1974), p. 26.
21. Alan Ware, "The Concept of Manipulation," *British Journal of Political Science* 11, no. 2 (1981): 165.
22. As Bachrach and Baratz put it, in manipulation "A seeks to disguise the nature and source of his demands upon B and, if A is successful, B is totally unaware that something is being demanded of him." See also Bachrach & Baratz, *Power and Poverty*, p. 31. Robert Goodin, *Manipulatory Politics* (New Haven, CT: Yale University Press, 1980) and Ware, "The Concept of Manipulation"; For an account of manipulation that leaves open the possibility of overt manipulation, see Joel Rudinow, "Manipulation," *Ethics* 88, no. 4 (1978).
23. For empirical cases of manipulation see Amy Gutmann and Dennis Thompson, *Ethics and Politics: Cases and Comments* (New York: Wadsworth Publishing, 2005), p. 160.
24. Gutmann and Thompson also refer to this ad as a case of manipulation; see Gutmann and Thompson, *Ethics and Politics: Cases and Comments*, p. 162.
25. In rare cases, manipulation may also arise from intentional negligence. In these cases, actors intentionally neglect to assess whether their actions might exert indirect control over others. Imagine that my town is debating an ordinance prohibiting smoking in restaurants and bars. I oppose this ordinance. After a few minutes of Internet research, I find a study showing that secondhand smoke benefits health. While I realize this study may be flawed, I accept its conclusions because it strengthens my argument. I use this study to influence my fellow townspeople to oppose the proposed ordinance. Is this a case of manipulation? I do not consciously intend to deceive. I have evidence, however questionable, that secondhand smoke has important health benefits. We might consider my actions manipulative on the basis of their intentionally negligent character. I may have "manipulated" fellow citizens because I intentionally neglected to scrutinize information that I knew to be questionable in order to strengthen my arguments. Thus agents also satisfy the third condition of manipulation if they intentionally avoid

scrutinizing information that they have good reason to believe is unreliable. This qualification to the intentionality condition is similar to Ware's point that manipulation can occur when "a rational person would have expected" that his or her actions would result in a covert form of influence. This condition does not implicate agents who are ignorant. If I were ignorant of the general scientific consensus that smoking has harmful effects and had no reason to doubt the Internet study, my actions would not constitute manipulation. The intentionality condition is only satisfied when negligence is intentional—that is, when agents know their information is questionable or that their actions may influence others covertly, but intentionally avoid any critical inquiry. See Ware, "The Concept of Manipulation," p. 173.

26. Sissela Bok, *Lying* (New York: Vintage Books, 1989), p. 19.
27. Peter Baker and John F. Harris, "Clinton Admits to Lewinsky Relationship; Challenges Starr to end personal 'prying'," *Washington Post*, August 18, 1998, p. A1.
28. While concealment is often viewed as a lesser evil than lying, these two forms of manipulation have the potential to be equally deceptive. In fraud and securities law in the United States, for instance, deliberate efforts to conceal material facts are punished with the same severity as deliberate efforts to propagate falsehoods. "Fraud," *American Jurisprudence*, 37 (2001): 32–56.
29. Bok, *Lying*, p. 4.
30. Sara Diamond, *Not by Politics Alone* (New York: Guilford Press, 1998); Matthew Freeman, *The San Diego Model: A Community Battles the Religious Right* (Washington, DC: People for the American Way, 1993); Jean Hardisty, "Constructing Homophobia: Colorado's right-wing attack on homosexuals," *Eyes Right!*, ed. Chip Berlet (Boston: South End Press, 1995); Clyde Wilcox and Carin Larson, *Onward Christian Soldiers?* (Boulder, CO: Westview Press, 2006); James Penning, "Pat Robertson and the Gop: 1988 and beyond," *Sociology of Religion*, 55, no. 3 (1994).
31. "How to Participate in a Political Party," internal memo obtained by People for the American Way and used at the Iowa Republican County Caucus, March 1986. On file with author.
32. Hardisty, *Mobilizing Resentment*, p. 110.
33. Goodin, *Manipulatory Politics*, p. 58.
34. Skinner, *Reason and Rhetoric in the Philosophy of Hobbes*, p. 121.
35. Tali Mendelberg, *The Race Card* (Princeton, NJ: Princeton University Press, 2001), p. 3.
36. Mendelberg, *The Race Card*, pp. 134–68.
37. Joshua Cohen, "Deliberation and Democratic Legitimacy," *Democracy*, ed. David Estlund (Oxford: Blackwell Publishers, 2002), p. 93.
38. Jurgen Habermas, *The Theory of Communicative Action*, trans. Thomas McCarthy (Boston: Beacon Press, 1984), p. 25.
39. For criticisms of this rational emphasis of deliberative democrats, see Nancy Fraser, "Rethinking the Public Sphere: A contribution to the critique of actually existing democracy," *Habermas and the Public Sphere*, ed. Craig Calhoun (Cambridge, MA: The MIT Press, 1992); Jane Mansbridge, "Practice-Thought-Practice," *Deepening Democracy*, eds. Archon Fung and Erik Olin Wright (London: Verso, 2003); Lynn M. Sanders, "Against Deliberation," *Political Theory* 25, no. 3 (1997); Young, "Communication and the Other: Beyond deliberative democracy," *Democracy and Difference*; Young, *Inclusion and Democracy*.
40. See, for instance, John Dryzek, *Deliberative Democracy and Beyond* (Oxford University Press, 2002); Jane Mansbridge, "Everyday Talk in the Delib-

erative System," *Deliberative Politics,* ed. Stephen Macedo (Oxford University Press, 1999); Amy Gutmann and Dennis Thompson, *Democracy and Disagreement* (Cambridge, MA: The Belknap Press of Harvard University, 1996); Amy Gutmann and Dennis Thompson, *Why Deliberative Democracy?.*

41. Gutmann and Thompson, *Why Deliberative Democracy?,* p. 51.
42. Dryzek, *Deliberative Democracy and Beyond,* p. 53.
43. For more on this insight see, Cheryl Hall "Recognizing the Passion in Deliberation: Toward a more democratic theory of deliberative democracy," *Hypatia* 22 (2007): 4; See also "Where is the Passion in Deliberative Democracy?" (Presentation at the Annual Meeting of the American Political Science Association, September, 2005)
44. Dryzek, *Deliberative Democracy and Beyond,* p. 53.
45. Dryzek, *Deliberative Democracy and Beyond,* p. 52.
46. Dryzek, *Deliberative Democracy and Beyond,* p. 53.
47. "Persuasion," *Oxford English Dictionary* (2007).
48. Aristotle, "Rhetoric," *The Complete Works of Aristotle,* ed. Jonathan Barnes (Princeton, NJ: Princeton University Press, 1984), 2153, 1355a5.
49. Aristotle, "Rhetoric," 2155, 1358b18–21.
50. Aristotle, "Rhetoric," 2155, 1358b6–7.
51. Benjamin R. Barber, *Strong Democracy* (University of Berkeley Press, 2003), p. 174.
52. Barber, *Strong Democracy,* p. 175.
53. Habermas, *The Theory of Communicative Action,* p. 86.
54. Habermas, *The Theory of Communicative Action,* p. 88.
55. In my formulation of deliberative and strategic persuasion, I am indebted to Habermas' notion that communicative actions are oriented toward understanding while strategic actions are oriented toward success. While my categories differ from Habermas' in important ways (see the discussion at the end of this section), they are inspired in part by his distinction between speech acts oriented toward understanding and success. For Habermas' discussions of these categories, see, Habermas, *The Theory of Communicative Action.*
56. I am grateful to Bernard Manin's paper on promoting debate as a form of deliberation for this definition; see Bernard Manin, "Democratic Deliberation: Why We Should Promote Debate Rather Than Discussion," *Working Paper* (2005), 15. For the original citation in Hobbes, see *De Cive,* XIII, 16.
57. Bernard Manin, "On Legitimacy and Political Deliberation," *Political Theory,* 15, no. 3 (1987): 351.
58. Joseph M. Bessette, *The Mild Voice of Reason* (Chicago: University of Chicago Press, 1994), p. 46.
59. "Strategy," *The Oxford English Dictionary,* 2007.
60. Bachrach and Baratz, *Power and Poverty,* p. 30.
61. For Kant's discussion of treating others as ends, see Immanuel Kant, *Grounding for the Metaphysics of Morals* (Cambridge, MA: Hackett Publishing, 1993).
62. "Sincerity," *Oxford English Dictionary,* 2008.
63. Bok and Goodin make similar claims on this point. See Bok, *Lying,* p. 30. Goodin, *Manipulatory Politics,* p. 26.
64. Kant, *Grounding for the Metaphysics of Morals.* Immanuel Kant, "What Is Enlightenment?," *Kant: Political Writings,* ed. H.S. Reiss (Cambridge University Press, 1991).
65. Kant, *Grounding for the Metaphysics of Morals.*

66. Korsgaard, "The Right to Lie: Kant on Dealing with Evil," p. 332.
67. Bok, *Lying*, p. 19.
68. Bok, *Lying*, p. 19.
69. Philip Pettit, *Republicanism* (Oxford University Press, 1997), p. 55.
70. For more on the epistemic effects of deliberation, see David Estlund, "Beyond Fairness and Deliberation," *Deliberative Democracy*, ed. James Bohman and William Rehg (Cambridge, MA: The MIT Press, 1997); Samuel Freeman, "Deliberative Democracy: A sympathetic comment," *Philosophy and Public Affairs* 29, no. 4 (2000); Cass Sunstein, *Infotopia* (Oxford University Press, 2006); Gutmann and Thompson, *Democracy and Disagreement*.
71. James Madison, *The Federalist Papers* (New York: Penguin Books, 1987), p. 313.
72. This worry is similar to Hobbes' concern that the use of rhetoric in democracy results in a de facto oligarchy, where skillful orators rule. As he puts it, "In a multitude of speakers therefore, where always, either one is eminent alone, or a few being equal amongst themselves, are eminent above the rest, that one or few must of necessity sway the whole; insomuch, that a democracy, in effect, is no more than an aristocracy of orators, interrupted sometimes with the temporary monarchy of one orator." See Thomas Hobbes, *The Elements of Law*, Part II, Ch.2.5.
73. Philip Pettit, "Democracy, Electoral and Contestatory," *Designing Democratic Institutions*, ed. Ian Shapiro and Stephen Macedo (New York University Press, 2000), pp. 117–19.
74. John Rawls, "The Idea of Public Reason Revisited," in Rawls, *The Law of Peoples With "The Idea of Public Reason Revisited"* (Cambridge Press: Harvard University Press, 1999), p. 138.
75. Bok, *Lying*, pp. 103–04.
76. Bok, *Lying*, pp. 103–04.
77. Arthur Isak Applbaum, *Ethics for Adversaries* (Princeton, NJ: Princeton University Press, 1999), pp. 116–17.
78. Applbaum, *Ethics for Adversaries*, p. 117; Bok, *Lying*, p. 104.
79. I am grateful to Jane Mansbridge for this insight.
80. Harvey Sacks, "Everyone Has to Lie," *Sociocultural Dimensions of Language Use*, eds. Mary Sanches and Ben G. Blount (New York: Academic Press, 1975), pp. 69–71.
81. Bok, *Lying*, p. 92.

Part II

Political Psychology

Introduction to Part II

In Parts II and III, we turn from analyzing the proper definition and scope of manipulation to the question of its mechanisms and effects. Whereas in the next section we will be concerned with the institutional mechanisms, which mediate and facilitate manipulative communication, in this section we are concerned instead with the raw material of humanity—its psychology. In order to understand what the possibilities and limitations surrounding manipulation truly are, we need to consider the cognitive aspects of how information is processed, how we form our worldviews, and how emotion plays a role in the process of decision making.

The essays in Part II each take a different approach to explaining the psychological mechanisms of manipulation. George Lakoff's essay "Changing Brains: Lessons from the Living Wage Campaign" takes a micro-level approach to the problems of political psychology. His interest is with the dynamics inside individual minds—how our brains habitually work to process communicated information, and how these habits in turn make us vulnerable to manipulation in certain specific areas. Lakoff uses the issue of a "living wage" to demonstrate how frames as components of our brains filter and shape our perceptions of the world as well as our political views, with corresponding implications for the possibilities and limitations of democratic deliberation. Where Lakoff's essay takes a micro-level approach, Rose McDermott's essay "Emotional Manipulation of Political Identity" focuses instead on the macro-level factors of social psychology that make human beings vulnerable to manipulation. While she does not neglect individual-level thought processes, her primary concern is with the effects of those processes upon the larger emotional dynamics of social groups. Finally, Christina Tarnopolsky's essay "Mimēsis, Persuasion, and Manipulation in Plato's *Republic*" takes a philosophical and historical approach to the same subject matter. Guiding us on a tour of ancient ideas regarding manipulation, Tarnopolsky breaks us out of our familiar contemporary assumptions regarding democratic conflict to point toward more deeply situated philosophical underpinnings of the problem of manipulation and its possible remedies.

Despite these differences of approach, however, Lakoff, McDermott, and Tarnopolsky converge upon similar accounts of the possibilities and limits of human rationality, agency, and emotion. Lakoff's political psychology implicitly challenges the essentially calculative depiction of rationality that animates the rational actor model. Instead, Lakoff argues our frameworks trump or even altogether replace the operation of our purported calculative faculties: that is, many of our responses never reach the point of calculating interest and advantage because we generally make decisions based on the cognitive apparatus that is operating in each individual. But second, Lakoff insists (in a manner reminiscent of Tarnopolsky's account of Plato) that the calculative model of rationality simply misses an important part of what reason consists of: what counts as reasonable is often merely part of the calculus of the framework that each of us carries. Part of the difficulty in deliberating on the ideals we should espouse in the polity is due to our cognitively generated attachment to our frameworks.

McDermott sees our reasoning processes as shot through with emotional complications. McDermott sees emotions as essential components of rationality and posits specific rational functions for many particular emotions. Like Lakoff, McDermott argues that emotions anchor our decision-making processes. For McDermott, many of our emotions must be understood as adaptive psychological mechanisms which have emerged to facilitate solving the persistent collective action problems which plague social life. Our emotional concern with identity thus drives our agency, but this is for a rational and calculated purpose (namely, solving the above-mentioned problems of collective action). Nevertheless, a variety of behaviors (e.g., many of the influence techniques such as "social proof") raise fundamental questions about how much rationality we can attribute to human actions at least at an individual level—though many other influence techniques (such as reciprocity and commitment) are clearly grounded in calculative, rational-choice considerations.

Tarnopolsky's interpretation of Plato, meanwhile, sees rationality as central to human life yet also limited in its scope and application. Some of the mimetic practices Plato considers, Tarnopolsky stresses, actually serve to encourage and enable deliberative rationality within democratic life. Nevertheless, Tarnopolsky approves of Plato's attempt to counter overly rationalistic deliberative models such as those associated today with Jürgen Habermas and John Rawls. The worldviews and paradigms crafted by our culture constitute significant constraints on our reasoning faculties which only the kind of philosophical self-criticism and self-awareness Plato praises in his dialogue can in the end hope to overcome.

The authors in Part II also converge in seeing frames and narratives as critical to understanding how human reasoning actually functions and how emotions mediate and modify that reasoning. For Lakoff, our brain takes information that is given to it and shapes a neural network that literally creates a framework through which we see the world. Every piece of information we acquire and every experience we have is filtered through an emotional apparatus and cognitive structure that is unique, in its own small way, to each individual. These frameworks, as Lakoff calls them, are continually reinforced through the adaptive and emotional structure that is our brain, and in particular through our brain's predisposition to make sense of the world around it through stories and narratives. Lakoff illustrates this process by describing the widely varying narratives that can be employed to examine the concepts of wages, economic relations, and fundamental fairness. What we find is that competing frameworks are stubborn and difficult to change or extricate due to the fact that they are fixed in individuals' brains.

The concepts we employ in public life collectively serve specific functions for us: they structure our reasoning and express and respond to our emotions. Consequently, to be viable our political concepts must fit into emotionally defined frames. These frames create built-in mechanisms through which issues come to be instilled with powerful emotional resonances going well beyond the instrumental functions they play in satisfying our rationally ordered preferences. The fact that our minds work this way has significant implications for the practice of our public life. Political advertising, television journalism, and similar forms of mass media all attempt to capitalize on this feature of our psychology in promoting their own distinctive ends. At the same time, however, these same mass media have crucial limits to the kinds of frames and narratives they can accommodate successfully. Some frames are simply too complex or too distant from our most powerful emotions to be communicated successfully through most forms of mass media.

McDermott too holds that frames and narratives are central to our political psychology, but she goes further to argue that the most significant frames and narratives for most political purposes are those connected to the dynamics of identity. Those frames and narratives which help to cement or undermine our sense of belonging to particular groups, and those frames and narratives which exalt or diminish specific groups as in-groups and out-groups, are those that hold the most power. It is for this reason that outrage plays such a central role in politics—because outrage is such a potent carrier of the emotions associated with in-group versus out-group dynamics. This is also why problems of identity and difference have reasserted themselves continuously throughout political life, as recent theorists from K. Anthony Appiah to William Connolly to Charles Taylor to Iris Marion Young have repeatedly emphasized. These techniques prey on our emotions, and use our deep-seated desire for identity and belonging as one of the most potent weapons in the manipulator's arsenal.

Throughout Tarnopolsky's essay, an account of frames emerges that bears some striking resemblances to Lakoff's and McDermott's theories: namely, that our worldviews or paradigms count as significant constraints on citizens' capacity for reasoning. Citizens, Tarnopolsky concurs, are emotionally invested in the worldviews that surround them, and these worldviews are shaped in turn by the practice of *mimēsis* or images whose uncritical use Plato sharply criticizes. But for Tarnopolsky, this indicates the special significance of the frame to which she devotes the most attention in her essay: that of Plato's conception of the "noble lie." This conception of Plato's offers a frame that is capable of becoming an anti-frame: a framework that encourages critical thinking by citizens about the regime in which they live and therefore offers an instrument for counteracting the vulnerability to manipulation which these features of human psychology seem to necessarily entail.

These constraints of human psychology bear directly upon the capacity of citizens for the kind of rational collective agency to which democratic theories tend to aspire. In most discussions concerning manipulation, there is a persistent assumption that actors in the polity have free will and the capacity to deliberate. Lakoff's model of psychology at the individual level suggests, however, that there are significant cognitive limits to what kinds of deliberations are possible. Consider for example the notion of a public's "putative will" that underlies critiques of manipulation as diverse as Robert Goodin's and James Fishkin's. Lakoff's psychology seems to suggest that, with respect to the idea of a pre-existing "putative will" independent of the factors manipulation makes use of, there may not in fact be any "there" there. This tends to lead us (employing the typology of forms of democracy developed by Fishkin) towards a more "contestatory" theory of democracy—one more open, as Ball's and Klemp's accounts are, to the idea that all rationalities are, to some degree, emotional and that all persuasions are, to some degree, strategic in character.

From a similar perspective, McDermott's analysis calls into question especially any democratic theory that is excessively reliant on a strong notion of public reasoning or citizen rationality in the conventional sense. Even more so, any democratic theory that relies on citizens sharing identities, values, or interests across the society are particularly suspect and almost certainly unworkable. Because citizens are driven by the in-group versus out-group dynamics that McDermott describes, any theory that relies on shared identity as its starting premise is ignoring the key fact of social psychology that we are oriented to divide along precisely the lines that such theorists would hope to unite us. Instead, "divide and conquer" is the inevitable motto of any effective political action, with severe consequences for any hope of shared, deliberative agency across the society as a whole.

Tarnopolsky's answer to this—or rather, Plato's answer, which to this extent she endorses—is the assertion that democracy requires continuous and vigorous philosophical contestation of society's core unquestioned assumptions. This idea requires its own form of "deliberative" democracy—but it is deliberative in a specific sense, namely, in the sense of the dialectic approach engaged in by the interlocutors in the dialogue of the *Republic*. Plato's unique contribution to democratic theory, Tarnopolsky argues, is his understanding that "manipulation works upon the minds of democratic citizens most insidiously in the spaces prior to and outside of their direct political activities of citizenship." This further explains the crucial importance which the *Republic* places on symbolic matters such as myths, role models, art, and similar matters. For it is the parts of politics that are second nature to us to the point that we do not *recognize* them as part of politics, Plato (along with Tarnopolsky) believes, that exert the most sinister and powerful forms of rule over our conduct.

The essays in this section provide tools for critically re-examining not only the concept of manipulation, but its relation to the philosophical ideals of deliberation and free will itself. Any traditional notion of manipulation holds that actors have volition to make their preferences known and to act upon those preferences. Yet taken together, these essays show (from varying perspectives) that our capacity for free choice is much different from what we have traditionally assumed. If democracy aspires to be the expression of our collective choices, then the limits which our psychology and cognition place on our capacity for free and rational decision making will in the end prove to be, at least in principle, limits on the possibility of democracy itself.

4   Changing Brains
Lessons from the Living Wage Campaign

George Lakoff

Framing in Everyday Life

Suppose you have a friend who doesn't spend his money very freely. You can understand his behavior in at least two very different ways. You might think of him as stingy. This contrasts with generous. These words raise the issue of how willing he is to part with his money to benefit someone else. Stingy says "not very" and imposes a negative judgment. But the same behavior might also be described by someone else as thrifty. Here, the opposite is wasteful, and the issue is how efficiently he manages his money. The judgment is positive.

What we have here is a case of framing. The same behavior can be framed positively as managing money efficiently or negatively as being unwilling to help someone in need. Opposites like "stingy" and "generous" are defined as opposing values in the same conceptual frame.

A frame is a mental structure that we normally use in thinking, usually without being aware of it. All words are defined in terms of frames.

Framing can be extremely important to your life. Framing matters. Frames characterize the way you understand a situation and they affect how you live.

Tax Relief

On the day that President George W. Bush took office, the words *tax relief* started appearing in White House communiqués to the press and in official speeches and reports by conservatives. Let us look in detail at the framing evoked by this term because it offers an excellent perspective on how issues in the public debate can be framed with political and media consequences.

The word *relief* evokes a frame in which there is a blameless afflicted person who we identify with and who has some affliction, some pain or harm that is imposed by some external cause-of-pain. Relief is the taking away of the pain or harm, and it is brought about by some reliever-of-pain.

The Relief frame is an instance of a more general rescue scenario, in which there is a hero (the reliever-of-pain), a victim (the afflicted), a crime (the affliction), a villain (the cause-of-affliction), and a rescue (the pain relief). The hero is inherently good, the villain is evil, and the victim after the rescue owes gratitude to the Hero.

The term *tax relief* evokes all of this and more. Taxes, in this phrase, are the affliction (the crime). Proponents of taxes are the causes-of affliction (the villains), the taxpayer is the afflicted victim, and the proponents of tax relief are the heroes who deserve the taxpayers' gratitude.

The more the term tax relief is used and heard or read by millions of people, the more this view of taxation as an affliction and conservatives as heroes gets reinforced. President Bush used the slogan, "Tax relief creates jobs." Looking at the Relief frame, we see that afflictions and pain can be quantified, and there can be more or less relief. By the logic of framing (*not* the logic of economics), if tax relief creates jobs, then more tax relief creates more jobs.

Conservatives have worked for decades to establish the metaphors of taxation as a burden, an affliction, and an unfair punishment—all of which require relief. They have also, over decades, built up the frame in which the wealthy create jobs and giving them more wealth creates more jobs.

The Power of Framing and Reframing

Indeed, conservative think tanks frame the full range of issues from their perspective. Today, conservative framings dominate our political discourse. Democrats too talk about tax relief, although the frame contradicts everything they are trying to do economically. That is the power of framing.

Framing is central to what politics is, and struggles over framing are as old as politics itself. It is only in recent decades, though, that cognitive scientists have begun to understand precisely what framing is, what its parameters are, and what these parameters mean for the practice of democracy.

Frames are in your brain, physically in the synapses. What we call thought is the result of physical changes in the brain, changes both powerful and durable. Their power lies in our utter dependence on them: we need frames to understand any new fact or to address any new problem. Just as we cannot see color without the color cones in our eyes and the color circuitry in our brains, so also we cannot take in ideas without frames, which are neural circuits in our brains. They determine what we can and cannot understand in the world of thought, what information we can and cannot accept, what beliefs we can and cannot sustain.

Frames are powerful; they are also durable. Once our brains have been changed to accommodate a particular frame, it is hard, if not impossible, to undo that frame. Several years ago I wrote a book called *Don't Think of an Elephant!*, the title of which captures this feature of frames. "Don't think of an elephant!" is a command with which you cannot comply, even if you want to. Why? Because the concept of an elephant is already there, physically in the synapses of your brain, waiting to be activated. And just by invoking the word *elephant*, a process in your brain is triggered that leads directly to the activation of that concept. There is circuitry in your brain, physically, for the concept of an elephant, and once I speak the word, neural activation is going to head straight for that circuit in your brain. Only when that frame-circuit is activated can the word be understood. Frames are thus normal and natural. You can't think or communicate without them—and their operation is 98 percent unconscious. Most of the time we are not aware of the frames we are using to think with. All communication is, thus, brain change; and learning new ideas is acquiring new frame-circuits, largely unconsciously.

Frames once created are impossible to eliminate entirely. One of the great challenges facing contemporary democracies arises from the fact that frames can be installed in your brain without you realizing it. The mechanism is *repetition*. Every time a word or phrase is repeated, the synapses in its frame-circuit get stronger. A catchy idea—even a transparently dumb one—if repeated often enough, will make its home in your brain and never leave. It may or may not be marked as being dumb, but it will be there. As any marketing expert knows, repetition can change brains. Political marketers know this and use it effectively to change the brains of others. That may sound like science fiction, but I am afraid it is all science, no fiction.

Much of thought is metaphoric. The metaphors can be so deep as to be constitutive of ideas. One version of morality, for example, is constituted in part by the metaphor of moral accounting, according to which helping someone is metaphorically giving someone money and hurting someone is taking money away. When someone helps you, you can say, "I'm in your debt" or "I owe you one." When you hurt someone, it is as if you metaphorically took money from them and you owe them recompense. "It's payback time!" Moral judgments—and even murders and wars—arise from the use of this metaphor, as does the concept of justice itself.

Real reason operates to a large extent by means of metaphor—and therefore so does political reason. Confronted with choices in a complex social world, we invariably proceed by means of ordinary frame-based and metaphorical reasoning more than by deductive or scientific reasoning.

What is crucial to understand is that the metaphorical reasoning that pervades all of political life is both largely unconscious and deeply laden with emotion. When we say the president's poll numbers are down, we don't notice that we are invoking a metaphor: that happens at a wholly unconscious level. But once invoked, that metaphor carries with it all the many emotional associations we may connect with it. Think about what you associate with the word *down*: debasement, dejection, perhaps even damnation. Now think about the president whose poll numbers are down—even if his approval rating merely fell from 58 to 53 percent, that almost statistically insignificant drop in his ratings may, by means of the metaphor, evoke our feelings of discouragement, contempt, or condemnation.

If the microscopic answer to the question is framing and metaphor, the telescopic answer is *worldviews*—what we might call the "deep frames" or cultural narratives which bundle metaphors into comprehensive stories guide our understanding and our behavior. Frames constitute all our thoughts, but not all frames are created equal. The words tax relief evoke a relatively specific frame in which taxation is a metaphorical affliction that should be eliminated. Sometimes progressives talk as though all they need to do is come up with some clever slogans like this to promote their own policies and all will be well. But cognitive science shows the problem lies much deeper than this. Tax relief has its power because it is embedded in a larger deep frame: the conservative worldview in which the market is the final authority, natural and moral—the decider, who rightly rewards fiscal discipline and punishes the lack of it. From the perspective of this metaphor, the government is acting immorally when it exercises authority over the market in one of four ways: regulation, taxation, unionization, and tort cases.

That worldview may in turn be embedded in a cultural narrative that is even more fundamental. The worldviews I discussed at length in *Moral Politics* and elsewhere—the strict father narrative underlying the contemporary conservative mindset versus the nurturing parent narrative underlying the progressive worldview—are examples of these deep frames.[1] These cultural narratives serve to ground and justify the more specific framings of particular political issues, and also to give them their emotional power. The deep-seated beliefs and emotions on which these specific framings can draw when they are properly embedded in cultural narratives of great power are why framing matters so much to our contemporary democratic politics.

Taken together, these facts about our brains explain why aspirations for a politics based purely on deliberative reasoning regarding commonly recognized facts is dangerously naïve. Our brains do not work like that. We need frames to make sense of facts. Just telling people facts that contradict the frames they already have will usually not have any effect. The frames stay, the facts just bounce off. Statistics and numbers won't matter. Even negating a frame just reinforces the frame. If you say, "I'm against tax relief," you are still evoking the tax relief frame, with taxation as an affliction. You might give facts and figures indicating that costs from federal tax cuts will just be passed down to the local level and to private costs, providing no relief, but the word "relief" still evokes the same frame.

Instead, what you have to do is reframe. Either find another frame that better fits the reality you are talking about, or create one. Finding an existing one is by far the better choice. If it exists, people already have it in their brains and you just have to find the language to evoke it. If you have to create a new frame, you have to get people to learn that frame, which takes time and effort and may not work.

Framing in Living Wage Campaigns

Let me illustrate how this process works with an example I have studied over many years—the struggle over frames employed in the campaign for a living wage.

Living Wage Frame

When advocates talk about a living wage, they assume what I call a Working-for-a-Living frame. The frame has certain elements—the basic parts of the frame:

An employee (whose viewpoint we take)
An employer (either a person or a business)
A job (e.g., waiting on tables, trimming trees)
A salary (for performing the job)
Basic needs of the employee (that the salary is to pay for)

This frame also has certain internal truths—that is, what is taken to be true of a situation when this frame is used. These include:

The employee does the job.
The employer pays the salary to the employee for doing the job.
The employee deserves the salary.
The salary is sufficient for the employee's basic needs.

Conservative's Frame

Meanwhile, business interests that oppose a living wage frame the conceptual issue very differently, with contrasting elements. Their frame could be called the Conservative Business frame. Frame elements include:

Business owners (whose viewpoint is taken by the opposition as paramount)
Employees
Products
Customers
Revenue
Expenses
Profit

Inherent in the opposition's frame are their truths:

> Owners own the business (not workers).
> The purpose of the business is to make maximum profit for the owners, who deserve the profits.
> Jobs must be done to produce the products sold by the business.
> Employees are paid to do the jobs.
> The less paid the employees, the higher the profits.
> To maximize profits, owners must maximize revenues and minimize costs.
> That's the American way of doing business, and we should not interfere with it (with living wage laws and other measures).

A note about the Conservative Business frame: I use the term *conservative* to contrast it with a socially responsible business frame, or the family-business frame. A word of caution should be used at this point. Real conceptual frames that people use are far more complex than those we are discussing here. I discuss the simple business frame for two reasons: (1) most people have it and understand it, and (2) it is commonly used in arguments against living wage legislation.

Unfortunately, in many areas of our society influenced by a conservative-controlled Congress, right wing dominated state legislators, and big business—not to mention many of those who are just wealthy—the Conservative Business frame is the dominant frame that rings true. Such "truths" may not actually be true at all, or maybe rarely. What is important is that when the frame is used to structure a situation and then communicated to the public through the media, it is assumed to be true—unless explicitly contradicted. And even then they may reappear as assumed truths.

Living Wage Campaigns and the Market

The Conservative Business frame does not stand alone. It is supported by the idea of the market, as economists often understand it and teach about it. The idea of the market is the basis of the entire American economy. It is framed in a way that distorts radically how it really operates, and that frame stands in the way of living wage campaigns. Here's what the Natural Market frame looks like:

Entities

> Businesses
> Commodities
> Customers
> Prices

Internal truths of this frame are:

Commodities are relatively scarce; they are not freely available.

Businesses sell commodities to customers at prices.

Businesses seek to maximize prices for commodities sold.

Customers seek to minimize prices for commodities bought.

The market is part of nature; its operation is inescapable.

If left alone, it works best and maximizes profit for everyone in the market.

Prices are determined by a law of nature, the Law of Supply and Demand.

Supply increases tend to make prices drop.

Demand increases tend to make them rise.

The operation of the market is fair, since nature is unbiased.

Prices determined by the market are fair prices.

For optimal results, the market should be left alone.

Externally imposed constraints on prices are not optimal and mess things up for everybody.

This frame is, of course, a myth, but living wage advocates encounter it everywhere. You need to recognize it, know its problems, and know how to reframe. Frames are embedded in the brains of those you want to convince, and shape how they perceive the world. Without the ability to change the relevant frames, you are likely to lose the debate.

One of the most insidious aspects of the Natural Market frame is its use as metaphor for the basis of labor and wages. Note that neither labor nor wages are in the market frame itself. Labor and wages are brought into the Natural Market frame via the metaphor that labor is a resource (a kind of commodity), where wages are prices for labor and employers are customers.

This is an extremely insidious metaphor—and it is everywhere. For example, the name *Human Resources* assumes the metaphor. When labor is made a resource, the fact that the resource is a human being is hidden by the metaphor. Human values and human relationships are hidden. Individual qualities are hidden—one worker is as good as another who fulfills the same function.

And of course, the very question of a living wage is outside the metaphor, as if it didn't exist. Resources don't have families, needs, health problems, and so on. A "fair wage" becomes a "fair price" determined by the "labor market."

The concept of skill is important in this metaphor. Skill is seen as a measure of value, with highly skilled labor worth more and unskilled labor worth the least. This idea, as it works in the frame, is also insidious. In the metaphor, high skill is assumed to be in short supply and needed. But this defines skill in terms of the law of supply and demand. A teacher may be highly skilled, but those skills will have low value if teachers are in great supply, or if there is no way to profit from those skills.

There is one more important issue here: Who sells labor to the employer? There are two answers. The worker either sells his own labor, or a union sells it for him, as an agent. If the worker sells his own labor, he is usually put at a big disadvantage by the law of supply and demand. Since he controls only a supply of one, he can't drive up the price. The individual is at another disadvantage as well—coercion, that is, sexual harassment, bad working conditions, demeaning treatment, predatory lending, and so on. Unions control a greater labor supply, and so can drive up the price and defend workers against coercion.

We can see why conservatives hate unions. They see them as interfering in the natural labor market. And worse, they see them as immoral—giving workers things they haven't earned and undermining discipline.

This puts unions in a difficult position. With their workers they use the working-for-a-living metaphor, which is their whole reason for being. But with employers, they use the employers' metaphor—the labor market metaphor. These are conflicting frames, and that makes for a hard balancing act. The fact that our emotions are tied so closely to our frames is what makes the debate so heated as well. It is not that we are merely arguing over policy; people feel that their very worldviews are being attacked and that the facts are being wrongly construed when others questions the frames through which they see the world.

The Conservative Moral Frame

Conservatives have a very different view of morality than progressives do. At the center of conservative morality is the idea of discipline.

The Moral Discipline Frame

People naturally tend to follow their desires rather than to do always what it is right. If people are to do right, they have to learn discipline. People who are not disciplined will not act morally.

Scarcity and difficulty in the world imposes a form of discipline. Market-based competition and unfettered free enterprise thus contribute to morality by imposing discipline. If people did not have to compete, if they were just given what they need, there would be no reason to be disciplined, and so no one would follow moral rules. People would just do what feels right.

Getting payments not earned (according to need, not worth) promotes immorality and is itself immoral. Moreover, it upsets the market and leads away from the maximization of the interests of all, thus hurting people in general.

An important consequence of The Moral Discipline frame is that there will always be winners and losers. The more disciplined people will win and they will deserve it. The losers will serve the winners. Those who accept the frame assume this is as it should be. Otherwise, there would be no need for discipline and all morality would break down. A saying like, "The poor will always be with us," expresses this clearly. Notice that the "us" in this saying does not include the poor.

The economic application of this moral frame derives from the specter of scarcity: If resources are scarce, then people who don't work to produce them don't deserve a share. They just take from those who are productive, creating the threat that there may not be enough for those who are productive. In the U.S. society, there is such abundance, there is no real specter of scarcity; there is only the lack of money to buy on the part of many people. Yet the frames have ossified in the brains of much of the population and are being taught to a new generation.

These frames do not accurately portray our reality, but that does not make them less real frames. Whether a frame accurately portrays the world has little to do with the fact that it is fixed in our brains and is difficult to change, let alone remove.

Real Arguments: Conservative Frames and Words

These dominant conservative frames illustrate what the living wage activist is up against. Let us look at how these frames create a logic—a mode of reasoning that living wage advocates constantly encounter.

The website of the conservative think tank, The Employment Policies Institute (*The Living Wage Policy: The Basics,* available at http://www. epionline.org/studies/epi_livingwage_08-2000.pdf), provides the following characterization of the living wage.

What is the Living Wage?

Since the mid-1990s, the American Left has been assembling a new Economic and Social Justice movement that works to implement so-called "living wage" ordinances in cities throughout the United States.

What is the living wage campaign? It is an organized effort to force employers to inject a welfare mentality into the workplace. The goal is to set pay wage rates to each according to their need rather than their skills. This means doubling, tripling, and even quadrupling the current minimum wage—at a huge cost to consumers and taxpayers.

In this debate, "need" is defined not by independent experts but by the living wage movement itself. Far from subsistence wages, various living wage proponents have endorsed mandatory wages as high as $48,000 per year, mandatory vacation of four to five weeks per year, health care coverage for all employees, and more.

The living wage movement did not start out with such large demands. The first successful campaign for a living wage, in Baltimore in 1994, sought a living wage of $6.10 an hour, rising to $7.90 within five years and thereafter adjusted to inflation. This ordinance applied only to companies that provided contracted services for a city or county (e.g., landscaping public grounds, providing meals to senior citizens or busing children to public schools).

Contrast that with a living wage ordinance pushed through in Santa Monica, California, in 1999. That ordinance required a $10.69-an-hour minimum wage for all businesses with 50 or more employees in the city's coastal zone business district, plus 24 paid vacation days each year.

Even that is not the limit. Help The Homeless, a pro-living wage organization, has suggested the following hourly minimum wages for select U.S. cities:

Boston $19.27
Santa Cruz $16.93
New York $16.81
Washington $15.46
Newark $14.58
Chicago $14.37
Boulder $13.62

As the living wage movement grew throughout the 1990s, proponents sought coverage of living wage laws to include companies that had received tax abatements, or incentive grants or that lease property from a city or county. Many businesses, whose "customer" was the general public—and NOT the city or county government, were now required to pay living wage rates to their employees, yet they were unable to pass along the cost of the mandated increase to the government body that mandated them

As the scope of the living wage coverage widened, the proposed living wage rates skyrocketed to $11, $12, even $15 an hour, plus full benefits packages for what were heretofore entry-level jobs. One group recommended a $48,000 living wage for a single parent with two children living in Washington, DC. That works out to $24 per hour—if the parent works full-time.

That's more than four times the current minimum wage, and that money has to come from somewhere. It will come from employers and their customers, or from government and taxpayers. In both cases, that means it will come from you. Or, the costs will be shouldered by employees who lose their jobs, or applicants who cannot get hired.

The living wage movement is now expanding its reach with, in the words of advocate Robert Pollin, "a more ambitious aim: to create a living wage policy with a national scope." (*The Living Wage Policy*, p. 4)

After reading the EPI's argument, it should be clear that they see the world through different frames than do supporters of the living wage movement. Let's take a closer look at how their frames structure their arguments.

Let us begin with the term *welfare mentality*. For conservatives, a welfare mentality violates The Moral Discipline frame. It assumes the idea behind the welfare state: Every human being inherently deserves to have basic needs met (regardless of whether they are earned through the discipline of the market).

The term *mentality* is condescending. It uses a frame in which some people have intellects superior to others, and in which those with inferior intellects have modes of thought that are wrong—false or immoral, or both. The word mentality refers to such modes of thought.

Other Uses of Conservative Frames

The conservative argument is an elaboration of the frames adopted above.

The phrase *to each according to his needs* is part of a Marxist slogan. By using that phrase, it is indirectly suggested that the living wage campaign is a form of communism. They refer elsewhere to living wage advocates as "Marxoids."[3]

The idea here is that the very concept of a living wage violates the idea of the labor market, which is taken to be literal, not metaphorically constructed. The labor market is assumed to be a special case of the market in general, which is taken as defining capitalism, assumed to be in contrast with socialism. A living wage, therefore, is seen as a threat to very idea of the American economy and conservative morality. It is not just anti-business, it is communist, un-American, and immoral. The frame that says socialism is immoral has been laid for years and reinforced in such a way that the very invocation of the idea brings about very strong emotions for most Americans.

The Pay-according-to-Skill frame assumes that the pay-skill hierarchy is a natural constraint governing the labor market. The implication is that, without it, the market would not function correctly to maximize the profits of all, and that therefore everyone would be hurt financially.

The phrase *This means doubling, tripling, and even quadrupling the current minimum wage—at a huge cost to consumers and taxpayers* is, of course, an exaggeration, a rhetorical trick.

What is interesting here *is at a huge cost to consumers and taxpayers*. This reasoning follows from using the Conservative Business frame. Note what is not mentioned in these passages:

- Community payments to corporations (in the form of tax breaks, development subsidies, zoning changes, local education, local infrastructure, and so on). These payments are made invisible by accounting methods.

- Lowered community service expenses (emergency health care, food programs, housing programs, and so on). These too are invisible, since they are saved, not paid.
- Increased profits due to improved corporate efficiency and lowered expenses for recruitment and training. These also do not appear overtly in budgets as living wage effects.
- The moral structuring of the economy. Economies are claimed to be "amoral," despite all sorts of moral structuring (e.g., no child labor, no assassinations of competitors). Entrepreneurs are expected to work within moral limits.
- Lowered but still reasonable profits (return to stockholders, stock price, bonuses to management, etc.). Profit relative to previous wages is taken as fixed, as if by a law of nature.
- Profits with a living wage are always considered relative to profits without a living wage taken as a norm. Non-living-wage profits are held fixed and other alternatives not considered: raising prices, firing employees, asking for more tax breaks, and so on.

We will discuss these in detail below. I mention them here because they cannot be considered—or even perceived—because they stand outside of the conservative frames. The conservative frames hide everything the living wage advocates are talking about.

Consider the response, "Times are tough. There isn't enough money to pay for a Living Wage!" The lack of money depends on how you keep the books, and the conservative frames dictate only one way of keeping the books.

Finally, a last argument is worth considering: Proponents sought coverage of living wage laws to include companies that had received tax abatements, or incentive grants, or that lease property from a city or county. Many businesses serving the general public and not the city or county government "were now required to pay living wage rates to their employees, yet they were unable to pass along the cost of the mandated increase to the government body that mandated them."

The assumption again is that living wages are externally imposed additional costs that should be passed on. Profits without a living wage are considered not only as a financial base line, but as a moral base line.

The Living Wage Frames

The Ideal vs. the Norm

The Working-for-a-Living frame, mentioned earlier as the living wage movement's frame, has an interesting mental status. For most Americans, it characterizes an ideal: working a job should pay enough to meet basic needs. It also has the mental status of a norm. In other words, many Americans commonly assume that, in this land of opportunity, a job will pay enough to live on. That is, the frame is both taken as ideal and normal. The ideal status of this frame is an advantage to the living wage movement. The norm status of this frame contradicts the living wage campaign as many people assume that jobs already pay a living wage.

That is why books like Barbara Ehrenreich's *Nickel and Dimed*, which exposes the reality of working Americans just trying to get by, have been so shocking to so many people; most Americans believed that simply going from welfare to work would allow someone to earn a living wage.

Living wage campaigns not only have to counter-frame the opposition, but also have to confront the fallacy that the ideal has not been achieved—it's not even close, but most people don't know that.

The Progressive Moral Worldview

Living wage campaigns exist within a moral perspective that is fundamentally at odds with the conservative moral worldview. They assume a progressive moral worldview that centers on:

Empathy: caring about, identifying with, and connecting with others; and

Responsibility: actually carrying out what empathy requires—that includes taking care of yourself so that you can carry out your responsibility to others.

From this moral center, a great deal more follows: fairness, protection of those who need it, cooperation, honesty and trust, open two-way communication, competence, education, fulfillment in life, and the development of communities that live by these values.

It is from this moral perspective that the Working-for-a-Living frame makes sense as an ideal. The fact that most Americans accept it as an ideal is testimony to the fact that most Americans accept the moral worldview that underlies it.

But people are not necessarily logical. Many Americans accept both the Working-for-a-Living frame and the conservative frames, even though they may contradict each other. Recall that frames are complex and difficult to remove. It is possible to hold two differing frames that pull at our emotions in different ways. This is something that political actors know and why the battle to find ways to reiterate, repeat, and reinforce a particular frame over and over is so important.

The job of the living wage campaign is to bring the living wage frames into American life, and with them, the progressive moral worldview. Unless that moral worldview and those frames become dominant in the American cognitive landscape, there will be little hope for economic justice in general and living wages in particular.

More Living Wage Frames

The genius of the living wage campaign has been to provide specific framings that highlight oft-hidden economic realities and fit progressive morality. Some of these are implicit, some explicit. We have already seen the Working-for-a-Living Frame; the others are discussed below.

The Constructed Market Frame

Markets are constructed to fit practical considerations, moral principles, and specific interests. For example, the Securities and Exchange Commission structures the stock market. The World Trade Organization has almost 1,000 pages of regulations, mostly favoring international corporate interests. Slavery is excluded from the labor market as is child labor. These are all externally imposed constraints, and they exist in all markets. This realistic view of markets is entirely at odds with the view that the market is a force of nature, entirely free, amoral, and optimal.

Once one sees that markets are constructed in this way, the question arises: How can the market best serve the public interest and progressive moral values? The living wage movement is providing some answers to this question.

Living wage advocates are not just pointing out the benefits of the living wage to communities, they are creating a new frame.

The Community Benefit Frame

The more businesses pay living wages, then the more:
The cost of community services will go down,
The economy will improve (more money spent),
The self-respect of low-income residents will rise,
The general quality of life in the community will rise
(less crime, drugs, homelessness),
The moral level and reputation of the community will rise,
Property care and property values will rise, and
Businesses will do better.

This frame takes the focus away from business alone and puts it on the community as a whole and the people who live within it. From this perspective, certain otherwise hidden things can be seen, namely, that businesses do better as their communities do better and that communities do better when businesses do better, and both do better with a living wage ordinance in place.

The Business Benefit Frame

If a business pays living wages, then:

Morale will rise,
Turnover will fall,
Recruitment and training costs will fall, and
Efficiency will rise.

This frame focuses on things that are left out of the conservative frames: Morale, turnover, recruiting, and efficiency. It is based on studies by distinguished economists Janet Yellen (a former presidential advisor to Bill Clinton) and George Akerlof (a Nobel Prize winner).

The Payment to Corporations Frame

Tax breaks and subsidies from cities to corporations are wealth redistributions; taxpayers' taxes are going from cities to corporations.

Zoning changes for corporations are wealth redistributions from taxpayers to corporations. The reason is that zoning changes lower property values for taxpayers and raise property values for corporations.

If corporations are receiving payments from communities, it seems reasonable for the communities to get something in return. What, exactly, makes this seem reasonable?

There are actually two different versions: one involves fairness, and one involves a social contract.

The Fiscal Fairness Frame

It is only fair to balance part of the flow of wealth from taxpayers to corporations with a flow of wealth and well-being (health, safety, etc.) to the community.

It's a bargain for the corporations; they spend only 1 to 4 percent of revenues on living wages, while they get much more than that in wealth redistribution from the tax payers and future profits.

The Social Contract Frame

We allow corporations certain privileges, protections, and even payments, and we expect certain ethical behavior in return: paying taxes, honest accounting, environmental responsibility, and paying employees a living wage.

One reason that living wage campaigns are difficult is that these frames are mostly novel and have to be introduced and repeated over and over, while there is no ready-made language for them. On the other hand, opponents can use commonplace, everyday, familiar frames with familiar language and patterns of reasoning.

We can now see the basic argument for living wage ordinances, given these frames.

The Basic Argument for Living Wages

Everybody who works for a living deserves a living wage. No one who works a full-time job should be mired below the poverty line and be unable to support a family. It is simply immoral (i.e., Working-for-a-Living frame).

Markets are structured morally. Child labor is not permitted, because it is immoral exploitation. Slavery is not permitted. Nor are whippings and beatings of employees. So increasing profits by driving wages below the poverty line should be outlawed on moral grounds; impoverishing people should not be permitted.

Moreover, markets are structured to serve special interests. Oil and coal subsidies are examples of how special interests structure markets. These subsidies are huge payments from taxpayers to such companies. The effect is to keep oil and coal low in price, thus allowing more to be sold with the result that the country has become more dependent on oil and coal. This serves the interests of those companies, since it structures the market in their favor.

We believe that markets should be structured to serve the public interest (Constructed Markets frame).

Local communities make payments out of taxpayers' money to businesses in many forms: tax breaks, development subsidies, zoning changes that raise the value of businesses, local education and infrastructure development that contribute to business profitability, and most obviously, contracts (Payment-to-Corporations frame). It is only fair that businesses return some of these payments in the form of living wages to employees (Fiscal Fairness frame). They have that responsibility (Social Contract frame).

Living wages benefit communities in many ways. First, they lower the cost of community services to the indigent by allowing those working to move out of poverty. Those costly services include emergency medical care, food programs, housing programs, drug and alcohol programs, and so on. Living wages make communities better places to live and result in less poverty, less crime, less homelessness, less addiction and more self-respect, more community pride, and better-kept communities. When communities are better places to live, more people want to live there and more businesses want to locate there. Living wages are infectious in their benefits to communities (Community Benefit frame).

Living wages also benefit businesses. As economists Yellen and Akerlof have found, businesses benefit from paying living wages in the following ways: the wages increase morale, they increase productivity (workers who are financially better off and are not regularly changing jobs work better), and because such workers tend to stay on the job, businesses save on recruitment and training costs (Business Benefit frame).

In some cases, businesses may face the possibility of lower profits. Well run businesses can cope with the moral limits set on markets. Effective entrepreneurs have coped without slavery, child labor, and the beating of workers. If they are competent, they can cope without paying below poverty level wages (Constructed Markets frame).

But they shouldn't have to. The cost to business of paying living wages has been found to be extremely low. Between payments by the community and the benefits of increased productivity and lowered costs, living wage costs should be easily absorbed when accounting practices make the trade-offs clear. Businesses can both do good and do well. That is how the living wage frames are put into practice.

Beyond Living Wage Campaigns: A Moral Economy

Conservatives are right to be afraid of living wage campaigns. They are just one step to a moral economy.

Living wage advocates sometimes get a bit dejected with the thought that their efforts are on behalf of such a small portion of the population. But the results of their efforts go far beyond the often modest wage increases they win for others.

Living wage campaigns are changing the framing of the economic system.

Each of the frames introduced by advocates of living wage frames makes the conservative frames weaker. I want to mention two new frames beyond the living wage that I think we will need in creating a moral economy.

The Two-Tier Economy

In Greek mythology, Atlas was the Titan whose job was to hold up the heavens to keep them from falling. He wound up stuck in this job, unable to move lest the heavens fall.

The Modern Atlas Frame

The United States has a two-tier economy, with about a quarter of the population in the lower tier. Those in the lower tier mostly work—often multiple jobs—but tend not to have health insurance or adequate housing, nutrition, education, child care, transportation, and so on. The jobs they do are absolutely necessary to our economy. For low wages they pick fruits and vegetables, care for children and the elderly, clean houses, cook, waitress, garden, bag groceries, work at check out stands, mop floors and clean up in office buildings, work as security guards and hospital orderlies, and so on. Without them, this society and this economy could not function. These Atlases support the life styles of the top three-quarters of the population and yet are financially enslaved. They are paid far less than their labor is worth to the economy. They deserve to be paid on the basis of their contribution to the economy.

The sentence, *They are paid less than their labor is worth to the economy*, makes no sense from a commonplace economic perspective. It violates a fundamental property of markets, namely, the exchange metaphor for value, the value of something is what buyers in a free market pay for it- and that includes labor. From this perspective, your labor is worth exactly what you are paid for it, no more, no less. Since the economy as a whole is not an employer (a buyer of labor), that sentence is nonsensical from a traditional economics perspective. That sentence can only make sense if one rejects the exchange metaphor for value and adopts another metaphor.

Our two-tier economy calls for a very different metaphor for the value of labor, a contribution metaphor for value: the value of labor is what it contributes to the economy as a whole. Given this metaphor, what you contribute is what you earn through your work. But you may be paid much less than you earn, that is, less than your labor contributes to the economy. This is unfair.

The living wage campaign and the Earned Income Tax Credit (EITC) are two ways to begin addressing this unfairness, at least minimally, by bringing what is paid a bit closer to what is earned, at least close enough to get working people out of abject poverty.

These two approaches share important common elements. Both have a moral component in that they make use of the Working-for-a-Living frame, and the fact that it is seen as a moral ideal. Both focus on hidden aspects of the economy. Advocates of living wage point to community payments to corporations and asks for equity in the form of wages paid above the poverty level, which provide community benefits. The money ultimately comes from taxpayers, though it is in the form of salaries and is seen as earned, since, according to the exchange metaphor for value, what is earned is what is paid by one's employer.

Under EITC, the money also comes ultimately from taxpayers, but it is not seen as earned from the company as it comes from the government in a lump sum, not from one's immediate employer.

The living wage campaign makes sense for many, but not all, workers. The American economy is structured so that, in all too many cases, the people or businesses paying employees cannot afford to pay them what they are really worth to our society and our economy. They are, in short, not able in this economy to be paid what they earn. Nannies and child care workers, for example, contribute much more than they can be paid by their employers—as do many others throughout American society.

They are working to support the economy as a whole, cannot be paid what they are worth by their employer, and so, one might argue, they should be paid by the economy. A far more serious EITC—a negative income tax—might be a fair way for these modern Atlases to be paid what they earn for holding up the sky.

Living wage and EITC are both needed as they both work to lift the poor into a standard of living that is acceptable. They have two different constituencies, which in some cases may overlap.

Note that I have framed both living wage and EITC not as social programs, but as the use of taxpayers' money for taxpayers' benefit. At no time have I argued for the *right* to a living wage. I have used an equity argument.

Toward Ethical Business

The business of America is business—ethical business. Business is central to American life, and American values demand that business be ethical. There is no shortage of ideas in this area. I am including one version—The Ethical Business frame. At the center is the distinction between a shareholder and a stakeholder. Stakeholders are more than shareholders as they include people who represent the interests of the employees, the community, and the environment. Corporations receive their charters from the state. The idea is to change those charters to turn corporations into better businesses.

The Ethical Business Frame

The shareholders own the business.

The stakeholders are the Shareholders plus representatives of the employees, the community, and the environment.

The purpose of the business is to maximize the interests of the stakeholders.

The board of directors represents the stakeholders.

All employees are paid a living wage plus a share of the profits.

Revenues minus costs equals profits, where employees' salaries are seen as part of profits, not costs.

Costs include costs previously unloaded onto the community, e.g., pollution cleanup costs.

Community infrastructure contributions, tax breaks, subsidies, etc. are recorded as community loans to the corporation.

The higher the profits, the greater the employees' salaries.

Employees share in the risks, as well as the profits.

The devil, of course, is in the details, which are to be worked out. There is more than one way to do it. But it's time to start.

Conclusion

Living wage campaigns are about much more than living wages. Ultimately, they are about what Fred Block has called a moral economy.[4] Living wage and EITC are just small first steps.

The actual gains made (e.g., moving the minimum wage from $6.25 to $8.50) are small compared to the gains that need to be made. What is important in the long run is changing the frames used in comprehending the economy. Replacing the Natural Market frame with the Constructed Market frame is crucial, as is replacing the exchange metaphor for value with the contribution metaphor for value.

Part of the process of making such cognitive changes must be to focus on the payments made by taxpayers to businesses—both in the form of money (e.g., subsidies, tax breaks) and in the form of common infrastructure provided by taxpayers. Businesses make use of such common assets as roads, airports, the airwaves, the Internet, the air traffic control system, and the technology developed largely with taxpayers' money (e.g., computer technology, biotechnology, and so on).

An important aim of such reframing should be to destroy a major economic and moral fallacy, the myth of the self-made entrepreneur. Nobody makes it alone. The American taxpayer has supplied a huge infrastructure and makes enormous payments that allow entrepreneurs to succeed. Entrepreneurs are given enormous resources by the taxpaying public. They are not operating in a free market. They owe a lot—morally if not legally. The market is skewed toward them—and away from ordinary working people.

Frames are not just ideas. They are very often ideas that get institutionalized and made real. Conservatives are in the process of institutionalizing their frames. We must stop them, undo the damage, and institutionalize ours instead.

Notes

1. See George Lakoff. *Moral Politics: How Liberals and Conservatives Think* (Chicago: University of Chicago Press, 2002).
2. See Barbara Ehrenreich. *Nickel and Dimed: On Not Getting By in America* (New York: Holt, 2008).
3. Steven Malanga, "Living Wage is Socialism," Manhattan Institute for Policy Research. Retrieved from http://www.manhattan-institute.org/html/miarticle.htm?id=3077
4. Fred Block, "A Moral Economy," *The Nation* (March 20, 1996).

5 Emotional Manipulation of Political Identity

Rose McDermott

During the 2008 presidential political campaign, academics and political pundits alike expressed concern that our current democratic system has become increasingly vulnerable to public manipulation. Yet aside from that assertion, little systematic discussion has been generated about the source or the purpose of such manipulation. Is it worse than in the past, or just different and more pervasive because of changes in the nature of the mass media? What kind of manipulation actually exerts an effect on outcomes that matter, such as voting and policy choice? Who benefits from such manipulation? Political participants see strategic action all the time, and yet it is often not conceptualized as such. If manipulation remains rife in political contexts, it must be because practitioners feel that it remains an effective strategy for obtaining desired outcomes. Thus, the key question that arises is why and how does it work? Here I will argue that manipulation works because it evokes adaptive psychological mechanisms designed to help solve classic collective action problems.

The notion of political manipulation takes on a particular meaning within the modern context of enormously expensive two-party elections. In popular books and academic literature designed to explain the bifurcated basis of American culture and society, authors such as Thomas Frank argue that politicians encourage poor citizens to vote against their economic self-interest by appealing to their conservative social values.[1] By using hate to insert social wedges between voters who might otherwise share natural economic alliances, leaders are able to rule with the consent of the many for the benefit of the few. To add further insult, these same leaders often fail to deliver on the conservative social agendas which motivated voters to support them initially. Others, such as Morris Fiorina, Samuel Abrams, and Jeremy Pope, claim that divides in American political culture are more apparent than real, that the country is more "purple" than either red or blue.[2]

Certainly the art and science of political manipulation and propaganda are nothing new. Hitler's propaganda minister Joseph Goebbels proved a master of the science long before any findings concerning the underpinnings of social influence were pursued in a more scientific context. Films such as *Triumph of the Will,* while perhaps appearing dated by today's media standards, nonetheless paved the way for students of persuasion to bring their skills to bear on the formulation and shaping of public opinion.

What perhaps represents a more novel form of political manipulation in the modern democratic context derives from the conscious, calculated use of emotional entrepreneurship by leaders to create and craft particular kinds of political identity. The structuring of such novel and distinct political identities serves the purposes of leaders who hope to open cleavages between groups which might otherwise organize against them. To be clear, the term *emotional entrepreneurship* refers to the process by which leaders strategically use outrage at opposition members to cue in-group members to participate in action against the out-group members who have committed the outrage. This argument places the politics of outrage front and center in the strategic manipulation of the political process. Transformative political leadership works by redefining coalitional goals and creating new visions for existing coalitions. Effective leaders locate existing adversaries, and put those opposition groups in a bad light. By so doing, such leaders tap into the underlying logic of psychological manipulation by highlighting the relative costs and benefits of in-group membership, threatening that inaction will lead to the loss of important goals and values, and increasing the perception that action will lead to the effective control of significant outcomes. Such signaling on the part of leaders serves the function of increasing group solidarity as well as recruitment into the party, group, or organization.

Why does this work? Why do people adopt such strategies? This paper explores the process by which leaders can manipulate both identity and emotion for particular political effect and partisan advantage. In order to understand this dynamic properly, this paper draws on three distinct literatures in psychology to examine the ways in which leaders strategically instill, manipulate, and encourage specific emotional responses in voters in order to advance their own personal political power and public agendas.

First, work in self-categorization theory illustrates how leaders can come to serve as identity entrepreneurs who, through their ability to define the boundaries of particular categories, can mobilize followers through uniquely effective mechanisms. Second, work on the psychological dynamics underlying effective techniques of social influence and persuasion helps explain the specific nature of the tactics employed by leaders in garnering such effective support. The third literature, deriving from work in evolutionary psychology and biological anthropology, examines the use of particular signal emotions such as outrage and fear to consolidate in-group cohesion and foster out-group discrimination. Such processes further strengthen leaders who can interpret, identify, and invent suitable emotional challenges in order to mobilize followers to engage in effective collective action as directed. This occurs, in particular, when various group leaders increasingly rely on the symbolic use of opposition "out-rages" to cue in-group members of the need for increased strength and cohesion in order to respond to out-group provocation. Together, these processes decrease the ability of in-group members to make adequately informed choices concerning leadership and policy because of the way in which the verity of information is screened depending on the relationship of the person to the source. The source itself comes to define both the relevant political identity and the appropriate emotional reaction, and thus the most appropriate collective action in response. In this way, the meaning of information becomes interpreted in profoundly different ways depending on the source.

The Construction of Political Identity

Obviously, a great deal of work has been done in psychology on social identity theory, and, indeed many applications of psychological models of identity to political processes draw on this model.[3] And yet there are a number of other psychological bases by which individuals might identify with political forces. After outlining a number of these models, a discussion of self-categorization theory and its relevance for understanding the psychological mechanisms behind entrepreneurial political identity follows.

Identity Theory

I begin here with a brief digression on identity theory in order to explain how identity development proceeds through the following stages; this will allow me to later explain how political manipulation builds on the structure of political identity development. This preliminary background establishes the foundation upon which the later argument concerning the activation of political identity rests. While this chapter concentrates on the emotional manipulation of political identity by entrepreneurial leaders, it remains useful to begin with this history of identity research in psychology in order to understand some potential psychological bases for political identification. These psychological adaptations, designed by natural selection to help individuals selectively cooperate in the face of threat, can be stimulated by leaders, through the strategic use of outrage and emotional manipulation, to generate support for more selfish or pedestrian ends. The most basic forms of identification may be personal, and involve decisions individuals make concerning who they are, or want to be, in the world. But the next level of identification involves choice over who individuals want to associate with, decisions that affect not only who a person wants to be with, but who a person wants to be like. This background provides a useful foundation for understanding the nature and motivation of individual attachment to groups.

Erik Erikson's work best illustrates the dynamics which underlie individual identity development. He is the father of identity theory in its broader conceptualization and history. As the first, and traditionally considered the most prominent, of the neo-Freudians, Erikson's contribution focused on introducing the social element into models of identity development. Unlike Freud, Erikson neither restricted his studies to internal manifestations of sex and aggression, nor did he limit his age of investigation to pre-pubescent activity. Importantly, Erikson provided the first fundamentally *social* definition and function of identity. As a result, Erikson developed a life-span model of *social* development that encompasses eight distinct stages.[4] Each stage is characterized by a central crisis in identity development which, if not fully or properly resolved, will hinder an individual's ability to successfully grow and develop through subsequent stages. For example, the central crisis for a young adult revolves around intimacy versus isolation. Individuals who fail to develop the capacity for complete emotional, moral, and sexual commitments to others will end up pursuing freedom at the expense of human connection. According to Erikson, this will lead to predictable deficiencies in the ability to successfully resolve later crises, such as the tension between generativity and stagnation later in life.

Erikson's model offered an important starting point for further theoretical developments in the conceptualization of identity. Various attempts to measure and explore social identity since that time have provided several different definitions and empirical operationalizations of particular constructs in order to illustrate the identity features and dimensions which given authors especially stress. These notions, while abstract, remain important because they point out the key areas of vulnerability individual leaders may target in order to effectively engage and transform the identities of their followers. In so doing, leaders can then manipulate followers, through the selective use of emotions such as anger and fear, to support policies and to engage in actions which the leader wishes.

As Schwartz writes in his comprehensive and careful review of Eriksonian identity theory and research, various measures of identity have been developed using different criteria and assumptions about the process and structure of identity.[5] This has led to great difficulty in obtaining acceptable levels of convergent validity in particular across measures. Obviously, such difficulties in measurement can compromise the quality of theoretical definition, development and testing. But this lack of careful empirical work and conceptual convergence does not, in and of itself, invalidate the central insights Erikson offered concerning the fundamentally social and emotional nature of psychological identification.

Identity Models

Marcia drew on Erikson to develop an alternative identity status model. This model combined elements of high and low identity exploration and commitment, producing four identity status categories in a 2 by 2 table.[6] Identity exploration refers to the way in which individuals may "try on" particular identities to see how well they fit; any parent of a teenager will be well familiar with such processes which can run the gamut from hair and clothing styles to peer group and activity preferences. Identity commitment happens as individuals find and consolidate those identities which work and fit best for them. Marcia labeled these four classifications identity diffusion, identity foreclosure, identity moratorium, and identity achievement; individuals high in commitment range from foreclosure (or prematurely shutting down various options) to achievement (or consolidating a comfortable identity). In one of the very few experimental studies in this tradition, Marcia manipulated self-esteem in 72 males and found that those who were low in ego-identity demonstrated a greater change in the manipulated direction than those subjects who were high in ego-identity, thus appearing more susceptible to manipulation at the hands of others who possessed stronger ego-identities.

Identity development remained key in the academic pursuit of identity theory. Berzonsky created an identity style model designed to focus precisely on this process.[7] Separating individuals according to how they solve problems and make decisions, Berzonsky discussed three distinct identity styles, which he called informational, normative and diffuse-avoidant.

Other scholars focused on how group identity relates to individual status. Harold Grotevant worked on empirical extensions of Marcia's work, including the use of a Q-sort methodology to assess identity status in individuals.[8] Grotevant wanted in particular to extend Marcia's work into interpersonal realms.[9] Grotevant's work remains largely consistent with Eriksonian notions of identity formation in its developmental and life-span approach.[10] However, Grotevant departs from Eriksonian theory in his emphasis on the adolescent process of identity exploration as the main process by which people formulate their identities. His identity framework incorporates four distinct elements, which include: individual characteristics, such as cognitive ability; context of development, which can include family issues; the identity process as it develops within specific domains, such as occupational or relational; and the level of interdependence among these different identity domains. He argues that identity exploration remains a function of individual abilities and orientations. These characteristics can be affected by five additional factors, including information seeking, satisfaction, willingness to explore, expectations, and competing forces.

Kerpelman, Pittman, and Lamke extended Grotevant's model of identity exploration into Identity Control theory, a revision which Grotevant accepted.[11] This modification of Grotevant's earlier model sought to examine the micro-processes which spurred and supported the process of identity exploration. This model places emphasis on the ways in which identity exploration mutually causes and becomes reinforced by interaction with, and feedback from, significant others who may approve, or disapprove, of particular identity trials.

Yet some obvious differences remain. Some individuals clearly derive more purpose from their identities than others; and certainly every individual has certain aspects of their identity that are more important to them than others. Waterman noticed that individuals responding to identity surveys tended to differ systematically between those who derived great personal meaning from their identity explorations, and those who seemed to feel that their behaviors had been driven by more external incentives.[12] In focusing on the differences individuals experienced in the meaning they attached to various dimensions of their identity, Waterman developed his personal expressiveness construct. In this model, personal meaning can serve as an avenue for self-discovery or self-actualization.[13]

Three additional, more extensive expansions of Marcia's identity status model deserve mention. Kurtines, Azmitia, and Alvarez's co-constructivist perspective provides an existentialist take on identity development, focusing on issues of choice, responsibility and control.[14] Kurtine et al. believe that identity evolves in a creative process between the individual and his or her social and cultural environment. In this way, the individual and society mutually construct each other. This individual model is conceptually similar to Wendt's constructivist theory of international relations which focuses on the interaction between the agent and the structure within the context of a particular kind of external environment.[15] Kurtines et al. focus on the ways in which individuals become active agents who choose their identities from the variety of choices that might be available; the individual thus remains conscious and responsible for all the choices she makes. In other words, identities are not foisted on a person unaware; she chooses which identities to adopt and which to reject in a conscious process of association and identification. Kurtines et al. note in particular the importance of socially desirable attributes, such as creativity, suspension of judgment, critical discussion, and integrity of character, which remain essential in the successful co-creation of identity.

Some scholars have attempted to blend work on identity theory, which mostly emerged from the literature in developmental psychology subfield, with the more group-related emphasis embedded within the subfield of social psychology. Adams and Marshall present a developmental social psychology of identity.[16] In their model, Adams and Marshall divide the social context into both micro and macro processes. They argue that the macro processes of a person's social and cultural environment become incorporated into their identity through the micro practices of interpersonal relationship. In this way, Adams and Marshall specify the "how" of Kurtines et al.s' model into more particular social processes. Both personal and social forces influence identity development, but the mechanism by which each evolves differs; distinguishing oneself from others requires a process of differentiation, while integration represents the social mechanism by which individuals connect with others. As a result, Adams and Marshall posit two forms of identity: personal and collective (or social).

Finally, some scholars have sought to examine not only the causes of identity, but also the consequences inherent in adopting particular identities. Cote presents an Identity Capital Model, which focuses primarily on social identity.[17] Unlike the previous identity theorists who emphasize the origins of identity, Cote concentrates on the consequences of identity formation. He sees the value of personal identity in the social utility it brings. He argues that individuals use their resources in order to negotiate and bargain for social resources. This model offers the most macro level analysis of identity formation in the non-experimental tradition.

Group Attachment

Coalitionary psychology has been key to human evolution and development. Humans were able to survive in the face of much physically stronger predators precisely because they proved able to band together to cooperate in finding food, avoiding predation, and building shelter. Thus, the process by which individuals attach to social groups remains an integral part of the human cognitive architecture. In exploring the mechanisms that drive social identity, some identity theorists place their emphasis less on individual identity development and more on how individuals make their attachments to such groups. Smith, Murphy, and Coats borrow their theoretical and measurement strategies for examining individual attachments to groups from the work on emotional attachment in close relationships.[18] They argue that people have cognitive ideas of themselves as members of a group, and derive identity and esteem from these notions. These ideas affect subsequent thoughts, emotions, and behaviors toward the group. They find two important and distinct components in individual attachments to groups, attachment anxiety and attachment avoidance.

While this may appear at first glance to recall Erikson's intimacy versus isolation divide, it reflects instead an entirely different tradition in the literature on social development which remained focused entirely on attachment, as opposed to intra-psychic development. Early work by Konrad Lorenz on imprinting and John Bowlby with orphaned infants during World War II, began this tradition.[19] In this paradigm, Mary Ainsworth et al. developed the Strange Situation test to discern attachment styles in young children.[20] They and others demonstrated the ways in which preferred attachment style, witnessed as early as fifteen months, and categorized as secure, avoidant or ambivalent, can accurately predict a wide range of social adjustments, including popularity, levels of social anxiety, and quality of attachment over a decade later. In this paradigm, a baby is brought into a strange room with its mother, who then leaves the room. If the baby is secure, he or she will explore the novel situation, returning to the mother if something happens that makes the baby scared. And when the mother leaves, the baby may display some initial upset, but will continue to explore, and be happy upon the mother's return. An avoidant baby will shy away from exploring the environment and will avoid contact with the mother, treating her little different than a stranger. An ambivalent baby will appear very upset once the mother leaves, but while seeking closeness upon the mother's return nonetheless makes it clear that she remains resentful of the prior absence. The reason this is important is that these childhood characteristics predict later adult attachment styles. Some people need a sense of community more than others. Some people are more comfortable with certain attachment styles in their leaders; attaching to one leader over another may result as much from the comfort a person feels in style than in substance. It is easy to imagine that a person who prefers an aloof attachment style will feel more comfortable with a leader who advocates for personal responsibility over state interference, for example.

Attachment style in childhood can predict a number of similarly important outcomes in adult attachment, including how much of a person's identity is invested in their attachment to others in a group. In Smith et al., group attachment similarly predicts significant outcomes, including emotional reactions to the group, how much time and what kinds of activities an individual shares with the group, social support, collective self-esteem, and conflict resolution strategies.[21] They argue that their measure of group attachment, based on the notion of group attachment anxiety and avoidance, remains distinct from individual relationship attachment styles such as those discussed by Ainsworth et al., or other measures of group identification.

Henry, Arrow, and Carini pose an alternative model of group identification in examining how individuals develop and maintain their social identities.[22] They define group identification as a member's identification with an interacting group. This process remains distinct from social identity. They argue that this sense of identification derives from three unique sources, which are cognitive, emotional, and behavioral in nature. The cognitive process relates to social categorization. The emotional dynamic rests on interpersonal attraction between group members. And the behavioral phenomenon results from levels of interdependence among group members. These authors provide a group identification scale based on this tripartite model.

Strategic Social Identity

Political identity constitutes a particular form of social identity. And self-categorization models provide a helpful way to conceptualize the development of such political beliefs and actions.[23] Self-categorization refers to the way in which individuals consciously choose particular political categories which they believe represent themselves and their interests in some meaningful way. Often, individuals choose these identities or groups on the basis of which categories they believe will help them to garner the greatest amount of political power or dominance over other social or political groups. One of the mechanisms that such individuals and groups use to solidify this control is by reifying categories in rigid terms, thus deciding who can belong, and therefore who must be excluded. Such clear categorization helps delimit those who can reasonably expect to benefit from group status or resources. This process of social exclusion not only serves to limit the number of individuals among whom potential benefits of dominance might be divided, but simultaneously disallows alternative constructions of individuals or social groups which might interfere with these pre-existing categorizations. Successful leaders act as political entrepreneurs by carefully defining group membership in this way, using often arbitrary criteria to cast out-group members in a bad light, and solidifying in-group membership by appealing to the rational self-interest of those who participate and wish to receive material and status benefits from such group identification.

Clearly, the process by which an individual comes to espouse a particular social or political identity occurs through a dynamic interchange between internal needs and external forces. In other words, political identity like any other is not given, but rather exists at least in part as a function of the individual's interaction with their specific external environment, which poses its own contingencies, constraints and incentives. This allows a space for an effective leader to serve as a kind of identity entrepreneur, a person whose ability to set the agenda and define the boundaries of a particular political identity becomes a very powerful tool in mobilizing followers toward a particular partisan goal or effect. Indeed, effective leadership results exactly from the ability to define and marshal political identities toward specific outcomes in this way. My point here is that the kind of leader who does not, or cannot, naturally mobilize people likely will resort to totalitarian control as a means to avoid opposition. Those who cannot rely on such authoritarian structures to maintain control because they operate in a democratic context must learn to mobilize people through the strategic use of outrage. Outrage represents a key component in consolidating support in democratic regimes if tyranny is to be avoided.[24]

To embrace this notion of leadership, the relationship between leaders and followers must be conceptualized in a mutually constitutive way. In other words, the strategic interaction between leaders and followers from this perspective is in no way zero sum, but rather interdependent in nature. This partnership creates and establishes both leadership and group social cohesion as intrinsic aspects of the process of mutual role definition. Reicher, Haslam, and Hopkins describe this interaction as "the way in which a shared sense of identity makes leadership possible and the way in which leaders act as entrepreneurs of identity in order to make particular forms of identity and their own leadership viable."[25] This does not mean that there is no external reality that constrains leadership. In fact, effective leaders must and do remain exquisitely aware of the external forces impinging on their communities. However, particularly strategic leaders can help to transform these forces into successful collective action through the effective mobilization and direction of their followers' interests in pursuit of their own political power.

Recent work in psychology conducted by Haslam and Reicher has demonstrated at least one process by which such identity entrepreneurship can occur.[26] In undertaking a BBC sponsored replication of the famous Stanford Prison Experiment, Haslam and Reicher designed strategies to increase the prisoners' shared sense of social identity.[27] In so doing, they managed to increase the prisoners' sense of efficacy while simultaneously diminishing the guards' ability to act in unison. In this variant of the prison study, the guards did not unthinkingly adopt the roles they were given; in fact, they resisted the identity category membership that others thrust upon them. Indeed, the authors argue that the very categories of "guard" and "prisoner," and their definitions, came under dispute and contestation over the course of the replication.

In this study, the authors illustrated a way in which leadership can create social identity among a particularly malleable group of individuals, and, in turn, how such social identity makes leadership itself possible. These individuals may have been particularly susceptible to such identity manipulation because they were operating in a novel, uncertain environment without clear goals or rules, and purposely detached from their established social support networks; it is not clear that everyone would adopt such leadership dynamics under more naturalistic settings. However, it is often the case that political leaders strive to encourage their constituents to follow them into unknown territory in pursuit of better collective outcomes. Indeed, these authors go so far as to argue that the long term success or failure of leaders depends fundamentally on the viability of their identity projects; in other words, a leader's ability turns on his acumen in devising compelling identifications among his followers. If leaders fail in establishing cohesive bonds of social identity among followers, according to these authors, authoritarian leaders will likely follow. This is because a shared sense of social identity remains the necessary prerequisite for any kind of successful group social mobilization; any such effective cooperative action must rest on shared goals and values, or the collective project is doomed to fall away into the cracks of internal division. As Haslam and Reicher state,

> it is only through a shared sense of social identity that people come to share common goals and are able to organize in such a way that their plans and priorities can be realized. Hence social identity provides both the means and the parameters of collective agency. Second, the

ability of an individual to influence the group and shape its collective fate depends upon the extent to which their position can be seen as representative of the group as a whole.[28]

Klein, Spears, and Reicher, in developing their social identity of de-individuation model (SIDE), argue that the active political construction of identity proves crucial because the public performance of such identity serves two essential, simultaneous purposes.[29] First, public demonstrations of identity can consolidate identity by affirming and strengthening an individual's ties to the collective. Second, such identity performance can also mobilize others by persuading observers to join in certain displays or activities, thus strengthening both group size and cohesion. They argue that such identity performance helps create stronger and more cohesive social identity by helping to coordinate social activity in both in-group and out-group contexts. In this way, political empowerment derives not from successful collective action per se but rather from the way in which such success serves to glorify, validate, and express a particular social identity.[30]

Thus, the psychological mechanism by which leaders can serve as entrepreneurs of identity takes place through several inter-locking processes. Recall that leaders who strategically manipulate identity, and invoke emotional responses to create and justify outrage, benefit by increasing social solidarity and recruitment within the group; as long as the leader defines the nature of in-group membership, that person can then control many of the activities of the group. First, and most importantly, leaders create social identity among followers by generating and reflecting a sense of solidarity. This depends crucially on how the boundaries of that identity are defined. In many cases, such boundaries focus on locating geographies of exclusion. In Northern Ireland, for example, a person may not be particularly religious as a Catholic, and may not even identify with the more theological aspects of the creed, but such a person will publicly identify as Catholic because while she is not sure she is really "Catholic" she knows for dead certain that she is not "one of those" Protestants.[31] Similarly, a secular Jew in Israel may not feel particularly spiritual, but knows beyond a shadow of a doubt that he is not Arab. In such cases, identity itself, defined negatively by what a participant is not rather than by what she is, can fuel the perceived discrimination often related to particular ethnic, religious, or racial identifications. In such circumstances, such processes of social identification serve the goal of the dominant group in preserving the extant status quo with its existing social status ordering and hierarchy.

Since social identities are often constructed, and not given, entrepreneurial leaders can use fear and anger, shaped by authentic experiences of hostility and discrimination, to shape group identification and mobilization. The specifics of this emotional process are discussed in greater detail in the final section. For now, suffice it to say that those leaders who can define the boundaries of group identification thus become very powerful as effective entrepreneurs of identity. They can then use this power to mobilize followers on behalf of that specific group identity.

The person who can define group identity serves a crucial role precisely because identity often constitutes the site of argumentation and contestation, and these boundaries delimit who is involved in constituting "us" and who comprises "them." Effective leaders thus define the boundaries of exclusion and inclusion, and use threat and virtue, and the discourse of evil and *glory*, to maintain their authority over such definitions. Note here the critical importance of glory, since the wealth and status benefits that accrue to successful warriors, for example, may garner for these individuals important resources, including mates to whom they might not otherwise have had access. In this way, consummate leaders reflect, create, and manifest entrepreneurial identity in service of maintaining control over both the glorification of in-group virtue, as well as the demonization of out-group outrages. The specific mechanisms that facilitate such processes of social influence and control follow in the next section.

Processes of Social Influence

In his brilliant book, *Influence*, Robert Cialdini outlined six major "weapons of influence," which he discovered and outlined while working in a wide variety of jobs whose purpose is to persuade people to do something or buy something.[32] In working as a car salesman, a waiter, and in other occupations, Cialdini noticed that the most effective forms of social influence strategies could be distilled into six basic types. These techniques are commonly employed by all sorts of individuals and organizations to induce compliance. Political entrepreneurs certainly represent some particularly creative and effective exemplars of these strategies.

These techniques begin with reciprocity, whereby people feel obligated to return a small favor or gift to the giver. In this strategy, agents of influence seek to capitalize on the normal human desire to cooperate with others in small groups to achieve goals that would be impossible to accomplish alone. We are all aware of these techniques from direct mail campaigns, which send everything from money to address labels in their requests for return donations, implicitly invoking the natural human desire to reciprocate generosity and act cooperatively toward those who appear to serve a larger public good. When a politician asks for your vote in return for promises of goods and services that will be delivered if he is elected, he too is preying on the same tendency. Here the problem is that the voter has to make the concession first, hoping that the politician will reciprocate their trust once in office. Such trust may or may not be warranted.

The second technique involves liking. We are much more susceptible to influence from people we like and who we believe like us. In advertising, this strategy is clearly invoked in campaigns employing beautiful, happy people, implying that if the observer were to use or buy a given product, he or she would not only be beautiful and happy too, but would be surrounded by such beautiful and happy people who would like him or her in return. But this strategy can elicit much more insidious manifestations, as when friends or neighbors ask us to buy Girl Scout cookies, Tupperware, or other products where refusal threatens a larger on-going social relationship of friendship or cooperation. Similarly, politicians try hard to get voters to like them. While kissing babies and smiling and shaking hands may offer only the most obvious examples of this desire, modifying physical appearance or policy positions to generate wider public appeal constitutes illustrations of this effect as well.

The third strategy refers to commitment and consistency. In most situations, once a person has made a commitment, verbally or in writing, to do or say a certain thing, he or she is more likely to follow through on the intended behavior. Even when the original motivation disappears, people remain consistent with their prior commitments because of the internal desire for consistency between beliefs and behaviors. Failing to do so causes undesirable cognitive dissonance in most people who remain uncomfortable when not honoring earlier commitments. Diet and substance abuse groups recognize this power when they encourage people to come to meetings and openly state their goals and intended changes in behavior. In politics, examples of the use of this strategy in fund-raising in particular abound. When someone asks for a small amount of money to support a campaign, for example, the person who offers a small amount will prove more likely to give more money later. In a particularly dramatic example of this kind of foot in the door technique, voters who agreed to have a lawn sign for a candidate placed on their yard were much more likely to give money and participate in other ways in support of that candidate than those who refused initially, even though these individuals did not differ significantly from each other prior to the intervention in their stated preference.[33]

The fourth technique is social proof, which refers to the phenomenon whereby people like to do things that lots of other people are doing. Many people find safety does exist in large numbers. People find some security in the group, taking their cues for proper behavior, dress and other norms from watching others who they think are like them. We are all familiar with the experience of looking up at the floor lights in an elevator when someone else does; this is a trivial example of this tactic of social influence which also provides the basis for canned laughter on television comedy shows, as well as a number of amusing episodes of *Candid Camera*. In politics, polling represents the consummate example of social proof; public opinion polls tell voters who everyone else is voting for, thus allowing each person to compare him or herself to others. It may also paralyze and disempower voters who wish to support an unpopular candidate, but do not think it is worth the effort since the person is likely to lose; at the theoretical margins, of course, if everyone felt this way, many potential winners would lose many elections. This is why, for example, election results are typically not reported until the last polling place is closed. Politicians don't want to discourage voters from showing up if they believe that their candidate is losing; self-fulfilling prophecies can turn beliefs into reality under such circumstances.

The fifth form of social influence relies on scarcity. Everyone wants to keep their options open by making sure they can have things they want. It is a natural human instinct to react against restrictions to our freedom, even if those restrictions can be artificially manipulated. Such a desire hinges on the perception of freedom; if something is gone, perhaps it was something valuable that the person might have wanted or needed later. Worse still, perhaps the valued object will now land in the hands of an enemy who can use it against the person who was too slow or indecisive to get the last resource. Such desires no doubt stem from evolutionary pressures to maximize the amount of food and mates that each individual could obtain. The most common examples in the modern world are television marketing ploys that tell the viewer that unless they call now, every one of those ginsu knives, or similarly valuable commodity, will vanish from the planet forever, so it is incumbent to call now or forever lose the opportunity to own this precious commodity. In politics, scarcity operates in many forms, at least some of which involve the manipulation of identity, as when voters are told that certain categories of voters, such as African Americans, are being prevented from reaching the voting booth. This may be true, but such a clear illustration of the scarcity of the right to vote should also serve to motivate demand elsewhere among similar voters who would be expected to react negatively to externally imposed scarcity.

Finally, the sixth and final weapon of influence derives from authority. People tend to look up to and admire authority figures and often do what they ask, even when those things may seem unreasonable or morally objectionable. Clearly, the Milgram experiment constituted the most graphic illustration of the pressure toward obedience most people experience in the presence of authority. In political settings, the use of powerful patriotic symbols such as the flag or the national anthem only enhance the power of the institution of the Presidency in terms of infusing the person with perceptions of rightful authority. Given that many individuals possess an active desire to like and admire and respect their leaders, the additional pull of authority provides a powerful mechanism by which leaders can persuade followers to mobilize on behalf of their policies and programs, ostensibly for the benefit of all who participate.

Signal Emotions as Consolidating Cues to Group Behavior

Why is it so important that leaders be able to increase group size and cohesion? Because, historically at least, larger groups were more likely to emerge victorious in war. The benefits that then accrued to the winning coalition included not only material resources, but also potential brides, either captured or seduced from the losing side, or secured through increased status and material benefits garnered in war.

Successful politicians can employ the strategies of persuasion outlined in the section above to secure larger and more cohesive group followings. To what purpose are such mechanisms used by politicians in the course of their strivings toward identity entrepreneurship? Two of the most important goals in creating and maintaining political leadership reside in the ability to establish and maintain in-group solidarity while fostering out-group hostility. But it remains critical that such purposes remain distinct, for leaders do not want extensive in-group violence any more than they want excessive passivity toward the out-group. The use of emotional means of persuasion in service of these goals allows effective politicians to essentially invoke emotional reactions on the part of citizens in order to sustain both these processes in service of a self-defined identity based cause. In other words, effective leaders manipulate and define political identity, including some while excluding others and invoking emotional triggers, in order to generate comprehensive collective action on the part of citizenry to *both* remain peaceful at home, accepting of established leadership, and fight effectively abroad.

The basis of much of social identity theory rests on the notion that in-group membership serves to bolster the self-esteem of individual members.[34] This certainly appears true. However, group membership also serves an additional, more strategic function as well. Larger groups are more likely to emerge victorious in conflict, particularly battle. In addition, larger and more powerful groups will more likely emerge victorious in situations of conflict and thus achieve social dominance over other groups, obtaining all the resources such control allows. Groups seek status in order to win such contests.

From the perspective of evolutionary psychology and biological anthropology, the ability to form and maintain coalitions against predators would have presented an evolutionary recurring adaptive problem, and victors able to overcome such challenges successfully would have achieved reproductive advantage. Amplification coalitions provided a key mechanism whose function would have been to magnify the coordinated action of individual members in order to achieve greater collective efficacy, particularly in conflicts with out-groups.[35] In such a scenario, if the group is too small, it will lose fights against opponents. But if the group is too large, it risks falling prey to internal divisions and social fractures, which can render such groups ineffective in battle as well. Simultaneously managing the problems posed by in-group division in the face of threats of external attack requiring marshaling maximum power posed a serious problem for leaders.

Richard Wrangham has made the argument that in-group solidarity and out-group hostility represent two fundamentally different adaptations designed to resolve these simultaneous challenges to effective group behavior in collectivities. This argument reconciles the two conflicting world views presented by prominent political philosophers: the world of Rousseau where aggressive killing is unnatural, versus the Hobbesian world where aggression represents the way of the world. In the Wrangham construction, the world of Rousseau supports in-group cooperation while Hobbes holds sway in behavior toward out-groups.

Drawing on ethnographic work with chimpanzees, Wrangham notes that a balance of power tends to suppress violence. It is only when an imbalance of power exists that individuals see an opportunity for political gain and access to greater resources through increased power. Indeed, in the hunter-gatherer societies in which humans evolved, more power leads to clear evolutionary advantages down the line, including more territory with better conditions, faster reproduction, and higher infant survival rates.[36] Under such circumstances, even if no immediate reward in terms of access to food or mates derived from the immediate coalitional victory in an uncertain world, natural selection would favor a drive toward inter-group dominance behaviors, by providing benefits to those who could successfully compete for territory. Thus, a psychology of inter-group hostility would have increased the likelihood of unprovoked attacks against strangers in service of clear reproductive advantages to the victor. Equally important, such a psychology would have placed inordinate value on status as one mechanism by which powerful members of a group could attain greater resources which while not necessarily immediately relevant, would nonetheless manifest reproductive advantages down the line.

Indeed, natural selection should have operated separately on premeditated, as opposed to impulsive, forms of aggression. In making calculated attacks against other groups, such predatory, premeditated attacks of aggression would have been frequent and would have created neural underpinnings distinct from those which operate impulsively in intra-group settings. In such inter-group attacks, impulsive actions might have proved counter-productive, by warning the enemy prior to attack for example. However, in intra-group settings, natural selection should operate to induce cooperation and tolerance in order to gain the enormous benefits that derive from successful collective action against out-groups.

The problem arises, of course, because collective action across many individuals can be enormously difficult to achieve and sustain. Free riding presents a common and difficult challenge to leaders who want to encourage participation in in-group activities where larger numbers are more likely to lead to victory. From an evolutionary perspective, the conundrum becomes even greater because natural selection should operate against those who sacrifice themselves for the group, only to leave behind fewer progeny on average, than those who shirked their duty to protect hearth and home. And yet clearly throughout human history, many examples exist of human males who appear quite enthusiastic about the possibility of fighting in war. What can explain this conundrum?

The Role of Emotional Entrepreneurship in Mobilizing Collective Action

When successful leaders wish to overcome the powerful tendency of individuals to free ride on one another's contribution to collective welfare, one of the most common and effective ways to do so is to invoke anger and fear as the proper emotional responses to what has happened to the group or collective at the hands of the out-group. Recall that a leader who successfully defines the boundaries of group identification can clearly precipitate the effective entrepreneurship of political identity, deciding what "they" did to "us." In so doing, such a leader, reflecting and representing a particular political identity, can use past discrimination, hostility and aggression on the part of one group toward another to both justify out-group threats *and* solidify and mobilize in-group cohesion and solidarity. In this way, perceived or real discrimination or hostility serves as a basis for both political identification with the in-group as well as motivation for exclusion and threats toward the out-group, however defined.

This process is possible precisely because identity remains fluid and boundaries serve as a site for contestation. In such an environment, groups in reality represent little more than a joint imagination which has no objective meaning outside the mutual representation in the minds of its members. Since the definition and boundary of the group remains fluid, members can easily feel threatened by those who wish to challenge their inclusiveness, and thus challenge control over territory, resources, food, property, and mates.

This site of contestation is precisely the location where effective leaders can strategically invoke the use of "outrages" on the part of out-group members to signal to in-group members the importance of their group membership, and the crucial nature of their contribution to group victory.[37] An outrage occurs when a member of an opposing group, in reality or through invention or exaggeration on the part of the in-group, takes an action or makes a statement, which members of the in-group perceive as a threat to status, by failing to take the others' values and wishes into account. By failing to show sufficient respect for the in-group, rivals in the out-group present a status challenge to in-group members, signaling that they believe they are more powerful and deserving of rights and resources than previously acknowledged or negotiated. The harm might indeed be more perceptual than real, a threat to status, as opposed to an actual loss of territory or resources. In particular, such an act would signal to the opponent that the out-group not only does not offer sufficient or appropriate deference to the in-group, but also challenges the in-group to define its relative position in the status hierarchy. If the in-group accedes to this request, the adversary has gained reputation, status, perhaps even real resource advantages. But a clever and creative leader would strategically utilize, or invent, such an outrage to mobilize the group by pointing to the ways in which the other group failed to offer sufficient respect and deference to in-group members, inviting challenge and demanding restitution.

John Tooby has proposed that humans possess a psychology of outrage which serves to overcome otherwise difficult challenges to collective action by inciting members of a group to join in cooperative action against enemies. As part of this evolved cognitive architecture, Tooby suggests that the evolved mechanisms of human psychology include the ability to detect adversaries whose exclusion might benefit the group, identify potential allies whose inclusion might benefit the coalition by making it bigger and therefore stronger, and find or create instances of outrage on the part of opponents that can be used to advantage in mobilizing in-group members in collective action against the out-group. Importantly, outrages serve to generate responses because it is assumed that the other side initially engaged in such egregious action precisely because they did not value the welfare of the other group sufficiently. Each member of the in-group should feel insulted by such treatment, and want to participate in action designed to elicit apology or recompense. If such action is allowed to stand, all involved then assume that the new status quo sets a baseline for future action, and interaction, between the group where the out-group can again treat the in-group with disrespect and disregard. If the offended group fails to respond, they essentially accede to their loss of status vis a vis the other group not just in the present, but in the future as well.

In this way, the discovery or successful fabrication of outrage serves as an important resource for in-group leaders who wish to overcome internal divisions and mobilize members behind a successful collective action on behalf of the group. Successfully fabricating such an outrage holds intrinsic value and helps explain, in part, the premium placed on such news items in media coverage.

Tooby, Cosmides, and Price argue that there are two reasons why outrages increase the probability of coordinated action. First, outrages themselves serve to mobilize latent sources of collective action because everyone recognizes that they might continue to suffer harm if such future disregard for their welfare by the opponent continues unabated. The threat of loss thus mobilizes greater collective action as individuals come to recognize that increased participation can help forestall future costs. Second, through the collective realization of this fact, the outrage itself becomes a "rallying point" or reference point around which group members can coordinate their efforts, overcome internal divisions, and fight for the over-arching group welfare.

The utility of outrage to a leader can be enhanced, of course, if that leader can personally benefit from a newly powerful or energized coalition; new leaders seeking power might be most likely to express outrage, for example. Further, the force of outrage becomes exacerbated to the extent that the offensive act really happened, involved vivid events, and represented a calculated deliberate act on the part of the perpetrator. In this way, leaders invoke outrages to mobilize opposition toward rivals who pose a status threat, not toward individuals or group who engage in morally reprehensible behavior per se. Thus leaders use emotional manipulation in service of political identity formation to create mobilized followers who will serve their personal political interests. In so doing, they need to accurately reflect the emotional and identity interests of the majority of their constituents at least some of the time, or they may find themselves falling victim to the impulsive aggression that can occur within groups when individuals become non-cooperative or exploitative toward their community.

Conclusions

The emotional manipulation of political identity is not an easy or automatic task. Certainly some leaders prove more effective and successful than others at inventing outrage toward a defined in-group in order to mobilize personal partisan political advantage. Leaders who create and sustain powerful political coalitions become effective masters of entrepreneurial identity, in part by defining and locating acceptable places for identity contestation, approving certain domains and excluding others as proper sites of boundary argumentation. Such leaders prove adept at locating potential sources of new allies who can be mobilized through the strategic use of emotional reactions such as fear and anger directed against the outrages, either real or imagined, perpetrated on them by outsiders. They also remain acutely aware of potential new adversaries who threaten the construction of internal boundaries of identity internally, or pose a threat to the survival of the group externally. These leaders can then employ the influence strategies mentioned above in order to elicit and maintain the support and compliance of in-group members toward the political goals they espouse. Such leaders reflect and shape the boundaries of political identity in ways which define in-group supporters as distinct from out-group rivals. Using past examples or imaginations of discrimination, hostility or aggression to create and define dominant political coalitions, emotional entrepreneurs serve to awaken potential constituencies to the importance of collective action by activating a sense of threat. By noting current examples of disrespect, group leaders can efficiently mobilize members to ward off future status devaluations, and benefit from group resources.

Of course, the discourse surrounding fear and anger does not comprise the only emotional means by which leaders gain the adherence of members. In addition, appeals to the virtue of in-group members and the glory of their cause can also serve to motivate and define included members and excluded outsiders. Again, the function of leadership in this domain represents not so much a function of external reality as a mechanism by which authority is consolidated through recognizing the power and force of collective action on behalf of group members. Indeed, the true promise of political authority lies less in the ability to control and distribute specific resources and more in the construction and control of internal political divides. Just as in-group members can cooperate to defeat out-group members, leaders themselves can consolidate power by dividing and conquering groups that might otherwise join forces to unseat the leader, if only they could see past the often artificial and arbitrary identity divides which the leader structures for his own personal political benefit.

Transformational leadership uses emotional entrepreneurship to redefine group membership and create new coalitional goals. By picking a vicarious out-group they already have in mind, effective political leaders can invoke the psychological mechanisms that exist in the mind of the consumer to increase group solidarity and recruitment. By tapping into the underlying logic of emotional manipulation, leaders use outrages, real or imagined, to signal supporters that unless they take action on behalf of the leaders, as defined by the leader, they will lose important things they value, such as status. And in fighting over nothing, followers come to believe they are fighting for everything.

Notes

1. V. O. Key, *Southern Politics* (New York: Knopf, 1949); Thomas Edsall and Mary Edsall, *Chain Reaction: The Impact of Race, Rights and Taxes on American Politics* (New York: W.W. Norton, 1992); Thomas Frank, *What's the Matter with Kansas? How Conservatives Won the Heart of America* (New York: Owl, 2004).
2. Morris Fiorina, Samuel Abrams, and Jeremy Pope, *Culture War: The Myth of a Polarized America* (New York: Longman, 2005).
3. John Turner, Rupert Brown, and Henri Tajfel, "Social Comparison and Group Interest in In-group Favoritism," *European Journal of Social Psychology* 2 (1976): 187–204; Rawi Abdelel, Yoshiko Herrera, Alistair Johnston, and Rose McDermott, "Identity as a Variable," *Perspectives on Politics* 4 (2006): 695–711.
4. Erik Erikson, *Childhood and Society* (New York: Norton, 1950).
5. Seth Schwartz, "The Evolution of Eriksonian and neo-Eriksonian Identity Theory and Research: A Review and Integration," *Identity* 1 (2001): 7–58.

6. James Marcia, "Development and Validation of Ego Identity Status," *Journal of Personality and Social Psychology* 5 (1966): 551–58.

7. Michael Berzonsky, "Self-Construction over the Lifespan: A Process Perspective on Identity Formation", in Greg Neimeyer and Robert Neimeyer, eds., *Advances in Personal Construct Theory*, vol. 1 (New York: JAI, 1990): pp. 155–86.

8. Harold Grotevant, "Assessment of Identity Development: Current Issues and Future Directions," *Journal of Adolescent Research* 1, no. 2 (1986): 175–81.

9. Harold Grotevant, William Thorbecke, and Margaret Meyer, "An Extension of Marcia's Identity Status Interview into the Interpersonal Domain," *Journal of Youth and Adolescence* 11 (1982): 33–47.

10. Harold Grotevant, "Toward a Process Model of Identity Formation," *Journal of Adolescent Research* 2, no. 3 (1987): 203–22.

11. Jennifer Kerpelman, Joe Pittman, and Leanne Lamke, "Toward a Microprocesses Perspective on Adolescent Identity Development: An Identity Control Theory Approach," *Journal of Adolescent Research* 12 (1997): 363–71.

12. Alan Waterman, "Personal Expressiveness: Philosophical and Psychological Foundations," *Journal of Mind and Behavior* 11 (1990): 47–74.

13. Schwartz, "Evolution."

14. Williams Kurtines, Margarita Azmitia, and Mildred Alvarez, "Science, Values, and Rationality: Philosophy of science from a co-constructionist perspective," in W. Kurtines, M. Azmitia, and J. Gewirtz, eds., *The Role of Values in Psychology and Human Development* (New York: Wiley, 1992), pp. 3–29.

15. Alexander Wendt, "Anarchy is What States Make of It: The Social Construction of Power Politics," *International Organization* 46, 2 (1992): 395–425.

16. Glenn Adams and Sheila Marshall, "A Developmental Social Psychology of Identity: Understanding the Person-In-Context," *Journal of Adolescence* 19 (1996): 429–42.

17. James Cote, "An Empirical Test of the Identity Capital Model," *Journal of Adolescence* 20 (1997): 421–37.

18. Eliot Smith, Julie Murphy, and Susan Coats, "Attachment to Groups: Theory and Management," *Journal of Personality and Social Psychology* 77, no. 1 (1999): 94–110.

19. N. Tinbergen, *The Study of Instinct* (New York: Oxford University Press, 1951); John Bowlby, *Attachment and Loss, Vol. 1: Attachment* (New York: Basic Books, 1969); John Bowlby, *Attachment and Loss, Vol 2: Separation, Anxiety and Anger* (London: Hogarth, 1973).

20. Mary Ainsworth, Mary Blehar, Everett Waters, and Sally Wall, *Patterns of Attachment* (Mahwah, NJ: Erlbaum, 1978).

21. Eliot Smith et al., "Attachment to Groups."

22. Kelly Henry, Holly Arrow, and Barbara Carini, "A Tripartite Model of Group Identification: Theory and Measurement," *Small Group Research* 30, no. 5 (1999): 558–81.

23. Stephen Reicher and Nick Hopkins, "Psychology and the End of History: A Critique and a Proposal for the Psychology of Social Categorization," *Political Psychology* 22, no. 2 (2001): 383–407.

24. Alexis de Tocqueville, *Democracy in America*, ed. Isaac Kramnick and Gerald Bevin (New York: Penguin, 2005).

25. Stephen Reicher, Alexander Haslam, and Nick Hopkins, "Social Identity and the Dynamics of Leadership: Leaders and Followers as Collaborative Agents in the Transformation of Social Reality," *Leadership Quarterly* 16, no. 4 (2005): 547–68.

26. Alexander Haslam and Stephen Reicher, "Identity Entrepreneurship and the Consequences of Identity Failure: The Dynamics of Leadership in the BBC Prison Study," *Social Psychology Quarterly* 70, no. 2 (2007): 125–147.

27. Philip Zimbardo, *The Lucifer Effect: Understanding How Good People Turn Bad* (New York: Random House, 2007).

28. Haslam & Reicher, "Identity Entrepreneurship," 547.

29. Oliver Klein, Russell Spears, and Stephen Reicher, "Social Identity Performance: Extending the Strategic Side of SIDE," *Personality and Social Psychology Review* 11, no. 1 (2007): 1–18.

30. John Drury and Steve Reicher, "Explaining Enduring Empowerment: A Comparative Study of Collective Action and Psychological Outcome," *European Journal of Social Psychology* 35, no. 1 (2005): 35–58.

31. Orla Muldoon, "Children of the Troubles: The Impact of Political Violence in Northern Ireland," *Journal of Social Issues* 60, no. 3 (2004): 453–68.

32. Robert Cialdini, *Influence: Science and Practice, 4th ed.* (Boston: Allyn & Bacon, 2000).

33. Jonathon Freedman and Scott Fraser, "Compliance Without Pressure: The Foot in the Door Technique," *Journal of Personality and Social Psychology* 4, no. 2 (1966): 195–202.

34. J. Turner, R. Brown, and H. Tafjel, "Social Comparison and Group Interest in In-Group Favoritism," *European Journal of Social Psychology* 9, no. 2 (1979): 187–204.

35. Robert Dahl, *On Democracy* (New Haven, CT: Yale University Press, 2000).

36. Michael Wilson and Richard Wrangham, "Intergroup Relations in Chimpanzees," *Annual Review of Anthropology* 32 (2003): 363–92; Richard Wrangham and Michael Wilson, "Collective Violence: Comparisons between Youths and Chimpanzees," *Annals of the New York Academy of Sciences, Youth Violence: Scientific Approaches to Prevention* 1036 (2006): 233–56; Michael Wilson, Richard Wrangham, and Martin Mueller, "Comparative Rates of Violence in Chimpanzees and Humans," *Primates* 47, no. 1 (2006): 14–26.

37. John Tooby, Leda Cosmides, and Michael Price, "Cognitive Adaptations for In-Person Exchange: The Evolutionary Roots of Organizational Behavior," *Managerial and Decision Economics* 27 (2006): 103–29.

6 Mimēsis, Persuasion, and Manipulation in Plato's *Republic*

Christina Tarnopolsky

When a country faces unprecedented economic and military crises, environmental challenges, and natural disasters to the degree that the United States has in the past few years, there are always going to be patriotic calls for unity from all sides of the political spectrum. And, of course, unified responses, both domestically and globally, *are* needed in order to respond to the threat of terrorism in the world, or the global economic crisis caused by the sub-prime mortgage debacle, or the ravages to our physical environment caused by global warming. However, it is important to ask what kind of unity or collective identity the politicians, spin doctors, pundits, and media are calling for, and whether this particular unity amounts to a subtle manipulation of the population that actually forecloses rather than fosters the deliberations necessary to solve these crises.

Connected to this are questions of psychology: Which emotions are ignited by these crises and which ones should guide our subsequent responses to these crises? What kinds of stories about our collective identity or images of the patriotic citizen should frame our way of coping with these traumatic experiences to the collective psyche of the polity? How should we frame the "threats" or challenges that we are now facing, and the solutions to meet them? It was not only the contents, but also the framing of, the $700 billion plan to combat the economic crisis as a "bail-out" package rather than a "rescue" package, that produced very different emotions towards and narratives about who was getting the money and who wasn't, e.g., envy and suspicion rather than compassion and caring towards anyone who might receive the funds, and a feeling of being ripped off, rather than of making a necessary sacrifice on the part of American tax-payers. Similarly, framing the response to 9/11 as a "War on Terror" suggests that the enemy is as ubiquitous as the very feelings of terror that are constantly being ignited by the media. If secrecy and dispatch are the two things most needed by a polity in times of war, then promoting a state of constant siege or danger fosters a climate of secrecy and suspicion amongst the citizenry. As Sheldon Wolin argues, the War on Terror has fostered a problematic kind of mobilization or unity of the American citizenry that is not that of joint sacrifice, but one of mutual suspicion that leads to an intolerance of dissent and a politics of sloganized patriotism.[1]

On a more positive note, these very crises have also prompted many of our political leaders and citizens to begin thinking about the different forms of collective unity and coalition building (both inside and outside the polity) that are necessary to deal with our current situation. An important part of this work requires exploring and dealing with many of the psychological issues outlined above. In this chapter, I turn to Plato's *Republic* in order to understand the political psychology behind the manipulative tactics that were used to envision a "world" that fostered a problematic atmosphere of suspicion and distrust amongst the American citizenry. I do so because Plato's *Republic* focuses on an empirical situation that has important parallels to our own. He critiques the manipulative tactics of his own democratic polity that led to a lengthy and costly war with Sparta (the Peloponnesian War). This long imperialistic war ended up sapping the very economic and political supremacy of Athens that the war was designed to preserve, and culminated in Athenian bankruptcy and the oligarchic rule of the Thirty Tyrants.[2] Plato's *Republic* is also one of the first political treatises to examine the complex psychology of fictions or frames in order to understand how authoritative myths of citizenship or national identity either foster suspicion, complacency and resignation; or caring, courage, and critical deliberation amongst the citizenry.

Of course, at first glance, Plato's *Republic* might seem like the ideal source for constructing a guidebook *in* political manipulation. The infamous "noble lie" (*gennaion pseudos*)[3] of *Republic* 3 has been interpreted as Plato's account of the lies and deception that he deems necessary for a healthy polity, in opposition to the very open and frank-speech (*parrhēsia*) so favored by fifth- and fourth-century democratic Athens and by contemporary liberal democracies.[4] More recently it has even been taken to be a precursor to the current politics of manipulation, where the American populace is deceived into fighting a never-ending War on Terror and thus duped into ignoring more pressing domestic issues and relinquishing precious civil and political rights.[5]

Instead, in this chapter I reinterpret Plato's seminal treatment of the concept of *mimēsis*[6] in the *Republic* as an examination of the aesthetic and psychological elements behind manipulation and persuasion and the differences between these two forms of democratic rhetoric.[7] Many casual readers of the *Republic* focus only on Plato's discussion of art as mirroring artifacts and natural objects in *Republic* 10 when they think about Platonic *mimēsis*, and thus think of it solely as an aesthetic doctrine.[8] However, his earlier accounts of *mimēsis* in *Republic* 2 and 3 show that his related concern was to understand the *psychology* of *mimēsis*, i.e., the ways in which human beings internalize the character (*ēthos*) of their own polity by emulating (*mimeisthai*) certain exemplary role-models (*Rep.* 3.395d), or by listening to the authoritative myths (*muthoi*) and fictions (*pseudea*) of what it is to be a good citizen (*Rep.* 2.377a-381e).[9] Far from counseling manipulation, Plato tries to encourage his fellow Athenians to engage in (i.e., create, perform, and spectate) the *right* kinds of mimetic practices that will cultivate rather than foreclose the deliberative skills necessary for critical democratic citizenship.[10] This Platonic teaching is both explained and exemplified in the dialogue in the exchanges that occur between Socrates, Glaucon, and Adeimantus and in the kinds of models (*paradeigmata*) or fictions (*pseudea*) that Socrates crafts for his Athenian interlocutors. One of these includes the "noble lie" (*gennaion pseudos*), which I argue is better understood as a fiction (*pseudos*) or frame that encourages critical thinking about one's regime and its normative paradigms of citizen behavior, rather than blind obedience to it.[11]

In the first two sections of the chapter, I turn to recent scholarship on Platonic *mimēsis* and the interconnections between aesthetic practices, political practices and the education of citizens in fifth- and fourth-century democratic Athens in order to re-situate Plato's *Republic* within this kind of project. In the third section of the chapter, I examine the problematic frame (or vision) of citizenship identity that Glaucon and Adeimantus have had inculcated in them by the poets and sophists (i.e., the media, pundits, and spin-doctors) of imperialistic democratic Athens, in order to show how they have been manipulated into apathy and resignation, as well as suspicion towards their fellow citizens. In the fourth section, I turn to the initial treatment of *mimēsis* in *Republic* 2 in order to show how the discussion of stories (*muthoi*), paradigms (*paradeigmata*), and fictions or falsehoods (*pseudea*) is meant both as a response to their predicament and as an attempt to cultivate within them the deliberative skills necessary for critical, philosophic citizenship. In the conclusion, I show how certain aspects of the noble falsehood (*gennaion pseudos*) at the end of *Republic* 3 actually encapsulate Plato's teaching about, and exemplify his creation of, a new collective identity or vision of philosophic citizenship that serves as an antidote to manipulation by fostering an *ēthos* of wakefulness and skepticism towards one's authoritative paradigms.

I: Politicizing Plato's Discussion of *Mimēsis*

For much of the twentieth century, scholarly studies of Plato's doctrine of *mimēsis* focused on whether or not there is a consistent doctrine or definition to be found in the *Republic*. To state the problem very briefly: In *Republic* 2 and 3, Plato seems to banish only some forms of *mimēsis* while allowing and even requiring his guardians to practice another form, i.e., they are to learn stories about new kinds of gods and to imitate or emulate only the actions of good men. *Republic* 10, however, opens with the statement that they (Socrates, Glaucon, and Adeimantus) have been correct to banish *all mimetic* poetry from their ideal republic (*Rep.* 10.595a). And yet even in this book Plato goes on to allow some forms of *mimēsis* back into their ideal republic, i.e., hymns to the gods and encomia of good men (*Rep.* 10.607a).[12] The range of meanings of the term, *mimēsis*, that have been identified by scholars trying to work out the puzzling character of Plato's account includes: replication, imitation, copy, impersonation, analogy, metaphor, emulation, dramatic enactment, identification, imitativeness, mimicking, likening, acting as if, resemblance, correspondence, equivalence, metaphysical conformity, representation, expression, approximation, participation, and simulation.

But, in recent years, there has been a change in the direction of analysis away from questions of *whether* Plato has a consistent doctrine of *mimēsis* to *what political work is being done* by Plato's definitions, examples, and uses of *mimēsis* in the *Republic*. What is Plato doing by defining and then re-defining *mimēsis*; censoring the poets in a dialogue that happens to exemplify the very style of delivery for which he censors them;[13] critiquing the production of images and then producing some of the most memorable images in the history of philosophy? The virtues of this approach are twofold. First, it explicitly foregrounds the historical, social, and political aspects of Plato's treatment of *mimēsis*.[14] As Gebauer and Wulf put it, "The history of *mimēsis* is a history of disputes over the power to make symbolic worlds, that is, the power to represent the self and others and interpret the world. To this extent *mimēsis* possesses a political dimension and is part of the history of power relations."[15] It thus allows us to see just how the ancient quarrel between philosophy and poetry (referred to at *Rep.* 10.607b) is actually re-staged in the dialogue itself as a contest (*agōn*) and as an implicitly political one. Plato's treatment of *mimēsis* is, at least in part, a political struggle (*agōn*) with the mimetic artists (both poets and painters) over the power to re-shape the symbolic world of his contemporary and future audiences.[16] It is also important to note that when Plato engages poetry in the *Republic*, he is engaging something that was as ubiquitous a communicative medium as television, cinema, and the Internet are for us today.[17] In other words, Plato's attack on the poets must be seen as an attack on the media elites and spin-doctors of his own day.

This new approach allows us to see Plato, not as a thinker who naively subordinates the aesthetic sphere to political considerations or the psyche to politics, but rather as a thinker who is interested in the interconnections between the aesthetic, the psychological and the political. The *Republic* is an investigation of the aesthetico-psychological practices that either facilitate or hinder the introduction of new meanings and contestation of old ones within one's collective worldview. As Danielle Allen puts it, "The *Republic* is itself a drama. It poses the question not only of how to define justice but also the question of how efforts to define justice impact the behavior of those people who are engaged in the enterprise of definition."[18] If we politicize Plato's treatment of *mimēsis,* then we can see that he is not only focusing on what poets, actors, and spectators do or ought to do in relation to a work of art or dramatic performance; he is also focusing on how participants in a deliberation enter into and contest a realm of shared meaning within a democratic polity.

Second, this new approach allows one to ask *what kind* of politics is being done by a thinker who doesn't actually present the reader with a "monolithic doctrine" but rather with a series of "exploratory, shifting and inconclusive arguments on the subject."[19] A number of theorists have recently argued that Plato's treatment of *mimēsis* is far more open and even self-subverting than the authoritarian and closed imposition of meaning it is often taken to be.[20] These theorists have focused primarily on how this is related to Plato's own attempt to introduce and in turn provoke the very activities of critical thinking and self-reflection so central to Platonic philosophizing. Similarly, in this chapter I focus on how his treatment of *mimēsis* is meant as both a critique of and engagement with the Athenian democratic politics of establishing authoritative meanings in the polis.[21] If, as Stephen Halliwell has recently argued, Plato's treatment of *mimēsis* has been fundamentally misunderstood as the monolithic notion of world-reflection or "mirroring," rather than as the complex exploration of the two poles of world-reflection and world-creation (i.e., creating new ways of seeing the world and thus new places [*topoi*] within the typology of the mind),[22] then translating this to the aesthetico-psychological dimension means coming to terms with a Plato who is simultaneously exploring the conservative (world-reflecting) and revolutionary (world-creating) potentials of the mimetic practices within his own democratic polity.

II: Situating the *Republic* in the Athenian Democratic Context

This political interpretation of Plato's treatment of *mimēsis* has been facilitated by recent scholarship, which has reconstructed the Athenian democratic normative imaginary that serves as the direct political background to Plato's dialogues.[23] One variant of this latter type of scholarship has illuminated the association between Athenian democracy and tragedy or theater-going more generally.[24] Much of this scholarship focuses on how Athenian tragedy served both as a representation of the Athenian political and social order and as an opportunity to subject this order to analysis and criticism. Not just the elite, but also a large portion of the Athenian population attended the dramatic festivals, especially the City (or Great) Dionysia.[25] Even prisoners were released on bail for the occasion, and full citizens on the deme register[26] received a subsidy (*theriōkon*) to cover the expenses of tickets for the tragedies and comedies and other festival expenses.[27] More importantly, seating at the theater replicated the seating in the assembly (*ekklēsia*), and certain portions of the theater were reserved for the council (*Boulē*).[28] Directly following the theatrical performances, the assembly (*ekklēsia*) actually held a meeting in the Dionysiac theater "at which officials' conduct of the festival was evaluated."[29] Such regular theater attendance facilitated the development of the psychological and deliberative skills necessary to be a citizen in democratic Athens: "self-criticism, empathy, appreciation of the complexity of moral issues, recognition that things are not always as they seem, and an ability to enter the thoughts of another."[30] Also the kind of active spectating that took place in the theater—where audience members made their judgments of the plays known through heckling, yelling, etc.—resembled the kinds of judgments encountered by anyone addressing the mass audience in either the assembly (*ekklēsia*) or the lawcourts (*dikasteria*).[31] The aesthetic and the political were thus intricately interconnected within the symbolic practices of democratic Athens. As Ober and Strauss put it, "Oratory drew on the audience's experience of theatre; drama drew on the audience's experience of political and legal speeches. By doing so, each genre implicitly taught its audience that being an Athenian was a comprehensive experience, that there was no compartmentalized division between [a]esthetics and politics."[32]

Plato's *Republic* alludes to these aesthetico-political practices at numerous points both in terms of its explicit setting and in terms of the discussion that occurs between Socrates, Glaucon, and Adeimantus. A number of commentators have noted that the dramatic setting of the *Republic* in the Piraeus, the port of Athens, points to one of the central themes of the dialogue: the relationship between philosophy and democratic politics.[33] More importantly, this connection is made specifically within the Athenian democratic practice of festival and theater-going. The opening line of the dialogue: *katebēn chthes eis Peiraia ... tēn heortēn boulomenos theasasthai tina tropon poiēsousin hate nun prōton agontes* ("I went down to the Piraeus yesterday... [because] I wanted to spectate/observe/contemplate [*theasasthai*] how they would put on the festival, since they were now holding it for the first time" [*Rep.* 1.372a]),[34] parallels the cave analogy where the philosopher is also said to go down to into the cave to spectate/observe/contemplate the dark things there (*katabateon ... ta skoteina theasasthai Rep.* 5.520c).[35] Socrates' desire to go down to the Piraeus to witness a new and foreign spectacle ties him to the Athenian democracy, which was also renowned for craving new and innovative spectacles and festivals.[36]

The narrative (as opposed to the dramatic) context of the *Republic* also suggests (perhaps even more directly) the theme of contesting meanings in the Athenian democratic setting of theater-going and festival attendance. We learn from the introduction to the *Timaeus* that the *Republic* is narrated by Socrates in the first person to four interlocutors: Critias, Timaeus, Hermocrates, and an unnamed fourth person. It recounts a conversation he had "yesterday" in the Piraeus, but the narrative itself falls on the day of the Lesser Panathanea, and its scene is thus likely to be the city or the Acropolis.[37] The Greater and Lesser Panathanea were two Athenian festivals in honor of Athena, the patron goddess of the city. As Simon Goldhill argues, the various ceremonies were meant to underscore the relationship between democratic ideology, the notions of war and fighting, and how a child is initiated into being a citizen and warrior.[38] As will be seen in what follows, this is one of the major themes explored in the *Republic*. The dialogue also contains numerous allusions to the processions, sacrifices, and athletic, poetic, and artistic contests that formed an integral part of these important civic and political festivals. For example, *Republic* 1 mentions the torch-races that were held in honor of the goddess at these festivals (*Rep.* 1.328a). In *Republic* 2 Socrates describes Glaucon's elaborate descriptions of the just and unjust man as polishing statues to be judged for a prize competition (*Rep.* 2.361d), and such competitions were also a part of the Panathenea. *Republic* 8 contains a reference to the richly embroidered cloak (*peplos*) that was carried through the streets of Athens to the Acropolis to clothe the statue of the goddess on the occasion of such festivals (*Rep.* 8.529c-d).[39]

Putting all of these allusions together, I believe that Plato writes the *Republic* as an offering to his fellow Athenians that is meant as a cure (*pharmakon*) to purge (*kathairein*) and transform what he takes to be problematic in their specific worldview and in the ways this worldview had been constructed and contested by the poets, sophists, and citizens in their aesthetico-psychological and political capacities as poet, actor, and spectator.[40] He introduces not only a brand new meaning of justice into their conceptual schema, but also a new poetic-philosophic activity that fashions new symbols and revises concepts central to their worldviews "to force them to conceive of what had been to them inconceivable,"[41] and he does this while simultaneously interrogating the aesthetic and psychological mechanisms by which such an activity is done. This new philosophic activity is meant to cure not only what ails the luxurious or "feverish city" (*phlegmainousan polin*) first introduced by Glaucon at *Rep.* 2.372e, but also the psychic ailments and perplexity suffered by the actual citizens of imperial democratic Athens.[42]

III: Glaucon and Adeimantus' Tragic Worldview

At the beginning of Book 2, Glaucon and Adeimantus enter the discussion with a bad case of psychic indigestion or perplexity (*aporia*): As Glaucon tells Socrates, "I'm not yet satisfied by the argument [for or against the just life] on either side.... I'm perplexed, indeed, and my ears are deafened listening to Thrasymachus and countless others. But I've yet to hear anyone defend justice in the way I want, proving that it is better than injustice. I want to hear it praised *by itself*, and I think that I'm most likely to hear this from you" (*Rep.* 2.358b-d).[43] Glaucon's psychic predicament is complex: He constructs an image of the unjust life that appears to be logically coherent to him but which he professes not to be able to fully believe, that is, he refuses to give assent to it as the model for his own actions. Borrowing images from the historian Herodotus and the poet Aeschylus, he gives a vivid description of the life of the unjust man that makes him "like a god among humans," and that includes his ability to confiscate property, have sex with anyone he wishes, and to kill anyone with impunity (*Rep.* 2.360b-c).[44] (Later in *Republic* 8, Adeimantus will also admit that Euripides and the other tragic poets "extol tyranny as a condition 'equal to that of a god'" [*Rep.* 8.568b], and this is one of the reasons that Socrates banishes them from his ideal city [*Rep.* 8.568b]).

Glaucon also constructs an image of the just life which he wishes were true and which he wants Socrates to defend even when this person has both his eyes burned out, is whipped, racked, bound, mutilated (and subjected to other unspecified evils), and is finally crucified (*Rep.* 2.361e-362a).[45] Both of his fantasy images of injustice and justice include the desire for a god-like self-sufficiency that would make the person invulnerable to those around him, either in the active sense of being a tyrant who does whatever he wishes to others, or in the passive sense of being the martyr who suffers the worst torments and still chooses this unfortunate way of life. When Adeimantus joins the discussion, he expresses related but slightly different concerns: he complains that the poets ultimately teach one that justice and happiness are at odds with one another and that it is better to be the wily and subtle fox who only pretends to be just and virtuous (*Rep.* 2. 362e-367e). To support this position he once again resorts to the poets and historians and thus makes ample use of quotations from Hesiod, Homer, and Simonides.

Of course, neither Glaucon nor Adeimantus have actually followed the poets' advice and become tyrants themselves so that they could enjoy the allegedly wonderful pleasures of killing, stealing and raping with impunity in the manner of the Greek gods. They have thus not been fully converted by the poets' or by the sophist Thrasymachus' praise of injustice in *Republic* 1 and instead they remain agnostic. They have not assented to or rejected either view, but these images or worldviews haunt their lives as possible ways of life that they cannot fully assent to and thus bring to life. The completely just and unjust men whom Glaucon depicts are like a pair of statues skillfully scoured for an art competition (*Rep.* 2.361d), which nevertheless remain lifeless works of art for him.

At this point, Glaucon and Adeimantus' view of the world is a tragic one because they feel that the answers to their predicament might not be within their reach and because they feel that the life of justice has no cosmic support, at least as these ultimate values are conveyed via the tragedies they have recited or witnessed.[46] Indeed, in a completely corrupt world, such fantasy images of justice might well be the *only* place where justice actually exists.[47] Glaucon and Adeimantus' fantasy about the perfectly just but tortured man serves as a realm of aesthetic repose that offers at least some respite from the corruptness of the world around them.[48] Thus, although most commentators see the *Republic* as offering a cure for Glaucon and Adeimantus' overweening political ambitions, I agree with G.R.F. Ferrari that what Socrates really hopes to cure them of is a tragic withdrawal from political life as hopelessly corrupt. As Ferrari argues, the two brothers seem to have already withdrawn from politics to focus on the cultivation of their souls and the reason Socrates begins to look at justice in the city is, in part, meant to get them re-engaged with its concerns and projects.[49] In their view, you either become a tyrant or become the victim of one when you choose to enter political life.

Interestingly enough, the situation in which Glaucon and Adeimantus find themselves at the beginning of *Republic* 2 is actually not that different from the one in which many contemporary Americans found themselves in the aftermath of 9/11, or now find themselves in the unfolding global credit crisis and world-wide Great Recession. With respect to 9/11, the American populace was not coerced into following a particular policy; rather the media almost unanimously painted a picture of the world which then legitimated what seemed like the only two alternatives for action: Either the United States could remain perpetually vulnerable to terrorists who would exact upon the nation the kinds of horrific cruelties that Glaucon's just man suffers at the hands of his tormentors; or the United States could reassert its invulnerability and omnipotence by launching a preemptive war against any and all countries suspected of harboring these terrorists. Just like certain sophists and poets of ancient Athens, the implicit message of the media and leaders in the United States was: act like a tyrant or you will become the victim of one. Moreover, in both cases, the readiness with which this over-simplistic and extremely pessimistic view of the world was accepted was facilitated by the fact that both the Athenians and Americans were faced with a new kind of war.[50] The Peloponnesian War "broke the standing rules of warfare that had been in effect since the eighth century BCE, causing major changes in the practice of war," "destabilizing hitherto settled rules of engagement and categories of identity," and "giving free rein to *pleonexia* [over-reaching] in all its registers, psychic, domestic, and imperial."[51] In the case of Glaucon and Adeimantus, this war served as the immediate backdrop that reinforced the worldview first conveyed to them as children in the poets' stories of warring and pillaging gods. It is not surprising then that theirs is a worldview in which inflicting or suffering violence at the hands of one's fellow citizens or at the hands of other polities seem like the only two realistic choices open to one. As Jill Frank puts it, "with both an aggressive and a defensive aspect, *pleonexia* generates the rule 'take from another before another takes from you,' a rule characteristic of 'apprehensive states of war of all kinds'."[52]

Painting a world in which perpetrating or suffering violence are the only two choices is not only directly opposed to the democratic ideal of discussion and debate as a means of solving problems, but it also works via a problematic dialectic of activating the population through de-activating and dividing them. An *ēthos* of suspicion towards their fellow citizens is prevalent in both Glaucon and Adeimantus because of the worldview they have had inculcated in them by the poets and have seen reiterated in the sophist Thrasymachus' view that justice is solely the advantage of the stronger (*Rep.* 1.344c). As Adeimantus tells Socrates, "since as the wise make plain to me, 'the seeming overpowers even the truth' and is the master of happiness, one must surely turn wholly to it. As façade and exterior I must draw a shadow painting of virtue all around me, while behind it I must trail the wily and subtle fox of the most wise Archilochus" (*Rep.* 2.365c). Similarly, in the aftermath of 9/11, the media and politicians on both the Left and the Right were quick to put up a façade of shallow patriotism and false virtue that foreclosed any kind of real debate about alternative policies and tactics for fighting this new kind of war. Instead, it only fostered an atmosphere of mutual suspicion amongst the citizens and towards anyone who tried to contest the need for an aggressive and preemptive war against Iraq. What was missing from both Glaucon and Adeimantus' Athens and contemporary America was the space for contesting and re-constructing the whole worldview that fosters mutual suspicion and predisposes citizens and leaders alike to think only in terms of militaristic strategies of offence and defense. If the great Greek tragedians were the first to recognize how tragedies could represent whole political orders and subject them to criticism, Plato was one of the first poet-philosophers to recognize how these tragedies could also transmit a completely pessimistic view of the world, which then indirectly influenced the political choices made by the citizens who greedily consumed these images and spectacles.[53]

Thus, even though Glaucon and Adeimantus claim to be skeptical or unable to fully believe and thus act upon either of their images of the life of complete justice or injustice, they do believe that these are the only two possibilities for how to live the good life. The two pictures of justice and injustice that they paint for Socrates depend on an already existing background that configures human existence in terms of these two possibilities. They don't want to give up their desire for omnipotence and self-sufficiency; they just want Socrates to show them how they can have this while leading the just life. Because they are no longer children, they do not literally believe in the stories of Achilles' wrath or Zeus' rape of various helpless maidens and they can recognize the allegorical character of these stories, but their perspective is still "Achillized" because their entire outlook or paradigm disposes them to see the world in terms of these kinds of existential possibilities.[54] In a certain sense simply reasoning with them would come too late because the paradigm that orients their lives already "predisposes them to recognize good and bad arguments in terms of that outlook."[55] Plato's solution to their predicament involves not simply reasoning with them, but getting them to engage in the kind of serious and imaginative play that is involved in pretending to be founders of a city in speech.[56] As will be seen in what follows, this activity is *playful* because they are not literally founding a city, but it is *serious* because it allows them to discern "in what way justice and injustice come into being in a city" (*Rep.* 2.376d),[57] so that they can then subsequently choose the way of life that most exemplifies justice.

What Socrates, Glaucon, and Adeimantus proceed to do is to construct an image of a city and a soul in speech which begins from the very education and upbringing that they have experienced in Athens, but which is continually altered or purged in response to their concerns as these are expressed at the end of *Republic* 1 and the beginning of *Republic* 2, and as they are altered and transformed in the course of the conversation. That this project is democratic is dramatized by the fact that the re-founding and re-framing happens as a response to the admissions of perplexity, interruptions, appeals, and criticisms of various interlocutors as they construct this model of the ideal city and citizen together (e.g. 1.354c, 2.357a, 2.362d, 4.419a, 5.499b, 6.506b-e).[58] The dialectical engagement between the interlocutors is itself an image of an interaction between citizens that becomes progressively different from the forceful impositions that open the dialogue (i.e., Thrasymachus' angry entrance at *Rep.* 1.336b), and the manipulative practices that were actually prevalent in Athens during the time-period in which Plato sets the dialogue (421 BC–404 BC). This is because both the content of the images they collectively produce and the way in which they relate to these images exemplify the kind of critical and reflective activity involved in being an active, philosophic citizen and not a passively manipulated one.[59] All of the participants in the dialogue, both silent and not-so-silent, end up imitating Socrates' critical-philosophical activity as gadfly to Athens so that they can better understand themselves and their own city.

IV: *Mimēsis* as World-Creation in Myths and Paradigms

If Glaucon and Adeimantus are both in some sense held captive by a picture,[60] i.e., the tragic worldview that has been constructed for them by the poets concerning justice and injustice, then it makes sense that Socrates examines the logic of just how these stories hold sway over human lives, while simultaneously getting them to join him in the construction of a new kind of story. Accordingly, the first detailed discussion of *mimēsis* in the *Republic* focuses on the stories, fictions, and accounts (*muthoi* and *logoi*) children are told as part of their education into the normative paradigms and patterns of their polity (*Rep.* 2.377a-382a).[61] As Socrates tells Adeimantus, "Don't you understand that first we tell tales to children? And surely they are, as a whole, false (*pseudos*), though there are true things in them too" (*Rep.* 2.377a2-5). The specific connection Plato wants to draw between *mimēsis* and these *pseudea* (fictions/falsehoods) is made at the end of *Republic* 2 where Socrates argues that such falsehoods or fictions (*psuedea*) can be an imitation (*mimēsis* of an affection in the soul (*Rep.* 2.382b).[62] What Plato constructs through the voice of Socrates is a new kind of fiction or frame that expresses the character (*ēthos*) of philosophical discussion and judgment, rather than the *ēthos* of war.[63]

In a sense Glaucon, Adeimantus, and Socrates all become like children again because they all pretend to be founders of a city in speech who legislate the patterns and models (*paradeigmata* and *tupoi*) to the poets (*Rep.* 3.379a). They engage in a form of serious play that exemplifies the way in which children first learn (and adults subsequently deepen or critique their understanding of) the *ēthos* of their culture from the various fictions and stories that they tell or are told about the world. As Stephen Halliwell puts it, "The discussion of poetic stories or myths (in *Republic* books 2-3, from 376e to 392c), is guided by a concern with the ethics and psychology of fiction. *This concern manifests itself in a setting that is ostensibly educational but whose underlying principles ... are applicable to all cultural and individual self-formation*" [my italics].[64] It is an investigation of the psychology of framing and re-framing that goes on in any attempt to persuade one's fellow citizens to adopt or reject a specific viewpoint upon or vision of the world that they all share now, but are also in the process of changing.[65]

These stories also operate at a very different level than the conscious first principles of action that the young guardians learn by impersonating or emulating the actions of good men in *Republic* 3 (which is the second sense of *mimēsis* that Plato subsequently investigates). They are at a lower level of consciousness, but for that very reason they reside at a higher-level of meaning. This is because they supply the paradigms or pictures (*paradeigmata*) that orient whatever specific strategic actions or true statements a person can subsequently choose to make in the world. In learning the story about the "wrath of Achilles" from Homer, the Athenian child is not (or not only) learning propositional or ethical facts about the world, but rather is acquiring an entire framework or paradigm for seeing the world in a specific way, which then grounds the very possibility of strategic and cognitive rationality.[66] Plato was thus one of the first thinkers to understand that manipulation works upon the minds of democratic citizens most insidiously in the spaces prior to and outside of their direct political activities of citizenship.

Moreover, far from reducing *all* forms of *mimēsis* to the monolithic doctrine of world-reflection or "mirroring," Plato's initial argument about *mimēsis* is that the models used by Homer, Hesiod, and the tragedians should be replaced by other stories and models because they simply reflect and even legitimate the facts of the empirical world around them (*Rep.* 3.377e-378e). Here Socrates says that even if certain stories are true about the world, they are inappropriate for children to hear (*Rep.* 3.378a).[67] Thus his standard for rejecting many of the stories and poems currently told to children about gods and heroes in Athens is that they are in fact too close to the way men actually behave and not to the way they ought to behave.[68] At this point in the discussion, the ability of poems or images to mirror the empirical world is clearly subordinated to their ability to convey moral lessons, express a new kind of *ēthos* and to open up new models (*paradeigmata*) or spaces (*topoi*) within the minds of one's audience. This is due to the fact that the discussion is now concerned with how new stories (*muthoi*) and fictions (*pseudea*) might be used to educate children and young men such as Glaucon and Adeimantus to reform the actual city of imperialistic Athens. The problem with the stories (*muthoi*) and fictions (*pseudea*) told by Homer and the tragedians (and the uncritical reception of these stories by citizens of an imperialistic polity) is that they simply reflect and thus conservatively reproduce the *ēthos* of martial virtue that eventually led to Athens' disastrous engagement in the Peloponnesian War.

Not surprisingly then, most of the stories and images that Socrates wants to censor involve the stories of war and strife amongst the gods and between the gods and heroes of Athens. As Socrates tells Adeimantus, "[Children] are far from needing to have tales told and embroideries woven about battles of giants and the many diverse disputes of gods and heroes with their family and kin" (*Rep.* 3.378c). Here it is important to remember that the Peloponnesian War "made foes of Greek cities that had fought as allies in earlier wars."[69] Socrates is not saying that children will simply ape the actions of the gods in these stories and that is why censorship is required (this sense of *mimēsis* as mimicking or imitativeness is not fully elaborated until *Republic* 3). Rather, "He is saying that such stories influence childhood fantasy, and fantasy has an effect on the development of character (*ēthos*). The sway of poetry over actions, then, is only indirect, insofar as action stems from character."[70] If children live in a world dominated by fantasy and imagination, then it is important to ensure that there is "method in this madness."[71] Otherwise, as was the case with imperialistic Athens, the myths of ethical corruption and violence that the Greek poets and tragedians depict will become a self-fulfilling prophecy because they turn out children and then adults motivated by these models of behavior.[72]

Accordingly, the models of action which Socrates, Glaucon and Adeimantus construct in *Republic* 2–3 are not empirically constructed nor are they meant to reflect the facts of the world around them. Instead, they involve a reformation of their dreams and images about what it means to be a god.[73] This model is in fact constructed counterfactually out of what humans don't do now, but what they ought to do. In a corrupt world, perfect justice might only be found in these sorts of ideal models, visions or dreams, and Socrates later reminds Glaucon of this fact: "it was, therefore, for the sake of a pattern (*paradeigma*) that we were seeking both for what justice by itself is like, and for the perfectly just man, if he should come into being, and what he would be like once come into being ... We were not seeking them for the sake of proving that it's possible for these things to come into being" (*Rep.* 5.472c-d). Modern parallels to this kind of utopian[74] or protreptic[75] speech-act include Martin Luther King's "I Have a Dream" speech and Barack Obama's campaign slogan "Yes, We Can." These are not meant to be descriptive models or images of the world as it exists *now*, but rather prescriptive and hortatory visions of what we should move towards and hope to become if we begin to follow these men and their vision, even though right *here and now* we don't really know where the path leads or how far along it we will be able to walk.

This means that such models can have a real effect on the world precisely because they are *not* making propositional truth claims. Part of the logic of *mimēsis* consists of the fact that the models, fantasies and stories we tell about justice have the potential to change the world because people can and do try to imitate or exemplify these ideals in their subsequent actions. The construction of the ideal city has the potential to educate the children of Athens to a better way of life (if Glaucon and Adeimantus were to become legislators in Athens), and to change Glaucon and Adeimantus *themselves* (if they choose to exemplify these ideals in their own lives as citizens of democratic Athens). As Jill Frank puts it, "By modeling interactions among political actors who do not resort to violence against the backdrop of an extremely violent war, the *Republic* depicts a different possible future while also arguing for the conditions necessary for such a change."[76] The discussion that Socrates has with Glaucon and Adeimantus (and the primarily silent, but still present, other interlocutors) in the *Republic* is thus therapeutic in the sense that it is meant to give them the space where they can question, contest and transform the authoritative paradigms and narratives of behavior that they have internalized from their own personal and political histories. But because Plato has placed this space in a writing that is without a set place (*a-topos*), it offers us today the best place (*eu-topos*) to see both back into our distant and not so distant past, and forward into our collective future.

Accordingly, their new gods (and ours?) are ones who do not make war with one another (*Rep.* 2.378c), and who do not deceive and trick other gods and human beings in order to satisfy their immoderate and tyrannical desires (*Rep.* 2.380d). Platonic *mimēsis* avoids the manipulative tactics of the tragedians and sophists (i.e., Thrasymachus) by opening up new possibilities for action rather than simply mirroring the corruptness of the world around Glaucon and Adeimantus, and then convincing them that this conservative activity of world-reflection is the key to a hard-nosed realism. Such creations in speech acts and images made the Athenians think that they were being realistic in their pessimism, but this realism was paradoxically illusory because it foreclosed the ever present possibility of creating a new world order that would foster rather than foreclose the kinds of discussions dramatized in the *Republic*.

VI: Conclusion

In the *Republic* Plato does not replace *mimēsis* with rational discussion, or poetry with philosophy, nor does he counsel a deceptive politics of manipulation that brainwashes its citizens with the use of noble lies. Instead, he dramatizes a new philosophical-poetic activity that involves the construction of authoritative models or fictions of citizenship-identity that open up rather than foreclose new possibilities for acting in the world we share with others. In forging his own alliance between poetry and philosophy, Plato suggests the kind of mediation or coalition-building that will be necessary to harmonize our relations with "others" both inside and outside the polity, as we engage in the ongoing work of creating a new world order. For Plato good models of citizen identity need to be simultaneously creative and reflective, conservative and revolutionary, idealistic and realistic, peaceful and agonistic. They need to present new possibilities that don't simply mirror the world around one, even while they reflect the kind of philosophic discussion by means of which new possibilities are introduced, critiqued, judged, and reformulated within one's own dynamic and collective worldview.

Some of the crucial differences between Platonic persuasion and the manipulation that he criticizes in the *Republic* are in fact encapsulated in two aspects of the *gennaion pseudos* (noble falsehood/fiction/lie) that are often *misinterpreted* or *overlooked* by commentators.[77] The *misinterpretation* that is important to clear up regarding this infamous "noble lie" is that it is *not told by the rulers to the citizens*.[78] The specific passages with which Socrates introduces it explicitly state that it is to be told to the guardians and auxiliaries and all of the other citizens (*Rep.* 3.414b, 3.414d). As Malcolm Schofield puts it, "The noble lie is very far from being simply a brazen piece of propaganda designed primarily to control the mass of the population of the ideal city...It is aimed at the rulers in the first instance, and its main purpose is to get them to be public-spirited."[79] In other words, it is completely opposed to the kind of fiction/falsehood/lie (*pseudos*) that has plagued many contemporary polities.[80]

The *oversight* made by most commentators[81] relates to Socrates' prefatory remarks about the *overall* character of the *gennaion pseudos*. These remarks are essential for understanding the fundamental difference between Platonic persuasion and the forms of manipulation he is criticizing. They are also important for understanding the connections between the *gennaion pseudos* of *Republic* 3 and the previous discussion of dreams, fictions, and gods in *Republic* 2, as well the subsequent discussion of the pathological waking-dream state that characterizes the tyrant in *Republic* 9 (9.574e). In these prefatory remarks, Socrates tells Glaucon that they will have to "persuade first the rulers and the soldiers, then the rest of the city, that the rearing and education they gave them were like dreams..." (*Rep.* 3.414d). In other words, the *gennaion pseudos* is a fiction (*pseudos*) about how *all* of the citizens of the ideal republic should treat their education as a dream (*Rep.* 3.414d).[82] It is thus "a dream about dreaming and waking up...it is an allegory told to us when we cannot recognize allegory as such but which *right on its surface* tells us that the other allegories we've already heard (and by hypothesis have not yet recognized as such) are really only dreams. In that way, the Noble Falsehood embeds an anti-foundationalist message about all other myths: none of them should be taken literally."[83] Taken out of its proper context, the *gennaion pseudos* might seem to encapsulate a Platonic teaching about the lies and deception needed to establish and maintain a moderate and unified polity,[84] but taken within its immediate context of the discussion of myths and fictions in *Republic* 2 and 3, it encapsulates Plato's teaching that the best citizens or guardians of a regime are those who continually question its authoritative myths and fictions.

It is an image that has much to offer us in a world that still seems to share dangerous similarities to Plato's Athens. As we rush to construct some kind of unified response with which to solve the many crises facing the world, Plato exhorts us all to become those gadflies with the golden souls who have the courage to question the authoritative myths and images of the "patriotic citizen" that have led to these crises in the first place, and that now limit our resources for thinking and acting differently.

Notes

1. Sheldon S. Wolin, *Democracy Incorporated: Managed Democracy and the Specter of Inverted Totalitarianism* (Princeton, NJ: Princeton University Press, 2008).
2. See Ryan Balot, *Greed and Injustice in Classical Athens* (Princeton, NJ: Princeton University Press, 2001); Jill Frank, "The Wages of War: On judgment in Plato's Republic," *Political Theory* 35 (2007): 443–67 for excellent accounts of how Plato's *Republic* responds to the greed (*pleonexia*) and injustice (*adikia*) that plagued Athens during the period of the Peloponnesian War and the oligarchic revolutions of the late fifth century B.C.
3. It is important to note that by Plato's time the Attic Greek noun, *pseudos*, could mean either a lie, falsehood, or fiction. Throughout the *Republic*, Plato constantly plays on the ambiguity between these meanings that gradually developed in both the noun *pseudos*, and the adjective *psuedēs*, beginning with Homer. See Stephen Halliwell, *The Aesthetics of Mimēsis: Ancient Texts and Modern Problems* (Princeton, NJ: Princeton University Press, 2002); Hannah Arendt, *Between Past and Future: Eight Exercises in Political Thought*, (New York: NYU Press, 1968).
4. For thinkers who see Plato as counseling deception and lying see Karl Popper, *The Open Society and Its Enemies, Volume 1: The Spell of Plato* (1945; repr., New York: G. Routledge and Sons, 1966); Leo Strauss, *The City and Man* (Chicago: Rand McNally, 1964), p. 102; Allan Bloom, "Interpretive Essay" in Allan Bloom, trans., *The Republic of Plato* (Basic Books, 1968), pp. 367–68; Malcolm Schofield, "The Noble Lie," in *The Cambridge Companion to Plato's Republic*, ed. G.R.F. (John) Ferrari (Cambridge: Cambridge University Press, 2007), pp. 138–164. (It is, however, important to

note that Strauss, Bloom, and Schofield offer much more nuanced versions of this argument than the one offered by Popper. For the importance of free or frank speech (*parrhēsia*) as an Athenian democratic ideal see Josiah Ober, *Mass and Elite in Democratic Athens: Rhetoric, Ideology and the Power of the People* (Princeton, NJ: Princeton University Press, 1989); Sara Monoson, *Plato's Democratic Entanglements: Athenian Politics and the Practice of Philosophy* (Princeton, NJ: Princeton University Press, 2000); Arlene Saxonhouse, *Free Speech and Democracy in Ancient Athens*, (Cambridge: Cambridge University Press, 2006); Schofield, "The Noble Lie," pp. 140–41; and Christina Tarnopolsky, "Plato on Shame and Frank Speech in Democratic Athens," in R. Kingston and L. Ferry, eds., *Bringing the Passions Back In: The Emotions in Political Philosophy* (Vancouver: University of British Columbia Press, 2008), pp. 40–59.

5. Earl Shorris, "Ignoble Liars: Leo Strauss, George Bush, and the Philosophy of Mass Deception," *Harper's Magazine* (2004): 65–80.

6. Although often translated as "imitation," Plato's use of the term has a far broader range of meanings. See section I below.

7. The *Republic* builds upon Plato's analysis of different forms of democratic rhetoric in the *Gorgias*. For an account of these different forms of democratic rhetoric in the *Gorgias*, see Christina Tarnopolsky, *Prudes, Perverts and Tyrants: Plato's Gorgias and the Politics of Shame* (Princeton, NJ: Princeton University Press, 2010), chapter 1.

8. Even the account in *Republic* 10 cannot be reduced to the view that art simply copies or mirrors objects in the world, and Halliwell, *The Aesthetics of Mimēsis*, shows that Plato is actually bringing up this conception of art to debunk it.

9. For scholarship on Platonic *mimēsis* that does emphasize the psychological dimensions of *Republic* 2 and 3 see for example Elizabeth Belfiore, "A Theory of Imitation in Plato's Republic," *Transactions of the American Philological Association* 114 (1984): 121–46; G.R.F. Ferrari, "Plato and Poetry," in *The Cambridge History of Literary Criticism, Volume One: Classical Criticism*, ed. George A. Kennedy (Cambridge: Cambridge University Press, 1989), 62–148; Christopher Janaway, *Images of Excellence: Plato's Critique of the Arts* (London: Clarendon Press, 1995); Halliwell, *The Aesthetics of Mimesis*; Jonathan Lear, "Allegory and Myth in Plato's Republic," in *The Blackwell Guide to Plato's Republic*, ed. G. Santas (London: Blackwell, 2006); Jill Frank, "Vying for Authority in Plato's *Republic*," presented to the 2008 Annual Meeting of the American Political Science Association Meeting.

10. Plato does not think that all forms of *mimēsis* are salutary for producing good democratic citizenship. His goal in the *Republic* is to look at how the mimetic tendency that all human beings share can have salutary or pernicious effects on their psyche and in their political lives. As will become clear in what follows, one can make a good or a bad copy (*mimēsa*) of the soul and there are good and bad ways of imitating (*mimeisthai*) others.

11. Arendt, *Between Past and Future*, p. 298, n. 5; Lear, "Allegory and Myth in Plato's Republic." See note 3 above for the range of meanings of *pseudos* in Attic Greek.

12. For a discussion of the inconsistencies or discontinuities see W.C. Greene, "Plato's View of Poetry," *Harvard Studies in Classical Philology* 29 (1918): 1–75; Ramona Naddaff, *Exiling the Poets: The Production of Censorship in Plato's Republic* (Chicago: University of Chicago Press, 2002); Alexander Nehamas, "Plato on Imitation and Poetry in Republic 10," in *Plato on Beauty, Wisdom and the Arts*, eds. Julius Moravcsik and Philip Temko

(Lanham, MD: Rowman and Littlefield, 1982), pp. 47–78; and J. Tate, "'Imitation' in Plato's Republic," *Classical Quarterly* 22 (1928): 16–23.

13. Naddaff, *Exiling the Poets*, focuses specifically on what political and philosophical work is being done by Plato's multiple acts of censorship in the *Republic*. Frank, "Vying for Authority in Plato's *Republic*," focuses specifically on what political and philosophical work is being done by the structural *mimēsis* of the *Republic* itself.

14. Indeed Gunter Gebauer and Cristopher Wolf, *Mimēsis: Culture-Art-Society*, trans. Don Reneau (Berkeley: University of California Press, 1995) fault Auerbach's seminal work, *Mimēsis*, for overlooking the social and historical background that made possible the changes in the senses of *mimēsis* that he surveys.

15. Gebauer and Wolf, *Mimēsis*, 3; Danielle S. Allen, "Envisaging the Body of the Condemned: The Power of Platonic Symbols," *Classical Philology* 95 (2000): 245–81, also argues that the *Republic* is political not because it gives us a blueprint for politics, but because it attempts to revise symbols and concepts that are fundamental to Athenian politics and it does this through offering new narratives and acts of *mimēsis*.

16. For the agonistic character of Plato's engagement with the poets see: Friedrich Nietzsche *The Birth of Tragedy and The Case of Wagner*, trans. Walter Kaufman (New York: Vintage, 1967); Nehamas, "Plato on Imitation and Poetry in *Republic* 10"; Naddaff, *Exiling the Poets*; and Monoson, *Plato's Democratic Entanglements*.

17. For the discussion of theater as a mass form of communication along the lines of television see Elizabeth Asmis, "Plato on Poetic Creativity," in *The Cambridge Companion to Plato*, ed. Richard Kraut (Cambridge: Cambridge University Press, 1992), pp. 338–64; Janaway, *Images of Excellence*, 81; Nehamas, "Plato on Imitation and Poetry in *Republic* 10m," 51; and Alexander Nehamas, *Virtues of Authenticity: Essays on Plato and Socrates* (Princeton, NJ: Princeton University Press, 1999).

18. Allen, "Envisioning the Body of the Condemned," 263. For an excellent account of how this works in Socrates' discussion with Polemarchus in *Republic* 1, see "Vying for Authority in Plato's *Republic*."

19. Halliwell, *The Aesthetics of Mimēsis*, p. 25. Halliwell argues, "one of the supreme myths of modern histories of aesthetics" is that Plato does present a monolithic doctrine of *mimēsis*.

20. See J. Angelo Corlett, "An Interpretation of Art as Mimēsis in the *Republic*," *Idealistic Studies* (1991): 155–69; Halliwell, *The Aesthetics of Mimēsis*; Lear, "Allegory and Myth in Plato's Republic"; and Naddaff, *Exiling the Poets*. In contrast Gebauer and Wulf, *Mimēsis*, 4, argue that Plato does try to close off rather than open up the meanings of *mimēsis*.

21. As Josiah Ober, *The Athenian Revolution: Essays on Ancient Greek Democracy and Political Theory* (Princeton, NJ: Princeton University Press, 1996), p. 11, argues, "classical Athenian politics operated quite overtly according to pragmatic, discursive, speech-act principles. By making proclamations in the Assembly and in the lawcourts, the Athenian demos self-consciously established and reiterated social and political realities, and it did so without worrying much about the ontological status of the realities so created."

22. Halliwell, *The Aesthetics of Mimēsis*, pp. 23–24. Glaucon first calls Socrates' image of the cave and the prisoners in it an *atopos* (strange or out of place) image (*Rep.* 7.515a).

23. See, for example, Josiah Ober, *The Athenian Revolution*; J. Peter Euben, *The Tragedy of Political Theory: The Road Not Taken* (Princeton, NJ: Princ-

eton University Press, 1990); Monoson, *Plato's Democratic Entanglements*; and Saxonhouse, *Free Speech and Democracy in Ancient Athens.*

24. See, for example, Euben, *The Tragedy of Political Theory*; Martha Nussbaum, *The Fragility of Goodness: Luck and Ethics in Greek Tragedy and Philosophy* (Cambridge: Cambridge University Press, 1986); Simon Goldhill, *Reading Greek Tragedy* (Cambridge: Cambridge University Press, 1986); Simon Goldhill, "The Great Dionysia and Civic Ideology" in *Nothing to Do with Dionysos?: Athenian Drama in its Social Context*, ed. John J. Winkler and Froma Zeitlin (Princeton, NJ: Princeton University Press, 1990), pp. 97–129; Susan Levin, *The Ancient Quarrel Between Philosophy and Poetry Revisited: Plato and the Greek Literary Tradition* (Oxford: Oxford University Press, 2001); Laura McClure, *Spoken Like a Woman: Speech and Gender in Athenian Drama* (Princeton, NJ: Princeton University Press, 1999); Monoson, *Plato's Democratic Entanglements*; Jean Pierre Vernant and Pierre Vidal-Naquet, *Myth and Tragedy in Ancient Greece*, trans. Janet Lloyd (Brooklyn, NY: Zone Books, 1988); John J. Winkler & Froma Zeitlin, eds. *Nothing to Do with Dionysos?*

25. Josiah Ober & Barry Strauss, "Drama, Political Rhetoric and the Discourse of Athenian Democracy" in *Nothing to Do with Dionysos?*, pp. 237–70, note that even non-citizens were allowed to attend the dramatic performances.

26. The register listing all males aged 18 years or older, who had full civic status and rights in the *demes* (districts or villages) into which Athens was divided.

27. Levin, *The Ancient Quarrel Between Philosophy and Poetry Revisited*, p. 9, n. 11.

28. The council or *Boulē* was an advisory citizen body consisting of 500 citizens over the age of 30, selected by lot from amongst the ten tribes of Athens. Their main business was to prepare resolutions (*probouleuma*) for the democratic assembly (*ekklēsia*).

29. Levin, *The Ancient Quarrel Between Philosophy and Poetry Revisited*, p. 9, n. 11. See also Monoson, *Plato's Democratic Entanglements*, 95-96; Oddone Longo, "The Theatre of the Polis" in *Nothing to Do with Dionysos?*, pp. 12–19; and John J. Winkler, "The Ephebes' Song: *Tragoidia* and *Polis*" in *Nothing to Do with Dionysos?*, pp. 20–62.

30. Monoson, *Plato's Democratic Entanglements*, p. 211.

31. I borrow the terminology of "active spectating" from Monoson, *Plato's Democratic Entanglements*, 206–207. Ober, *The Athenian Revolution*, 24, argues that "in both the Assembly and court the public speaker faced a mass audience of 'judges' ready and willing to shout him down if they did not like what they heard."

32. Ober and Strauss, "Drama, Political Rhetoric, and the Discourse of Athenian Democracy," 270. This should not be seen as something that sets democratic Athens apart from contemporary America. Think, for example, of how important it now is for political candidates to appear on the comedy shows that regularly imitate and mock their campaigns. These comedy shows are now a major source of political information for most Americans under the age of 35.

33. Bloom, "Interpretive Essay"; Frank, "The Wages of War"; Monoson, *Plato's Democratic Entanglements*; John Evan Seery, "Politics as Ironic Community: On the themes of descent and return in Plato's Republic", *Political Theory* 16 (1988): 229–56.

34. This translation follows the Bloom translation except that I have indicated the multiple senses of *theasasthai* to highlight the fact that Plato's own

word for contemplating is the same one as the word for spectating. Unless specifically noted, most references are from the Bloom edition. All references are to the Stephanus pages.

35. Monoson, *Plato's Democratic Entanglements*, p. 217. For extensive treatments of the *katabasis* ("going down") theme throughout the *Republic* see Seery, "Politics as Ironic Community," and Bruce Rosenstock, "Rereading the *Republic*," *Arethusa* 16 (1983): 219–46.

36. Bloom (1968), 311.

37. Paul Shorey, *The Republic* (Cambridge, MA: Harvard University Press, 1930), p. vii.

38. Goldhill, "The Great Dionysia and Civic Ideology," p. 107.

39. For a discussion of the significance of the richly embroidered cloak (*peplos*), see Monoson, *Plato's Democratic Entanglements*, chapter 8.

40. For Plato and Arendt, the notion of politics as performance entails theorizing three different moments or elements: the poet (and his genius), the actor (and his virtuosity) ,and the spectator (and his judgment). See Hannah Arendt, *Lectures on Kant's Political Philosophy* (Chicago: University of Chicago Press, 1982), p. 63.

41. Allen, "Envisioning the Body of the Condemned," p. 263.

42. Such a cure can also help us today to begin purging and transforming the anti-intellectualist populism and rampant consumerism that was put to such devastating use by the Bush regime.

43. This translation is from the Grube and Reeve edition of the *Republic*.

44. It is a description that will later be attributed to the lawless dream of the tyrant (*Rep.* 9.571d), which the tyrant then carries out in his waking life (*Rep.* 9.574e).

45. I leave it to the reader's imagination to construct a (perhaps less gruesome) image of what it felt like to be a just person under the Bush regime from 2000–2008.

46. Halliwell, *The Aesthetics of Mimēsis*, pp. 98–117, and Lear, "Allegory and Myth in Plato's Republic," both argue that Plato is concerned to counter the tragic worldview prevalent in democratic Athens, purveyed by the poets and exemplified by the comments of Glaucon and Adeimantus.

47. Their situation parallels the unprecedented lack of trust for any political leaders in the period immediately following the revelation of the global credit crisis. The media, bankers, and politicians of all countries manipulated their citizens into this mistrust either by pointing fingers at each other's greed or responsibility for deregulation, or by pulling figures like $700 billion out of a hat, instead of explaining the causes of the crisis and the possible courses of action to the public.

48. Many late night comedy shows also provided such temporary repose or comic relief during the unfolding of the 2008 financial crisis.

49. G.R.F. Ferrari, *City and Soul in Plato's Republic* (Chicago: University of Chicago Press, 2005), pp. 13, 27, 35. Commentators who see Plato as primarily offering a cure for political ambition include Strauss, *The City and Man*; Bloom, "Interpretive Essay"; Seth Benardete, *Socrates' Second Sailing: On Plato's Republic* (Chicago: University of Chicago Press, 1989); Jacob Howland, *The Republic: The Odyssey of Philosophy* (New York: Twayne Publishers, 1993); and Leon Harold Craig, *The War Lover: A Study of Plato's Republic* (Toronto: University of Toronto Press, 1994).

50. The completely rash execution of the $700 billion "bailout" package was also partially due to the panic generated by the unprecedented character of the situation. Although parallels to the Great Depression have been prolif-

erating in the media, there has also been a lot of talk about the mysterious, unprecedented, and terrifying character of the situation. A similar panic generated by the new and mysterious character of the AIDS crisis (it was dubbed the "Gay Plague" by some media outlets) created similar exclusionary reactions on the part of certain members of many governments around the world. See Christina Tarnopolsky, "Platonic Reflections on the Aesthetic Dimensions of Deliberative Democracy," *Political Theory* 35 (2007): 288–312, for the ways in which the disclosure of new challenges or "worlds" can lead either to justifications for new and subtler forms of tyranny, or to new and subtler forms of freedom.

51. Frank, "The Wages of War," p. 445.
52. Frank, "The Wages of War," p. 443. It is also an apt characterization of the *ēthos* of greed (*pleonexia*) behind the kind of lending and borrowing that had been going on for many years prior to the global credit crisis.
53. For an excellent treatment of Plato's contestation of the tragic view of the world purveyed by the poets see Halliwell, *The Aesthetics of Mimēsis*, pp. 98–117.
54. I borrow the term "Achillized" from Jonathan Lear, "Allegory and Myth in Plato's Republic," p. 30.
55. Lear, "Allegory and Myth in Plato's Republic," p. 25.
56. As Bloom, "Interpretive Essay," p. 343, puts it, "[Socrates] does not respond directly to the questions of his young companions. Rather than criticize their arguments or present a counter argument of his own, he invites them to share an adventure with him."
57. This activity of serious play begins at *Republic* 3.376d and Plato uses Socrates' assertions to explicitly remind the reader that it is ongoing at *Republic* 7.536c and *Republic* 10.595a.
58. Plato even has Thrasymachus, the spokesman for tyranny in *Republic* 1, use explicitly democratic language when agreeing to join the other interlocutors in asking Socrates to elaborate on his statement that there must be communism amongst the guardians (*Rep.* 5.450a).
59. For the purposes of this chapter, I focus more on the content of the new image that they produce and not the discussion of how to become a critical deliberator in *Republic* 3. See Christina Tarnopolsky, "Plato's Mimetic Republic: A Preliminary Treatment of Plato's Preliminary Treatment of the *Gennaion Pseudos*," presented to the 2009 Annual Meeting of the American Political Science Association; for a discussion of the complexities of *mimēsis*, as imitation or emulation and a fuller discussion of the *gennaion pseudos*.
60. The term is Wittgenstein's but, of course, Plato's image of the cave is the first picture to actually try to capture the problematic ways in which human beings can be held captive by pictures.
61. For treatments of *mimēsis* that focus on the discussion of allegory, myth, and fictions in *Republic* 2 see Ferrari, "Plato and Poetry"; Halliwell, *The Aesthetics of Mimēsis*; Janaway, *Images of Excellence*; and Naddaff, *Exiling the Poets*.
62. Schofield's account in "The Noble Lie" of the *gennaion pseudos* (noble lie/ falsehood/fiction) at the end of *Republic* 3 is one of the few that links it to this all-important discussion of "falsehoods in words" at the end of *Republic* 2.
63. For an excellent but different account of Plato's criticism of the Athenian education to war, see Frank, "The Wages of War."
64. Halliwell, *The Aesthetics of Mimēsis*, p. 108.

65. For an excellent treatment of this theme in Arendt's work see Patchen Markell, "The Rule of the People: Arendt, Archē and Democracy," *American Political Science Review* 100, 1 (February 2006): 1–14.
66. Ronald de Sousa, *The Rationality of Emotion* (Cambridge, MA: MIT Press, 2001) p. 203.
67. Here he alludes to the stories told in Hesiod's *Theogony* which relate Uranus' throwing his sons into Tartarus; Cronos' castration of his father, Uranus, in retaliation; and Cronos' eating of his own children (*Rep.* 3. 378a). It is important to note that this particular act of censorship is directed towards children not adults.
68. Cf. Schofield, "The Noble Lie," p. 143.
69. Frank, "The Wages of War," p. 245.
70. Ferrari, "Plato and Poetry," p. 111.
71. Jonathan Lear (inaugural lecture, "Freud's Death Drive and the Search for Meaning," University of Chicago, December 4, 1996).
72. Ferrari, "Plato and Poetry," p. 111.
73. Recall that their earlier view of the happy life of the tyrant involved being equal to a god among humans.
74. Utopia comes from *both* the Greek words for *a-topos* (no place) and *eu-topos* (best place).
75. As Harvey Yunis, "The Protreptic Rhetoric of the *Republic*" in *The Cambridge Companion to Plato's Republic*, ed. G.R.F. Ferrari (Cambride: Cambridge University Press, 2007) pp. 1–26, put it, the "protreptic discourse [of the *Republic*] aims to get education in virtue under way, to get the reader or auditor turned and moving in the right direction, and to make the acquisition of virtue an urgent priority."
76. Frank, "The Wages of War," p. 448.
77. For purposes of this chapter I focus only on these aspects of the *gennaion pseudos*. For a discussion of other important and overlooked aspects of the *gennaion pseudos* and their relationship to other parts of the work, and to the Athenian democratic context as a whole, see Tarnopolsky, "Plato's Mimetic Republic."
78. This mistake is made by Popper *The Open Society and Its Enemies*, vol. 1; Julia Annas, *An Introduction to Plato's Republic* (Oxford: Oxford University Press, 1981) p. 102; and Shorris, "Ignoble Liars."
79. Schofield, "The Noble Lie," p. 159.
80. *Contra* Shorris, "Ignoble Liars."
81. Lear, "Allegory and Myth in Plato's Republic," and Schofield, "The Noble Lie," are notable exceptions to this, although Lear takes this much further than Schofield.
82. Lear, "Allegory and Myth in Plato's Republic."
83. Lear, "Allegory and Myth in Plato's Republic," pp. 32–33. Cf. Arendt, *Between Past and Future*, p. 298, n. 5. *Contra* Schofield, "The Noble Lie," who criticizes the notion that the *pseudos* of the *gennaion pseudos* could mean fiction (pp. 138, 149). For a fuller discussion of how my interpretation of the *gennaion pseudos* relates to the accounts offered by Schofield, "The Noble Lie"; Bloom, "Interpretive Essay"; and Strauss, *The City and Man*, see Tarnopolsky, "Plato's Mimetic Republic." Plato's teaching is not a completely anti-foundational teaching, just a teaching about how to construct dynamic and regulative, immanent and transcendent foundations.
84. This is how Bloom "Interpretive Essay," p. 367, ultimately interprets the *gennaion pseudos* of *Republic* 3, even though his interpretation of the ironic character of the proposals in *Republic* 5 is far more nuanced.

Part III

Mass Media

Introduction to Part III

Part 3 focuses on manipulation's institutional context: the changes in media, technology, and journalistic and political practice that have made contemporary politics more susceptible to the manipulative strategies of political actors. With changes in media, in particular the massive increases in information sources that have sprouted up at the dawn of the new "information age," the possibilities for shaping the discourse and deliberative possibilities of the polity have multiplied as well. Perhaps no institutional innovation has driven these political changes more than those associated with communication technology. With the development of twenty-four-hour cable television, the Internet, and wireless communication, the ability to distract and deceive an audience both with information and through emotions has seen an exponential increase. These changes in turn have led to changes in journalistic practices regarding sourcing, verification, permissible content, balance and objectivity, and similar relics of the preceding media age. As Richard Fox and Amy Gangl, Lawrence Jacobs, Shanto Iyengar and Kyu Hahn, and Andrew Sabl describe in their essays, changes in media ownership, profit-driven content decisions, the culture of "infotainment," the use of polling by public officials, and the strategy of "overload" regarding the procedures of public deliberation and decision-making all constitute growing problems that make manipulation more likely.

As these chapters collectively observe, our connection to the world of politics has both grown and shrunk at the same time. For example, the ease with which we are able to access information about our representatives has never been greater. At the same time, the scope of information, the weakness of guidelines to help us determine what is important and what is merely distraction, and the power of partisan control over much of the media makes it difficult for the consumer of information to form a coherent worldview and therefore also to pursue precise and deliberative public action. As the new information bubble expands, we should expect that the information people do access will be more partisan and imprecise, and that professional politicians and their handlers will devise new ways to shape, mold, and, in short, manipulate the political world.

The authors in this section explore these phenomena by employing a range of methods and approaches not often seen working side by side. Fox and Gangl examine contemporary news practices and professional norms and motivations, but supplement this analysis with both historical case studies and experimental data to illustrate their findings. Jacobs offers an historical and archival reconstruction of the actions and intentions of presidents and their advisers, and combines this historical work with a larger quantitative study of the effects on public opinion associated with the presidential use of polling practices. Iyengar and Hahn bring a distinctively comparative focus to the problem, highlighting some of the peculiar features of manipulation in the case of the United States by comparing its practices with an institutional analysis in nations with very different media structures. Finally, Andrew Sabl brings philosophical analysis to bear on a set of concepts drawn from rational choice theory, returning us in some ways to the fundamental definitional questions with which our volume began, only now qualified more sharply by a set of institutional problems and constraints which further extend and complicate our normative definitions.

One common theme running through all the essays in this section is the decline of the neutral observer model of journalism and of the sense of "facticity" on which that model largely relied. As Fox and Gangl show, in the new media environment citizens seem to be seeking even less hard news information than before and instead are content merely with being entertained by news programming. Accompanying this decline in the centrality of hard news is a decline also in the journalistic practices associated with it: careful sourcing and verification of stories and an aspiration to neutrality and objectivity of coverage. The new media environment, by contrast, has reduced barriers to entry (anyone can write a blog), and this has led to a decline in standards of journalistic practices (with entrepreneurial figures like Matt Drudge leading the way). In their place we now find more "immediate, sensational, partisan, and fragmented" modes of news reporting, along with the rise of "brash punditry" as an institution that has taken ideological partisanship to new heights of intensity. As Fox and Gangl note, there are some advantages to the new media environment as well, even from the point of view of the old standards. With more information and consequently more news available to consumers, citizens now have greater access to inside political information than they ever have in the past—yet this has done little if anything to promote our actual deliberative capacities as a polity.

Jacobs's chapter shows how the seemingly innocuous change in polling practices he studies has serious consequences for the decline of facticity. In theory, polls purport to provide objective information for democratic decision making. In reality, they have been used increasingly to twist the information they acquire for partisan ends. In this way, Jacobs shows, polls can be used to craft a selective withholding of information which facilitates manipulation of the public. But their use in this way carries the consequence that citizens no longer have a shared basis of factual information on which to rely in public deliberation.

Iyengar and Hahn monitor a similar decline in the relevance of facticity and the neutral observer model of journalistic objectivity, concentrating in particular on a problem also mentioned by Fox and Gangl: the so-called "Daily Me" phenomenon associated with self-selection of news outlets. As citizens' exposure to news comes to be conditioned increasingly by self-selection, we observe a corresponding decline in the news content which most or all of the society shares in common. This in turn undermines the facticity at the heart of the neutral observer model: for without a basis of facts shared in common, it is in many ways as though citizens are living in entirely separate worlds. These tendencies are of course potentially exacerbated by the psychological predispositions toward such self-sorting examined by Lakoff and by McDermott in Part II. The audience fragmentation this describes is further facilitated by the demise of the "inadvertent audience" created in the older model by the limited number of news sources, for example the big three network news broadcasts. But in such a world, consumers hear only their own side of the issue, and they also use and consume news only with regard to issues they are interested in (leading for example to a decline in coverage of international news, an increased attention to coverage of ongoing scandals, and similar prejudices in coverage).

Sabl's analysis further expands the scope of the problem. In his view, not just a decline in shared facticity but also an explosion in "fact proliferation" constitutes a key part of the problem he designates with the term "heresthetic overload." A profusion of facts, as facilitated by the new media environment, makes us more dependent on the interpretive frameworks offered by heresthetic manipulators, and these in turn enable the manipulators to disguise what they are doing in influencing the direction of public choice. To this Sabl suggests that the news media themselves possess the resources and even the potential incentives (if only they would make use of them) to counteract some of these tendencies, since their ability to personalize and dramatize heresthetic manipulation as a struggle or conflict could help to overcome some of the limits on information processing defined by our political psychology.

A second shared concern of the essays in this section is how changes in the form of news and in its delivery systems have led to changes in content, with significant consequences for public discourse and policy. These authors show how this new "amorphous and multi-portal news world" has undermined aspects of our public discourse, particularly since, as Fox and Gangl demonstrate, its challenge to broadcast network news and newspapers has gone hand in hand with the rise of news as entertainment and the increased focus on scandal and celebrity at the expense of policy. The rapidity with which information can be circulated through sites such as The Drudge Report has made it easier to circumvent the journalistic standards of the mainstream media and led to a significant undermining of those standards.

In a similar fashion, Jacobs chronicles how the use of polling for priming and agenda setting is made possible only through the modern media's modes of news delivery and the limited audience attention span which these modes tend to promote. The contemporary media's focus on questions of image has further contributed to the use of polling for priming various aspects of presidential image, Jacobs shows, with the important consequence of consistently subordinating policy considerations to those of image.

Sabl likewise chronicles how changes in the forms of media delivery have helped to encourage the use of the heresthetic overload strategies he studies, since they have radically increased the scope and complexity of available and potentially relevant information. Yet because of the limits of most news forms in a commercial and entertainment driven media environment, in particular in terms of length of time available for news coverage, this new proliferation of information can be harnessed directly by elites to enhance their capacity for agenda control. In this world, our available sources of hard news frequently cannot or will not convey what really happened of true political significance even in horse-race style coverage, a loss that further strengthens the hand of political elites.

Iyengar and Hahn provide the most extensive focus on this particular cluster of issues, arguing that changes in the regulatory and economic frameworks surrounding news media are driving many of the other changes we observe with respect to their capacity for manipulation. In particular, the combination of an increasingly profit-driven, market-based orientation in the self-understanding of media companies, combined with the explosion in the quantity of available choices associated with twenty-four-hour cable and the Internet, have led to important changes such as the entertainment-driven orientation of news that Fox and Gangl study. Crucially, Iyengar and Hahn show why the information explosion associated with the rise of new media does not necessarily mean a more informed citizenry. Instead, the proliferation of information may easily contribute to information overload, of which the heresthetic overload phenomenon which Sabl studies is one but by no means the only example.

Finally, each of the essays in this section shares a concern for the impact of these institutional changes on the public and its capacity for meaningful democratic agency. If a polity is to be truly democratic, then its citizens must have access to information that is unbiased, unfiltered, and that provides all the relevant facts concerning the pertinent issues of the day. If this process is cut short or skewed at any point, then it is legitimate to ask, as these authors do, whether the members of the polity can make informed decisions based on their real preferences. As we saw from the essays in Part I, on the deliberative account of democracy one of the most important aims of manipulation is to circumvent deliberation. As a consequence, one of the crucial facets of a well-functioning democracy is the polity's ability to deliberate about the facts that pertain to important decisions. On this understanding, manipulation diminishes rather than enhances the autonomy of the individual, making her able to form preferences and make decisions based on accurate and pertinent information.

The problems posed by contemporary media institutions for the public's democratic agency is a theme repeatedly stressed by Fox and Gangl throughout their essay. In particular, they emphasize the idea that democracy requires mechanisms for accountability which in turn require considerable assurance of transparency. While more information may be available in the new media environment, this also means an increase in the capability to manipulate, as well as a greater unpredictability about the precise effects that any attempt at manipulation will in fact have. In general, Fox and Gangl stress how the contemporary media's focus on entertainment and amusement impedes the citizenry's capacity for exercising accountable and responsible self-government.

Jacobs's analysis of the use of polling by presidents carries with it a similar set of worries about the public's capacity for meaningful democratic agency. In theory, polling is supposed to provide objective information capable of facilitating deliberation, thereby securing the means for representative democracy (where representatives are understood as delegates reproducing their constituents' views in legislative deliberations). As Jacobs shows, however, the Oval Office has discovered that merely presenting facts and framing questions in a way that is favorable to the current administration's agenda can be sufficient to secure popular support. This changes the focus of polling efforts away from finding out what the polity actually wants and toward learning how to tell the polity what it should want, through the careful crafting of polls that are actually designed not to solicit the public's views but to advance a pre-determined agenda. In this way, polling reduces rather than enhances the responsiveness of elected officials to the public's will and facilitates the control of politics by extremes and interest groups rather than by the median voter.

Iyengar and Hahn also stress the need for informed citizenship as a central pre-requisite of democratic governance—since governments can only be accountable agents if their principals, the citizens, are aware of what they are doing. Yet changes in media economics, and in particular the explosion of choices available to the modern media consumer, has led to reduced public exposure to news programming, which has in turn led to more misinformed citizens and a more polarized electorate. Their findings carry several troubling implications for our assessment of the public's democratic agency. First, the insulation of the modern media consumer from perspectives contrary to their own leads to the perverse conclusion that voters may have their own prior views reinforced even by their own encounter with contradictory information (as evinced, for example. in the persistent attitudes toward the existence of weapons of mass destruction [WMDs] among conservative media consumers even after much contradictory evidence had been widely publicized). At the same time, however, the lack of exposure to news more generally means that citizens can be highly vulnerable to misinformation "during periods of high-profile and one-sided news coverage of particular issue," since they lack a comprehensive factual and interpretive framework which might serve to counteract attempted manipulation of this kind.

Finally, Andrew Sabl's analysis points to the phenomenon of "rational ignorance" as one of the most important handicaps regarding the public's democratic agency, particularly with respect to the complex political procedures of modern representative democracies. For Sabl, rational ignorance—the idea that it makes sense for citizens not to try to acquire political knowledge with limited practical utility for their daily lives—is a core fact of human psychology, but one that threatens to be thoroughly taken advantage of by means of heresthetic overload—the (purposeful) incomprehensibility of much modern political and specifically legislative procedural maneuvering. Due to the power of the heresthetic (or strategic) arts, key political actions—agenda setting, issue framing and priming, and similar matters—can be obscured by actors in such a way as to avoid accountability (and thereby threaten the public's democratic agency). Sabl's examples are from recent Republican tactics, but of course as he recognizes either party could (and presumably will eventually) exploit these techniques.

We must therefore seriously consider what effect it may have on the functioning of our democracy if the information we receive about the most important issues of the day is filtered, processed, and mediated in the variety of self-serving ways which these authors suggest. Rather than providing citizens with an informational basis for their deliberations, it would appear that the institutions studied in this section are in fact further confusing and degrading the public's capacity for collective choosing through infotainment, strategic polling, heresthetic overload, and similar tactics. We seem to be left with an unpalatable choice: between somehow restraining these seemingly unrestrainable and destructive tendencies of our institutions, or else diminishing our expectations for democracy to fit the limitations of the new media environment. Each alternative is dispiriting in its own fashion; but the first step toward circumventing these problems must surely be to better understand them.

7 "News You Can't Use"

Politics and Democracy in the New Media Environment

Richard L. Fox and Amy Gangl

We are creating a new universe, and it has all kinds of new laws and science and physics coming into play as well in this information world. And you've got planets out there colliding with each other, new life forms taking shape; others have drifted too close to the sun, and they've burned up. And we don't know how it's all going to settle down. And it has, now and forever more, a radiant effect.

Tom Brokaw, *NBC Nightly News* anchor from 1983–2004, speaking about the new media environment.[1]

In 1968, legendary *CBS Evening News* anchor Walter Cronkite returned from Vietnam and declared that the most likely outcome for the ongoing war was "stalemate." He delivered this assessment in a respectful and reserved tone that posited two possible alternatives for the future of the war: "real give and take negotiation" to end the war or "terrible escalation." At the time this was considered a dramatic deviation from the usual format of a news anchor simply delivering the facts. After watching the Cronkite broadcast, President Johnson reportedly responded, "That's it. If I've lost Cronkite, I've lost middle America." Cronkite's words were powerful and had resonance because he was viewed as a trusted and unbiased news reporter by a broad cross section of the American public.[2]

Flash forward forty years and Sean Hannity at Fox News tells his fragmented, partisan audience that there is reason to question whether President Obama, a Democrat, was born in the United States and thus is constitutionally qualified for his position. Switch over to MSNBC, and Keith Olbermann is telling his fragmented, partisan audience that Rush Limbaugh, the conservative radio talk show host, is both the current head of the Republican Party and the "Worst Person in the World."[3] As a result of the rise of cable programming like MSNBC and FOX, even the news anchors of network television are perceived by many as partisan, with none of the broad credibility that Cronkite enjoyed. Meanwhile, a 2007 Pew Research Center study found that *The Daily Show with Jon Stewart*, a satirical news program on the television network Comedy Central, offers more newsworthy political substance than the three major network newscasts.[4] From Cronkite to Hannity, Olbermann, and Stewart much has changed in how news and information are delivered to the public. In this chapter, we examine these changes and assess what this means in terms of manipulation and democratic legitimacy in the United States.

From a normative standpoint, we take the position that (attempted) manipulation in American politics is a constant. Powerful political actors almost always seek to manipulate citizens to support their respective political goals and desired policy outcomes. For our purposes the news media, or more broadly the information universe, is the primary means that political actors utilize in shaping or manipulating public attitudes. Of central concern in our analysis of the changing news environment is democratic legitimacy. A central premise of a democratic regime is that publicly elected officials are accountable to the citizens from whom they draw their political power. Transparent communication between government actors and the people is necessary for such accountability to be possible. Attempts to manipulate can threaten accountability because citizens may not have enough information to effectively evaluate or pressure political leaders. Throughout our analysis we gauge whether the changing norms and practices of political journalism and the news media have eroded the important democratic values of transparency and accountability that are required for democratic governance.

Historically, the primary source for political news was comprised of the mainstream media or hard news outlets, which focused on the reporting of serious national issues. Herbert J. Gans' famous study *Deciding What's News* identified hard news sources as those to which people turn to be made aware of the most important stories of the day. For most of the last half of the twentieth century the structure and the norms of the news media were fairly static.[5] The major television networks, daily newspapers, and wire services were the main sources of news and information for the public. The practice of journalism was well-defined. The Society of Professional Journalists (SPJ), for instance, adopted a full code of ethics including more than thirty topics pertaining to privacy, "sourcing" guidelines, and the maintenance of objectivity; and most journalists followed these rules of the trade. In this world, the practice of manipulation could be readily identified. Politicians, government officials, and institutions, through a series of leaks, press appearances, and press releases tried to manipulate members of the news media to provide good coverage for themselves and damaging coverage for their political opponents. The major actors in the news media competed amongst themselves to provide the "biggest" and "most important" breaking news stories in order to entice people to buy their papers or watch their news programs. The commercial imperatives of this competition were limited because there were relatively few outlets and the audience for the handful of major media outlets was quite high.

Although the mainstream television networks and major daily newspapers still exist in the same institutional forms, much has changed. Institutional media has lost a great deal of its influence and no longer has the audience or readership of years past. According to the blog Paper Cuts, which monitors the decline in traditional media, newspapers lost 15,974 jobs in 2008 and another 10,000 jobs in the first half of 2009. That translates into 26,000 fewer reporters, photographers, and editors to cover political issues in the United States and across the globe.[6]

The decline of the traditional news media has been precipitated in part by the rise of the new media framework: an environment where twenty-four hour cable news, Internet sites, blogs, and citizen produced videos are central tools of coverage and where individual citizens can and often do decide what constitutes media-worthy political news. The result has been the delivery of news that is more immediate, sensational, partisan, and fragmented.[7] We have very quickly moved away from a time when the more constrained and professional media of the mid- and late twentieth century provided a strong foundation for transparent communication between elected officials and the public. Not so long ago, a handful of national newspapers and three television news networks prioritized neutrality and objectivity, and offered the public a sort of "the buck stops here" approach to playing the media's critical role as a watchdog in American government. Today, the information environment is a chaotic and unmonitored playground of journalists, analysts, pundits, bloggers, and shock jocks, each offering up information, the veracity of which is challenged not by any kind of central news media institution, but only occasionally in the media columns of major newspapers, on a few cable news programs with small audiences, or, very tellingly, on Jon Stewart's *The Daily Show*.

Further, the new media technologies have created an information environment in which even the traditional news networks now help blur the lines between news reporting and partisan analysis. The media blur is particularly clear with the NBC News division. Brian Williams and David Gregory are marketed as the "journalists," hosting the *Nightly News* and *Meet the Press*, respectively. But over at MSNBC, the sister cable network with the marketing slogan "The Place for Politics," Joe Scarborough can spend weekday mornings on his news program railing against the Obama administration; and later in the day on the other side of the political spectrum, Chris Matthews, host of the program *Hardball*, can suggest that members of the Bush administration should be tried for war crimes. Nevertheless, Williams, Gregory, Scarborough, and Matthews are advertised on NBC and MSNBC as a political reporting team.

Manipulation in this new media world is much more complex both in its definition and in the means through which political actors seek to manipulate. In this media environment, the competition for audience has greatly intensified as news consumers are no longer limited to television news broadcasts or newspapers. The amorphous and multi-portal news world of today means that information outlets have to do more to encourage consumers to read, view, or listen to their product. One result is that all types of news outlets try to present a more attention grabbing style of news. Scandal has always been used by the news media to attract audiences. But in the contemporary environment where there is a camera on every candidate or celebrity virtually twenty-four/seven, there is much more trivial but entertaining content to present. Network executives and publishers can point to audience size to demonstrate that people are more interested in or entertained by details about Bill and Hillary Clinton's marital situation or 2008 vice presidential candidate Sarah Palin's wardrobe choices than in a discussion of candidates' competing health care plans.[8]

At the same time, those in power or seeking to be in power have a whole new universe of options as they attempt to manipulate public opinion to support their positions. They can still issue press releases or submit to interviews with mainstream outlets like the *New York Times*, but there are a limitless and still developing host of other options. Tactics can include posting videos on YouTube.com or having surrogates working as paid partisan pundits or relying on regular citizens who champion a particular point of view on the blogs to push public opinion in one direction or another on political issues. Indeed, Sarah Palin time and again invoked her desire to speak to the American people "without the filter of the mainstream media" which she felt was presenting a distorted picture of her to the voters. Democratic presidential candidate Barack Obama appeared to use the new media environment more effectively as a candidate, as he often circumvented traditional media channels by using Myspace.com and blogs on his own official website to speak personally to mass audiences. He even communicated with voters by sending text messages to their cell phones during the campaign.

In presenting our accounting of the current status of the institution of the news media, we focus on two central questions in this chapter. First, what exactly is the shape and style of the new media environment as we head further into the twenty-first century? In addressing this question we chronicle the transformation the news media has undergone in the past two decades and identify what we think are three of the central substantive characteristics of these changes. The second question we address concerns whether, given the changes in the new media environment, manipulation becomes more or less difficult for political actors to carry out. While manipulation has certainly been a constant of the intersection of news coverage and politics, we hope to explicate what the new environment means for manipulation within the context of a democratic society. In exploring the role of manipulation in the new media environment, we present two case studies. The first case study focuses on the 2008 presidential election and the ease with which spurious information travels between new and old media sources. Here we trace the origins and impact of the widely dispersed rumor during the campaign that Democratic Presidential candidate Barack Obama was a Muslim. The second case study involves an original experiment examining how infotainment and sensationalizing practices may influence citizens' expectations of and attitudes about government. Here we compare how people respond to information about the Federal Aviation Administration's (FAA) shutdown of several airlines in the spring of 2008 when it is presented on *The Daily Show* versus on a nightly news network, paying particular attention to public cynicism and attitudes toward government accountability.

Our analyses in this chapter advance two fundamental arguments. First, while there are now more means through which political actors might seek to manipulate the public, it is also more difficult for strategists to predict how the flow of information will play out and to what ends with respect to influencing public opinion. Our second and related conclusion engages the consequences of changes in the new media environment for democratic government. A public fed daily doses of news meant to make them laugh, gape with amazement, or go out and buy something is more easily manipulated away from demanding accountability and truth within the context of democratic government.

Shifting Information Environment: Goodbye TV News, Hello Podcasts

Throughout history the creation of new technologies has always precipitated broad changes in the style, delivery, and focus of the news. The Pew Research Center for the People and the Press offers a purely "technological" definition of new media—simply, cable television and the Internet. Media scholars Richard Davis and Diana Owen have asserted, however, that defining the "new media" is a difficult task, as the role that the media play in people's lives is now so much more multifaceted than in the past. They argue that a complicated mix of rapidly evolving technology, calls for increased pubic engagement, and a new potential to inform the public distinguishes the new media from the more traditional hard news outlets.[9]

In charting the changes to the news and information environment, the most significant developments are the dramatic decrease in both newspaper readership and the number of Americans who watch the "big three" network (ABC, CBS, and NBC) evening newscasts since the 1970s (see Table 7.1). The audience for local television news has also been steadily dropping since 2000. The decline of local and network news broadcasts has been accompanied by the expansion of the cable television industry. Currently, four cable channels (Fox News, MSNBC, CNN, and CNN Headline News) are devoted almost entirely to news.[10] Further, the Internet now plays a substantial role in the presentation and dissemination of news and information, with 24 percent of citizens in 2008 saying that it is

Table 7.1 The Decline of Traditional Media

	Circulation of Daily Newspapers (in millions)	Nightly Audience Size for Network News Broadcasts (in millions)	Local Television Newscasts (news share of voters)
1970	62.1	—	—
1980	62.2	42.3	—
1990	62.3	30.4	—
2000	55.8	23.5	17.4
2002	55.2	21.5	16.3
2004	54.6	20.2	15.9
2006	52.3	18.2	13.0
2007	51.0-	16.9	12.0

Note: Data compiled from Pew Research Center's Project for Excellence in Journalism's 2004, 2006, and 2008 State of the News Media Report. For local television, share indicates the percentage of the television sets in use that are tuned to a program at a given time.

one of the sources they regularly check for political news (see Table 7.2). This, of course, is tremendous growth considering the Internet did not become a fully viable source of news until the late 1990s. Tables 7.1 and 7.2 display several of the trends under discussion here.

Because the news environment has become so much more multidimensional, there is now fierce competition to attract an audience. To maintain ratings and attract viewers, structural, substantive, and especially stylistic changes have begun to overtake even the most traditional news outlets. All of the news organizations, both print and television, for example, have gone online with sophisticated, interactive websites. We live in an age where news (and every other imaginable type of information) is available at a moment's notice. Long gone are the days of awaiting the morning newspaper or evening newscast to learn what was going on in the world. Now, when the *New York Times* and the *Washington Post* break a big story, it is first posted on the website and likely to have been reported on the night before it appeared in print on a cable television news outlet such as CNN or MSNBC. John Temple, editor and writer for the *Rocky Mountain News*, the "paper of record" for the sensationalized and media obsessed JonBenet Ramsey murder investigation, illustrates the rise of the Internet. While that paper's Internet coverage was little more than an afterthought during the original investigation of the murder in 1997, with the arrest of John Mark Karr as a suspect in the unsolved murder case in 2006, the paper's website garnered almost twice as many hits as the paper's typical daily circulation. Temple notes that the public's thirst for information about the case apparently needed to be satisfied before the newspaper itself could be delivered each day.[11] Clearly, we live in an envi-

Table 7.2 News Habits for Political and Campaign News

	2000	*2004*	*2008*
Broadcast Television			
Local TV News	48%	42%	40%
Nightly Network News	45	35	32
TV News Magazines	29	25	22
Morning TV shows	18	20	22
Sunday Political TV	15	13	14
Cable & Other Television			
Cable News Networks	34	38	38
Political Talk Shows	14	14	15
Public TV Shows	12	11	12
Late-Night Talk Shows	9	9	9
C-Span	9	8	8
Comedy TV Shows	6	8	8
Print Media			
Daily Newspaper	40	31	31
News Magazines	15	10	11
Internet	9	13	24
Radio			
Talk Radio	15	17	16
National Public Radio	12	14	18
Religious Radio	7	5	9

Note: Adapted from Pew Research Report, "Internet's Broader Role in Campaign 2008." http://pewinternet.org/pdfs/Pew_MediaSources_jan08.pdf. Percentages indicate the number of citizens regularly using that source for political news.

ronment where we no longer wait for the news—today's news is immediate, and it permeates our lives.

Turning more specifically to the Internet, when citizens go online for information, where do they go? Pew reports people who rely on the Internet for campaign news often seek out the online version of news sources such as MSNBC (26 percent) and CNN (23 percent) (see Table 7.3). Importantly, Yahoo News with 22 percent is the third most frequently identified source for political news. Yahoo is not a news organization but a search engine that culls through and selects Associated Press (AP) stories to list on their site. In the new media environment, web search engines have become important sources of news and information. Perhaps countering concerns that the Internet does away with the accidental exposure to news stories a citizen might otherwise miss in paging through a newspaper on the way to the sports section, 52 percent of regular web users say they come across campaign news and information when they go online for reasons other than to seek out political information.[12] The question of what people are looking at online when it comes to political or campaign news is addressed in Table 7.4. According to Pew, 24 percent say they saw a speech, interview, commercial, or debate online in the 2008 presidential

Table 7.3 Sources of Political News on the Internet for Young People

	Total	18–29	30+
Cable Television Sites			
MSNBC.com	26%	30%	24%
CNN.com	23	30	21
Fox News	9	5	10
BBC	2	2	2
Web Browsers			
Yahoo News	22	27	19
Google News	9	10	9
AOL News	7	5	8
Newspaper Sites			
New York Times	6	5	6
USA Today	1	0	1
Washington Post	1	1	1
Internet Based Sources			
Drudge Report	3	1	4
MySpace	3	8	<1
YouTube	2	6	<1

Note: Adapted from Pew Research Report, "Internet's Broader Role in Campaign 2008." http://pewinternet.org/pdfs/Pew_MediaSources_jan08.pdf. Percentages indicate the number of citizens regularly using that source for political news.

election. Accessing candidate speeches or advertisements online would have been unthinkable just a few short years ago—YouTube.com, a staple of current news culture, was founded in April 2005.

More and more citizens are turning to hybrid political blog/news websites that usually have an ideological orientation. The Huffington Post, which identifies itself on masthead as the "The Internet Newspaper: News - Blogs - Video Community," reports almost 3 million visitors a month, many of whom are daily visitors to the site.[13] The site is left-leaning and partisan, and strongly supported Senator Obama throughout the 2008 presidential election. With direct links to news clips, campaign commercials, and a host of political and celebrity bloggers, The Huffington Post also offers updates on the latest tawdry entertainment industry news. The site, however, could not exist without the traditional press, at least in the service it provides to users who come to expect its "reporters" to seek out articles, quotes, and events reported in other news sources. This is true of many of the websites that traverse the old and new media divide. Former *New Republic* editor Andrew Sullivan runs a popular blog, The Daily Dish, that relies on links to mainstream and traditional media sources. Sullivan's audience can read the latest analysis on a presidential campaign or the status of health care legislation, and then scroll down to play and vote on their favorite '80s music videos, distinguishing themselves from

Table 7.4 Campaign Videos Watched On-Line in 2008 Presidential Election

	Total	*18–29*	*30–39*	*40–49*	*50–64*	*> 65*
Candidate Speeches	13%	22%	17%	13 %	10%	5%
Interviews with Candidates	13	23	18	11	9	3
Campaign Commercials	12	25	9	10	10	4
Candidate Debates	12	20	16	10	9	2
Any of the Above	24	41	28	20	21	7

Note: Adapted from Pew Research Report, "Internet's Broader Role in Campaign 2008." http://pewinternet.org/pdfs/Pew_MediaSources_jan08.pdf. Percentages indicate number of citizens who have watched on-line videos for each entry.

people who limit their news gathering to *NBC Nightly News*. Sullivan's political media mixed with elements of entertainment, it seems, is what many citizens have come to want (and perhaps expect) from their information sources.

In analyzing the substantive changes that have dominated this new media environment, we will explore three fundamental and interrelated characteristics that have emerged in the new media environment. First, the professional journalistic norm of neutrality is giving way to news that fits the preconceived views of the audience or works to advance a particular agenda. Second, there is an ever increasing emphasis on making news entertaining. Conversely, the news has become a central source of material for a number of comedy programs, and has thus blurred the lines between news and entertainment. And, finally, because of the lack of any information filters, a messy populist democracy exists on the web and has the potential to both bolster and undermine democratic representation and accountability in the coming years. Together, these characteristics make it easier for politicians and partisan pundits to manipulate citizens. Without a centralized system of filters, political actors can claim that they have the truth, and that what others are saying is purely political posturing.

Objectivity is Out, Brash Punditry In

A central criterion of quality journalism for most of the latter half of the twentieth century was objectivity. For instance, major newspapers and the television networks prohibited reporters from participating in interviews where they would provide their own opinions, as that might reduce the credibility of their work as journalists. By contrast, in the new media environment of the early twenty-first century, journalists are regularly turned into pundits and entire cable news channels have become identified with particular partisan leanings. In this new media environment, a news consumer can tailor the substance and style of the news to fit their own ideological preferences. A conservative can listen to Rush Limbaugh on the radio during the day, turn on Fox News in the evening, and search conservative websites such as drudgereport.com and townhall.com in their spare time. A liberal might start with the *New York Times* in the morning, turn on MSNBC in the evening to watch Keith Olbermann rail against conservatives and the Republican party (more about this later), and then surf the Net, getting more news and analysis from the liberal dailykos.com.

This self-styled fitting of news to the individual consumer has led to considerable fragmentation among the public, a concern Todd Gitlin raised a decade ago.[14] In a trenchant analysis of the infusion of electronic media into contemporary politics, Gitlin argued that contemporary media offers the possibility for and has created "public sphericules," or segmented spheres of ideologically similar deliberation and critique of political matters. Americans of different ideological stripes no longer have to talk to each other or even hear the foundation for an opposing point of view. Likewise, in Republic.com, Cass Sunstein similarly worries about the elevation of the "Daily Me," an information environment in which individual citizens can use new technologies and new media to filter their news environments in a discriminatory manner, only seeking sources that reflect and reinforce their ideological predispositions and beliefs.[15]

Fox News Channel, which is widely perceived as a purveyor of conservative news to a conservative audience, has lead the way in helping citizens tailor the news to their views. In their 2007 book, *Echo Chamber*, Kathleen Hall Jamieson and Joseph Cappella chronicle the tripartite role Fox News, *The Wall Street Journal,* and Rush Limbaugh's talk radio program played in tearing down 2008 Republican presidential candidate Mike Huckabee for being too much of a populist on economic issues. More generally, citing 2004 survey data, Jamieson and Cappella argue that Fox News viewers who are also likely to listen to Rush Limbaugh "are better able to confine themselves in an insulating, protective media space filled with reassuring information and opinion … It also inculcates frames of interpretation that blunt the persuasive power of antagonistic views."[16]

Other networks and programs are following suit in offering up a heightened partisan take on the news of the day, and in many cases the result is a blurring of partisan advocacy and straight news. On MSNBC, for instance, liberal commentator Keith Olbermann, who hosts the nightly program *Countdown,* could tell former President George W. Bush to "shut the hell up" on his nightly show and then double as a news anchor for the same channel during an election or for other major news events. Historically, news producers have explicitly distinguished traditional news on their network news programs from political commentary and analysis on their cable spin-offs. Network news played a foundational role in creating objective, neutral journalism, and the respective news departments insist they strive to maintain such values on the major network channels. In contrast, MSNBC is perceived as a different enterprise in so much that opinion and advocacy are permitted.

Olbermann's nightly *Countdown* sign-off, "Good night and good luck," is, of course, a rip-off from the legendary journalist Edward R. Murrow. A Murrow admirer, Olbermann believes his nightly news segments, often followed by analysis and commentary, are a throw-back to traditional news coverage of the kind Murrow offered at CBS in the 1950s. This is hardly the case. Where Murrow offered a cautious and thoughtful analysis at the end of his show that he clearly labeled and set aside from his reporting of the news as "commentary," Olbermann, though also using a commentary label periodically, often mixes news, commentary, and ridicule throughout the entire hour of his nightly show. Edward R. Murrow never did voice impersonations as Olbermann does in his tirades against former President George W. Bush or his Fox News competitor Bill O'Reilly. And in his era Murrow's commentary segments were not viewed by millions of Internet users and dissected in the combative world of political blogging.

Shortly before his death in the summer of 2008, NBC's chief political correspondent and *Meet the Press* host Tim Russert distinguished his brand of traditional reporting from Olbermann: "Keith and I have each carved out our roles in this vast information spectrum. What cable emphasizes more and more is opinion or even advocacy ... I try very, very hard not to come up and say to people, 'This is what I believe' ... But rather, 'This is what I'm learning in my reporting'."[17] In the end, though, media critics, political actors, and many working at the major news organizations lament the decline of traditional news reporting on the networks. Yet there appears to be no end in sight as network executives at Fox and MSNBC have composed primetime lineups with commentators who are decidedly partisan in their approach to covering political news. The jury is out and more research needs to be devoted to examining the impact of partisan journalism on public attitudes. Our concern would be that in an environment where citizens choose the type of news they want, manipulation or at least distortion becomes much easier to propagate. This creates a world with little common ground, where each side in a political debate is armed with their own version of the facts.

Again, though, more work in this area needs to be conducted— indeed, much of the so-called new media is anything but new to today's younger generations, as the role of blogs, YouTube, and MySpace.com that is so critical to younger generations is not well understood and is still evolving.

Moreover, there are some signs that journalism can develop and thrive in the blogosphere. Josh Marshall started Talking Points Memo, a popular left leaning blog, in 2000 when he was the Washington editor of *The American Prospect*. Bolstered by his coverage of U.S. Senate Minority leader Trent Lott's racist-tinged comments in 2002, Marshall's blog has become famous for not only commenting on news but breaking it as well. In 2007, Marshall offered some investigatory stories on the Bush administration's firing of U.S. attorneys, showing a pattern that led to a congressional hearing and earned Marshall a George Polk Award for journalism.

Though Andrew Sullivan of The Daily Dish does not engage in conventional reporting, his links and multiple sources offer sometimes new, radical, and original takes on the world. After the dramatically contested Iranian elections in 2009, for example, his site offered up-to-the minute presentations of e-mails, Twitter feeds, and YouTube videos from Tehran. Though Sullivan offered no pretence of balance, supporting the overthrow of Iranian president Mahmoud Ahmadinejad, he nevertheless offered a wealth of information not available to the more muzzled institutional media.

Let's Make Them Laugh: Turning the News into Entertainment

In the fierce competition for audiences, it is not surprising that news organizations have tried to make their broadcasts more entertaining. In fact, a number of analyses have chronicled the increasing sensationalism and tabloid fervor that have come to dominate all forms of news media.[18] It wasn't just *People Magazine*, but the major networks and cable shows that focused on the personal characteristics of 2008 Republican vice presidential nominee Sarah Palin. Sources ranging in credibility from the *New York Times* to cable news to gossipy websites all discussed Palin's looks, her pregnant teenage daughter, and her baby with Downs Syndrome rather than her positions on the major issues of the day. Ultimately, news organizations have tried many ways to present a more entertaining broadcast, but here we focus on the use of comedy and satire in news broadcasts. Especially notable has been the corresponding rise of humor based political satire programming.

This trend of adding humor to news broadcasts has been readily apparent in the past few years as traditional news outlets increasingly include popular political and news satire sources such as Jon Stewart's *The Daily Show* and Stephen Colbert's *Colbert Report*. Network news broadcasts and their sister cable shows routinely offer clips from entertainment sources as a foundation for or a complement to their own stories about political issues. After George Stephanopolous took over the reins of ABC News' long-running Sunday political show *This Week* in 2002, for example, the program introduced a new section called "The Funnies," which highlights the week's top political comedy lines. Indeed infotainment—news presented in a manner intended to be entertaining—is everywhere in the political information environment. In a move to entertain with news, the venerated cable news channel CNN actually added a program to their lineup in late 2008 called *D.L. Hughley Breaks the News*, a current events program hosted by stand-up comedian D.L. Hughley.

But beyond the news trying to add humor, programs on Comedy Central and the late-night talk shows have become venues for news that is taken seriously. PBS's Bill Moyers has suggested that Jon Stewart is a more thoughtful chronicler of contemporary politics than most journalists working in the mainstream media today. Tom Brokaw has also gone on record suggesting that Stewart's satirical take on the media is smart viewing for the informed citizen.[19] Moyers asked Stewart what he saw that "other journalists" did not, Stewart replied:

> I think we see exactly what you see. And ... but for some reason, don't analyze it in that manner or put it on the air in that manner. I can't tell you how many times we'll run into a journalist and he'll go, 'Boy that's ... I wish we could be saying that ... That's exactly the way we see it and that's exactly the way we'd like to be saying that.' And I always think, 'Well, why don't you'.[20]

Worth noting is Stewart's popularity given that the typical targets of his critiques and analyses are the mainstream media. Stewart highlights both the focus on the trivial in network coverage of American politics and the inconsistencies and absurdities of the commentary and analysis of major media figures like Fox's Bill O'Reilly and Sean Hannity. Stewart mocks traditional anchors relentlessly for hyping and sensationalizing news events. And he ridicules political candidates who feel like they have to prove themselves athletic and folksy and the media that plays along. Likewise, Stephen Colbert, whose show follows Stewart's program four nights a week, offers excoriating satire of the conservative media machine. Much of the public sees the circus of American media and enjoys laughing at it on Comedy Central. The problem, we believe (and engage further later in the chapter), is that the invitation to laugh in an information environment that does not provide us with much beyond the trivial, or turns serious issues into comedy, likely leads to cynicism and apathy more than meaningful and effective demands for change. As evidence of the seriousness and relevance of *The Daily Show* in today's information environment, Table 7.5 shows a summary of important political figures who have appeared on the program between 2006–2008. Regularly hosting presidential candidates, U.S. Senators, and former heads of state, the guest list for the program resembles the traditional Sunday morning political talk shows *Face the Nation* or *Meet the Press*. Serious news and entertainment feed off one another.

Thus, we have a new media environment in which ABC's George Stephanopoulos and CNN's Wolf Blitzer replay Jay Leno and Jon Stewart clips, encouraging citizens to laugh at things like poor post-war planning in Iraq or even the use of torture at Guantanomo Bay. Jon Stewart's regular "This Week in Torture" segment has noted how perversely hilarious it is that U.S. Senator Arlen Specter (R-PA) was more concerned about

Table 7.5 Political Guests on The Daily Show, 2006–2008

2008 Presidential Candidates	10
McCain (4), Obama (3), Dodd, Clinton, Edwards, Biden (2), Huckabee (2), Richardson, Paul, Nader (2)	
Current and Former Heads of State/Government	6
Carter (US), Clinton (US), Blair (UK), Morales (Bolivia), Fox (Mexico), Musharraf (Pakistan)	
Current and Former U.S. Senators	26
U.S. Cabinet Secretaries	11
Ambassadors, Governors, and Other Federal Officials	19

Note: Data complied from The Internet Movie Database at http://www.imdb.com/title/ tt0115147/episodes. Parentheses indicate number of appearances or country of leader. Includes guests through November 4, 2008.

the New England Patriots Spy-Gate scandal in which the Patriots coach was accused of stealing opposing teams' play calls than the missing CIA torture tapes. It's funny—almost unbelievably funny. The focus on the funny is further reinforced with the technologically sophisticated audiences that go to YouTube to watch the latest satirical hit piece on the bumbling U.S. Congress or have a MySpace friend send them a link to the previous nights' Stephen Colbert riff on George W. Bush. Consequently, we the people come to feel that this is normal, this is the way our government works, and there is not much we can do about it but laugh. Pew Research data suggests that young adults increasingly prefer sardonic satire akin to MSNBC's Olbermann or news as a mockery with Jon Stewart and Stephen Colbert.[21] Today's younger generations appear to find ostensibly objective mainstream news sources as less and less convincing and entirely uninteresting. As generations of news consumers age, more and more citizens will come to expect partisan analysis and a few laughs with their political news.

The End of Facts: No Information Filters on the Internet

The third change the new media environment has created is a messy populist democracy on the web that is inhabited by citizens more concerned with propagating their ideological version of contemporary events than the truth. The blurring of truth and distortion of facts is made possible on the web because it is an unregulated universe without journalistic standards. Citizens, political pundits, and media personalities alike can say whatever they want, true or untrue. It is difficult to find checks and balances within this information environment as the more traditional news outlets are overwhelmed by the information being put forward on the Internet. Online, there are no industry filters or any entity serving as an arbiter of fact and fiction. Perry Bacon, a *Washington Post* reporter, found in in-depth interviews with "average" voters that many are conflicted about whether to believe mainstream media reporting or rumors floating on the web.[22]

Rumors and distortions have been a staple of modern presidential politics. In 1988 rumors swirled that Democratic candidate Michael Dukakis had been in therapy for mental health issues. In 2000, during the Republican primary season, operatives for the campaign of George W. Bush put out the rumor that John McCain had fathered a black child out of wedlock. In 2004, right as John Kerry was locking up the 2004 Democratic nomination, rumors of his having an affair with an intern starting circulating on the Internet. Rumors as a tool to manipulate the preferences of voters in presidential politics are not new. In the election of 1884, Grover Cleveland, for instance, was met with the phrase "Ma, ma, where's my pa?" from Republicans backing James Blaine who were advancing the rumor that Cleveland had fathered a child out of wedlock. Rumors and scandal are thus not new, but the speed with which they can now reach an entire nation of potential voters must rattle even the most private and disciplined political candidate.

Matt Drudge of DrudgeReport.com was a pioneer in using rumors in the new media environment. In a 1998 speech to the National Press Club in Washington, he told the assemblage of traditional media members that he believed the publishing and disseminating of rumors from reliable sources was a perfectly acceptable practice. In his career Drudge has broken notable stories, such as the existence of Monica Lewinsky's blue dress stained with President Clinton's "genetic material," which ultimately became the key piece of evidence in the Clinton impeachment proceedings in 1998. He has also had major flops, such as his touting of a 2008 story about a McCain campaign worker who was allegedly attacked by an Obama supporter and had a "B" for Barack carved into her face. The story turned out to be a hoax, though it received considerable attention for a few days during the campaign. The new media world of the Internet has sacrificed the importance and even relevance of truth in contemporary politics.

In the new media environment, the rules of reporting have been exploded as journalistic norms regarding balance, sourcing, and accuracy have been discarded. Now there is often simply a rush to put out information as quickly as possible. In the 2004 election, *CBS Evening News* anchor Dan Rather was in such a rush to break a story about President George W. Bush's delinquent National Guard service during the Vietnam War that the network ended up relying on unverified documents that were likely forgeries. Another prominent example of changing journalistic norms occurred during the 2008 Democratic primaries when presidential candidate Barack Obama held a closed-door fund-raiser in San Francisco. Mayhill Fowler, a member of the audience, used her cell phone to record comments in which Obama described some voters in Pennsylvania as being "bitter" about hard economic times and consequently "clinging to guns or religion." Fowler, a Huffington Post blogger and an unpublished, self-proclaimed "failed writer," posted the comments to the popular liberal site. Though Obama believed his remarks were made in an informal, off-the-record setting with supporters, networks and newspapers nevertheless scrutinized the statements in the national press for weeks. In another example, in the 2006 U.S. Senate race in Virginia between incumbent George Allen and challenger James Webb, a Webb campaign worker videotaped Allen at a campaign rally directing an ethnic slur at him. Allen referred to the campaign worker, who was an American Indian attending the University of Virginia, as "macaca." The incident created a new transitive verb, to "YouTube," when the video was uploaded to the popular site and became widely cited as the infamous "macaca moment" that propelled Webb to a very narrow upset victory and ultimately shifted control of the U.S. Senate to the Democrats. As Larry Prior, University of Southern California journalism professor, states, "We have entered new territory and the rules are not all clear. You have to assume that every-thing is on the record. There's no getting around that anymore."[23]

The three substantive changes we have identified are illustrated more thoroughly in our two case studies presented below.

"Obama is a Muslim:" Manipulation and Misinformation in the 2008 Presidential Election

In our first case study, we focus on the spread of misinformation in the new media environment in the 2008 presidential election. Certainly the use of rumors as identified above is a widespread practice in the history of U.S. politics. What is new is the degree to which the contemporary media environment allows for the broad and unchecked dissemination of information. In the 2008 presidential election there were a number of particularly elaborate and pervasive rumors. Most of the rumors focused on Democratic candidate Barack Obama and Republican vice presiden-tial candidate Sarah Palin. Some of the more widely cited rumors about Governor Palin suggested that she was not the mother of her youngest child, that she cut funding for special needs children as governor, and that she presented a list of books to be banned to the librarian in the city of which she was mayor—all of which are demonstrably false. Rumors about Obama included that he is not a U.S. citizen, that he attended a Madrassa as a young boy, and that a tape exists showing Michelle Obama using the slur "whitey." But no rumor was more pervasive and perhaps more dam-aging to the Obama campaign than the claim that he is a Muslim.

According to the *New York Times* the rumor that Barack Obama is a Muslim was first advanced in a press release by conservative author and activist Andy Martin in August of 2004 (two weeks after Obama's speech at the Democratic National Convention).[24] The rumor was designed to play on fears that voters have about Islamic extremists and their connection to terrorism, stirring up the latent racism or xenophobic sentiment of some voters. The rumor did not gain much traction until early 2007 when it became clear that Obama was running for president. The conservative website FreeRepublic.com published Martin's press release, and the story took off. The rumor was sent around in email chains throughout the United States and became the fodder of discussion throughout almost all types of news outlets, but found particular resonance on the Internet. Table 7.6 shows the broad dissemination of the rumor online and its first appearance as a possible story on cable television. Also identified in Table 7.6 are some of the most pervasive videos and stories circulating on the Internet that purport that Obama is a Muslim.

The pervasiveness of the Obama/Muslim rumor demonstrates how the total lack of filters on the Internet and the ready army of partisan pundits make manipulation through the use of misinformation easier in the new media environment. The Obama/Muslim rumor was so widely circulated that by March of 2008, a Pew Center survey found that 79 percent of citi-

Table 7.6 Obama/Muslim Rumor Across the Media Spectrum

Origin: Rumor initially circulated in a press release by Andy Martin; rumor first reported on news source at FreeRepublic.com on January 8, 2007.

Traditional Media

Number of times mentioned in major U.S. and world publications (between January 8, 2008 and October 2, 2008)	1,424
Number of times mentioned in TV broadcasts (between January 8, 2007 and October 2, 2008)	
Network:	
ABC	528
NBC	315
CBS	261
Cable:	
Fox News Network	419
MSNBC	243
CNN	495

New Media

Google blog search for "Obama is a Muslim" (number of blogs)	187,937
Google search for "Obama is a Muslim" (number of entries)	10,300,000
Number of YouTube videos for "Obama is a Muslim"	2,040
Number of views for top five videos in "Obama is a Muslim" search on YouTube	1,281,641

Notes: Searches conducted between September 8, 2008 and October 23, 2008.

zens had heard the rumor, and 38 percent had heard about it "a lot." The story was not simply the purview of blogs, websites, and partisan cable news programming. The pattern of misinformation in the new media environment is as follows: something might begin as a rumor published on a partisan website; then it is circulated via millions of emails; and then it becomes the topic of discussion in cable news before major newspapers and television investigate the claim. When the traditional news organizations debunk the rumor or report its existence, this often serves to continue the national dialogue about the topic. In the case of the Obama/ Muslim rumor, the story had gained such traction that in a Democratic presidential debate right after the New Hampshire primary, NBC news anchor and debate host Brian Williams, noted that he had received an email claiming Obama was Muslim three times in the week leading up to the debate. Table 7.7 shows the media convergence of the Obama/Muslim rumor as it was reported on and discussed, not just in the new media, but across all spectrums of news media.

Perhaps not surprisingly, polls conducted across 2008 began showing that a substantial number of voters were unsure about Obama's religious beliefs. A Fox News poll from July 2008 found that 10 percent of voters thought Obama was a Muslim and 27 percent said that they did not know whether he was Muslim or Christian. These results were confirmed by a Pew survey, also taken in July 2008, that found 12 percent thought he was a Muslim and an additional 24 percent were uncertain of Obama's religion. A University of Texas poll conducted just weeks before election day in November 2008 found that 23 percent of citizens in Texas thought

Table 7.7 Dissemination of Obama/Muslim Rumor

Free Republic website	
Origin of rumor (average page views per month)	25–50 million
Fox and Friends television program	
First television network program to report rumor (average for Quarter 1, 2007)	769,000
"The Jihad Candidate"	
Widely circulated email spreading rumor (number of results for Google search)	303,000
Prominently viewed You Tube videos for "Obama is a Muslim" (number of views):	
"Obama: 'My Muslim Faith'"	623,771
"Red State Update: Obama Admits He's a Muslim"	223,879
"Was He Muslim?"	174,042
"Gaddafi: Obama is a Muslim – Foreign Donations to the Obama Campaign"	157, 772
"Obama Admits He is a Muslim"	102,177

Note: Searches conducted between September 8, 2008, and October 10, 2008.

Obama was a Muslim. A Kentucky poll from the same time period found that 28 percent of Republicans in the state thought Obama was a Muslim. In a close election, this is a substantial number of citizens holding a belief about a candidate that for many voters would disqualify him for the presidency of the United States. The intent of this manipulation was clear: to make voters fear Barack Obama's candidacy and support John McCain. Importantly, the Pew Survey found that Democrats who believed Obama to be a Muslim were more likely to support his Republican rival. Clearly, there was a political benefit to manipulating voters into believing that Obama was a Muslim.

As a result of this and other rumors, the Obama campaign created a website, StopTheSmears.org, to counter this and other claims. Everyday citizens could visit the site, send links to friends, and try to rebut the claim that Obama is a Muslim. In the end, though, two factors helped to facilitate the spreading of misinformation. First, much of what goes up on the Internet lacks the filters of professional news editors. Twenty years ago there would have been no way to publish and disseminate to millions of people a series of lies about a presidential candidate. Media organizations would not have allowed it, and the mainstream media would have uniformly squashed the story. Second, there is a ready and willing group of partisan pundits, both professional and non-professional, who discuss rumors and spread misinformation if it is in the best interests of their agenda. Before the early-1990s there were simply no openly partisan news broadcasters hosting widely watched programs or writing in mainstream publications who could advance a story akin to the Obama is a Muslim story. Ultimately, one of the great ironies of the dawning of the information age is that while it has made facts more readily available, it has also made it easier to spread misinformation and distortions.

"Government Oversight of Airlines: That Is a Funny Topic"

In our second case study, we examine the influence of different information sources on people's political attitudes. A challenge for media and politics scholars in the coming years will be to try to understand the individual level effects of the new and rapidly evolving information environment. To address one aspect of how different types of information affect citizens in the new news environment, we conducted an original experiment on 180 undergraduates in the spring of 2008. Our goal in crafting the experiment was to explore the ways in which different political coverage might influence the accountability citizens expected from government.[25] The less accountable citizens hold the government through voicing opinions, the more easily they are misled or manipulated or just ignored. As might be the case with a culture that is amusing itself to death, as Neil Postman famously asserted in his 1986 book, the less people care or think they should care about political issues the easier it is for leaders to serve their own interests.[26]

To this end, we created two experimental conditions comprised of different kinds of media coverage of the Federal Aviation Administration (FAA) grounding of hundreds of American Airlines flights in April 2008. Half of the students were exposed to an *ABC World News* story that ran the day that many flights were cancelled. The story began with the traditional press discussion of facts and information about the reasons for the cancellations and the likely duration, but the reporter also added a bit of sensationalism in focusing on outraged passengers criticizing American Airlines and the FAA. The clip ended with an ABC News airline industry expert suggesting that the groundings were akin to receiving a parking ticket thirty seconds after you get to your car and begin pulling away from the expired meter.

The other half of the students were shown the ABC News clip as well as an additional four minute clip of Jon Stewart's *Daily Show* segment discussing the reasons for and the impact of the cancelled flights on public trust in government and corporate regulation. *The Daily Show* clip began by mocking media coverage of major journalists creating and feigning their own fear of flying. It went on to show FAA officials testifying before Congress that they were told by their bosses that they might lose their jobs if they persisted in pursuing airlines with substandard planes. Stewart concluded:

> When you fly, you are inspected quite thoroughly, whereas the plane itself is perhaps occasionally vacuumed. See with this Administration, if a passenger blows up a plane, it is a failure of the War on Terror, but if the plane blows up on itself, it is the market self-regulating (Jon Stewart, *The Daily Show*, April 8, 2008).

We included both ABC News and *The Daily Show* in this condition because research indicates that people who watch *The Daily Show* typically watch or read other news as well, and that Jon Stewart is rarely their only source of news.[27]

Following the exposure to either of the conditions, students were given a short survey that assessed their perception of who was accountable for the airline groundings. In particular, we included a question that measured evaluations of whether the FAA or American Airlines were responsible for and should be held accountable for the airline groundings and the delay in travel and stress caused to thousands of citizens. We included items to pick up affective reactions to the shutdown as depicted in the news stories as well. Additionally, we asked students about how the stories they were exposed to might influence their likelihood of discussing the story with others, their support of government regulation of the airlines, and their confidence in government more generally. As controls we used party identification, ideology, and self-reported interest in politics.

Our expectations were that people exposed to the traditional ABC News story would be more likely to identify the government as accountable for the groundings, would be more likely to be angry with the FAA, and would report being more anxious to fly. In contrast, we expected that the added mix of Stewart's irony and satirical take on government, corporations, and citizens combined would make respondents more likely to discuss the issues with others, but less likely to think that it was anyone's fault and less likely to be very concerned about the issue. If everyone is behaving absurdly, as Stewart's critiques of government and politics commonly suggest, it's just the way things are and, once again, there is not much to do but sit back and laugh. Thus, in essence, we expected stronger behavioral and affective responses to the mainstream ABC clip compared to responses to ABC News combined with *The Daily Show* clip.

Our findings suggest that satire and comedic presentations of the news may lead to more discussion of political issues, but also to more cynicism and political disengagement. The results, presented in Table 7.8, did not turn up any significant differences in perceptions of accountability or anger toward the FAA. Descriptive statistics suggest a majority of people

Table 7.8 ANOVA Results

	Who is Accountable — FAA (1) or American Airlines	Angry With FAA	Discuss Story with Others	More Likely To Support Gov. Regulation of Airlines	More Anxious to Fly	Confidence in Government Generally
Just ABC	1.6	2.36	2.30	2.21	2.4	2.61
ABC & Daily Show	1.54	2.36	2.45	2.43	2.4	2.54
Sign	.25	.17	.01	.06	.62	.07

Notes: Accountability was measured with the question, "Some people say that American Airlines should be held primarily responsible for the cancellations and delays due to Federation Aviation Administration (FAA) officials' findings of faulty wirings on some if its airplanes. Others suggest that the government should have been more persistent in its testing and grounding of the company's planes. Which position is closer to your own?... 1.American Airlines should be held accountable for the delays and cancellations. 2.The government should be held accountable for the delays and cancellations." Angry with FAA was measured with the question, "To what extent does this story make you angry at the FAA?" Discuss Story With Others was assessed by asking, "To what extent does this story make you likely to discuss this issue with other people?" "Support for Government Regulation asked," "To what extent does this story make you likely to support government regulation of the airlines." ... Anxious to Fly was assessed with, "To what extent does this story make you more anxious about airline travel?" Finally, confidence in government asked, "Does this story make you more or less confident in government?" All of the responses were recoded in such a way that higher numbers in the cells represent more support for that statement or question.

in both conditions were more likely to hold the government account-able than American Airlines, which is consistent with evidence suggesting Americans increasingly prefer market to government forces.[28] Addition-ally, respondents were no more or less anxious to fly in either condition.

However, as expected, we did find that people who watched *The Daily Show* along with ABC News were more likely to say that they were likely to discuss the issue with others as a result of watching the clip (p < .05). *Daily Show* watchers also were more likely to say that they believed that the airlines should be regulated by government (p < .10). Finally, respon-dents who watched both *The Daily Show* and ABC News said that the story made them less confident in government generally (p < .10). The infusion of irony, critique, and satire provided by Stewart seemed to make people even more cynical and jaded about government than exposure to just the ABC News clip.[29] People are more likely to talk about a political issue presented in an entertaining manner and to think that something should be done about it (in this case government should do a better job of regulating the airlines). However, the belief that something should be done becomes more of a gripe than a call to action because people in the new media environment are less confident that government will do anything effective as manifested in lower confidence in government. The notion that people complain about lack of government oversight, but then quickly move on because nothing is going to be done right anyway, seems to be an attitude presented on *The Daily Show* and manifested in the results presented here.

The mock U.S. politics textbook that was spun off *The Daily Show*, entitled *America (The Book): A Citizen's Guide to Democracy Inaction*, best exemplifies the show's attitude toward and portrayal of the media. Chapter 7 of the book is entitled: "The Media: Democracy's Guardian Angel" (in the table of contents the subheading of the chapter is "The Media: Democracy's Valiant Vulgarians"). The chapter begins with the following:

> A free and independent press is essential to the health of a function-ing democracy. It serves to inform the voting public on matters rel-evant to its well-being. Why they've stopped doing that is a mystery. I mean, 300 camera crews outside a courthouse to see what Kobe Bryant is wearing when the judge sets his hearing date, while false information used to send our country to war goes unchecked? What the fuck happened?... And the excuses [by the media]. My God, the excuses! "Hey, we just give the people what they want." "What can we do, this administration is secretive." "But the last season of *Friends* really is news."[30]

Daily Show viewers get a nightly dose of Stewart's populist rhetoric suggesting the political process is absurd, but not as absurd as the media that covers it and, well, there is not a damn thing that can be done but shrug our shoulders and laugh.

Though there is an expectation for infotainment among the public, this same trend has led to a wary and cynical public. Many want to be entertained, to laugh, but in a manner that potentially undermines democratic accountability. In this way, it may be easier to manipulate a public á la Huxley's predictions in *Brave New World* that contemporary culture would come to love its distractions. Increasingly, we are seemingly incapable of distinguishing between what is serious and what is trivial. As long as public officials can create convincing and entertaining truths, transparent communication between political actors and their government can be both manipulative and fun. In the end, Stewart offers an analysis of the news of the day that suggests that as corrupt or ridiculous as democracy might seem sometimes, mass media is even more silly and laughable. We the people, Stewart's show suggests, do best by sitting back and laughing at a government and communications apparatus we cannot control. If it is true we lack such power, the message seems to be, why not have a little fun laughing at the people who do?

Conclusion

We began our analysis by identifying two tasks: first, identifying the shape and substance of the new media environment; and second, identifying whether the new environment as currently evolving would allow for heightened degrees of manipulation.

As to the first task, the uncertain and transitory nature of the contemporary media environment can be seen in both positive and negative lights. On the positive side, there is more information than ever before, and because journalists and inside-the-beltway-players like Joe Klein and Wolf Blitzer blog about their day-to-day conversations with their sources, citizens now have unprecedented access to the political world. That, it might be argued, is a net plus for democracy, especially given that people can converse amongst themselves as well as with the very journalists who act as fourth branch of government watchdogs. In the abstract, almost everyone applauds more direct democratic engagement by the people and the possibilities of the Internet. In this way, new technologies could offer average citizens unprecedented voice in the creation of laws and budgets that govern their day-to-day lives. As the Pew Project for Journalistic Evidence put it in 2009:

> Power is shifting to the individual journalist and away, by degrees from journalistic institutions… Through search, e-mail, blogs, social media and more, consumers are gravitating to the work of individual writers and voices and away somewhat from institutional brand.

Journalists who have left legacy news organizations are attracting funding to created their own websites.[31]

On the negative side, the demise of newspapers and the essential reporting they provide is the most devastating consequence of the new media era. Indeed there is a website entitled Newspaper Death Watch that is documenting the declining ad revenue and audience for print newspapers. Internet news, in recent years, has dramatically eclipsed print news use by younger audiences. Thirty-nine percent of those under the age of thirty-five told Carnegie Corporation's study entitled "Abandoning the News" that they expected to use the Internet in the future for news purposes. A mere 8 percent said they would rely on a newspaper.[32] Even online newspapers, like the cable counterparts to the network television news, have less revenue, offer less reporting, and rely on more blogging and commentary. In the new media era, the *New York Times, Washington Post*, and *Los Angeles Times* have all made drastic cutbacks in their editorial and reporting staff, with cuts in international reporting the most drastic. The changes in media technology will not be just about the news business but democracy itself. What becomes of democratically informed citizens when the primary news sources no longer invest resources in helping the public learn what we need to know about our world here and abroad?[33] *New York Times* Executive Editor Bill Keller also laments the "serendipitous encounters that are hard to replicate in the quicker, reader-driven format of a Web-site."[34] A hard copy of the *New York Times* might include a front-page election story with smaller stories on the atrocities in Darfur. If we lose the reporters who cover that area of the world and a public that is made aware (and some who will be made interested enough to act), we lose the documenting of places and events across the globe in the interest of an informed democracy.

Even though newspapers have been the bedrock of journalism in the United States for the past half century, somewhere along the way the public lost trust in newspapers. Sacred Heart University published a 2008 study showing that less than 20 percent said they could believe "all or most" media reporting, down from 27 percent in 2003. Philip Meyer predicts that the final copy of the final newspaper will be sometime in 2043.[35] Some papers are moving increasingly online as market research tells them that is where the audiences are looking for news. Madison, Wisconsin's *Capital Times* became the second of two newspapers in the country to move exclusively to online coverage. As we look to the future, then, one can only be concerned about the quality of news endeavors. The survival of high quality reporting and investigative journalism may rely upon traditional news outlets figuring a way to become profitable using the new media technologies.

In terms of our second task, the preponderance of the evidence at this point suggests that in the current information environment in which the media is increasingly focused on the trivial and has few filters on the information presented, we are experiencing an increasing ability for the public to be manipulated by political actors. The less we know about what is really going on and the more we seek out information that is either entertaining or primarily consistent with our own ideological views (or both), the easier it is for political actors to blur the line between what is true and what is merely desired as policy regardless of veracity. The amorphous, profit-oriented information environment of today makes it easier for people to believe what they want, as there is a market for every niche. In the end, though, we certainly recognize that the role of blogs, YouTube, and Myspace type forums are only in the beginning stages of taking on integral and likely unstoppable roles in the political process. As we continue to move forward into this unpredictable and amorphous information world, we think there is much to be concerned about in terms of the decline in transparency and corresponding accountability that serve as foundations for democratic legitimacy in the United States.

Notes

1. Paul J. Boyer, "One Angry Man...Is Keith Olbermann Changing TV News," *The New Yorker* (June 23, 2008), retrieved from http://www.newyorker.com.
2. Stepehn L. Vaughan, *The Encyclopedia of American Journalism* (New York: Taylor and Francis, 2008).
3. Each night, as part of his show, Olbermann included a "Worst Person in the World" segment where he calls out people he loathes for something they've done or said in recent days. More often than not, Olbermann calls out high-profile conservatives.
4. Julia R. Fox, Glory Koloen, and Volkan Sahin, "No Joke: A Comparison of Substance in The Daily Show with Jon Stewart and Broadcast Network Television Coverage of the 2004 Presidential Election Campaign," *Journal of Broadcasting Electronic Media* 5, no. 2 (June 2007): 213–27.
5. Herbert J. Gans, *Deciding What's News: A Study of CBS Evening News, NBC Nightly News, Newsweek, and Time* (New York: Vintage, 1980).
6. Michael Massing, "The News About the Internet," *The New York Review of Books* (August 13, 2009) (56), p. 13.
7. Of course, the rise of the partisan press is a return to the early years of the Republic when newspapers were entirely partisan. Political rivals Alexander Hamilton and Thomas Jefferson, for instance, wrote for politically competing newspapers while both working for President George Washington's administration. For a discussion of the early partisan press, see Jeffrey L. Pasley, *The Tyranny of Printers: Newspaper Politics in the Early American Republic* (Charlottesville: University of Virginia Press, 2003).
8. Richard Fox, Robert Van Sickle, and Thomas Steiger, *Tabloid Justice*, 2nd ed. (Boulder, CO: Lynne Rienner, 2007).
9. Richard Davis and Diana Owen, *New Media and American Politics* (Oxford: Oxford University Press, 1998), pp. 7–9.
10. There are numerous other sources of news on cable, such as the business news channels CNBC, Fox News Business, and Bloomberg News. Also, a number of cities, such as Charlotte, New York, and Austin now have local

twenty-four hour news stations. The most watched cable news programs, however, are Fox, CNN, and MSNBC.

11. The *Rocky Mountain News* could not keep up with techonological changes and after almost 150 years of service went out of business on February 27, 2009. John Temple, "Story Shifts from Cable to Internet," *Rocky Mountain News* (August 19, 2006), p. 8A.

12. The Pew Research Center for People and the Press, "Internet's Broader Role in Campaign 2008: Social networking and online videos take off" (January 11, 2008).

13. For a list of the most popular political blogs see http://www.ebizmba.com/articles/political-sites.

14. Todd Gitlin, "Public Sphere or Public Sphericules?", in *Media, Ritual, Identity* eds. Tamar Liebes and James Curran (New York: Routledge, 1998), pp. 168-75. Todd Gitlin, *Media Unlimited: How the Torrent of Images and Sounds Overwhelms Our Lives* (New York: Macmillan, 2001).

15. Cass R. Sunstein, *Republic.com* (Princeton, NJ: Princeton University Press, 2001).

16. Kathleen Hall Jamieson and Joseph N. Cappella, *Echo Chamber* (Oxford: Oxford University Press, 2007), p. xiii.

17. Boyer, "One Angry Man."

18. Tom Fenton, *Bad News: The Decline of Reporting, the Business of News, and the Danger to Us All* (New York: HarperCollins, 2005); David Mindich, *Tuned Out* (Oxford: Oxford University Press, 2004); Richard Krajicek, *Scooped* (New York: Columbia University Press, 1998).

19. Bill Moyers Journal. *Bill Moyers talks with Jon Stewart* (July, 2003).

20. Bill Moyers Journal. *Bill Moyers talks with Jon Stewart* (April 27, 2003).

21. Mark Lebovich, "The Aria of Chris Matthews," *The New York Times Magazine* (April 13, 2008).

22. Perry Bacon Jr., "Foes Use Obama's Muslim Ties to Fuel Rumors About Him," *Washington Post* (November, 29, 2007), p. A01.

23. James Rainey, "Barack Obama Can Thank 'Citizen Journalist' for 'Bitter Tempest'," *Los Angeles Times* (April 15, 2008). Retrieved August 10, 2008, from http://articles.latimes.com/2008/apr/15/nation/na-bitter15

24. Jim Rutenberg, "The Man Behind the Whispers about Obama," *New York Times* (October 13, 2008), p. A1.

25. The sample was drawn from undergraduate students in political science classes at Union College, Schenectady, New York, and Loyola Marymount University, Los Angeles, California. Fifty percent of the sample consisted of self-reported Democrats, 35 percent Republicans, and 15 percent Independents. Men comprised 55 percent of the sample and 45 percent were women. The average age of the respondents was 20 years.

26. Neil Postman, *Amusing Ourselves to Death: Public Discourse in the Age of Show Business* (20th anniversary ed.) (New York: Penguin, 2006).

27. Fox, Koloen, and Sahin, "No Joke."

28. Sunstein, *Republic.com*.

29. We tested these conclusions further in regression analyses. The results (not presented) show that our findings of differences across exposure to different media formats hold when controlling for party, ideology, sex, and the extent to which people follow politics. Of course these results are only suggestive, and we hope much more research will be conducted in the near future to enhance our understanding of the individual-level effects of new media on political attitudes, beliefs and behaviors.

30. Jon Stewart, Ben Karlin, and David Javerbaum, *America (the Book): A Citizen's Guide to Democracy Inaction* (New York: Grand Central Publishing, 2004), p. 131.
31. Pew Research Center for the People and the Press, "State of the News Media: An Annual Report on American Journalism" (March 16, 2009). Retrieved June 1, 2009, from http://www.stateofthemedia.org/2009/narrative_overview_majortrends.php?media=1
32. Eric Alterman, "Out of Print: The Death and Life of the American Newspaper," *The New Yorker* (March 31, 2008).
33. Boyer, "One Angry Man."
34. Boyer, "One Angry Man."
35. Philip Meyer, *The Vanishing Newspaper: Saving Journalism in the Information Age* (Columbia, MO: University of Missouri Press, 2004).

8   The Betrayal of Democracy

The Purpose of Public Opinion Survey Research and its Misuse by Presidents

Lawrence R. Jacobs

Survey research has long been considered a tool to establish and strengthen democracy. In particular, it has been charged with objectively identifying the general public's policy preferences and informing government officials of those views in order to facilitate greater responsiveness to public opinion.[1]

Indeed, this conventional view has fuelled the presumption that the use of polling by politicians is evidence of pandering and the notion that public opinion routinely drives policy decisions. The alliance of polling and hyperresponsiveness to the general public's policy preferences has generated fears that politicians will compromise their independent judgment to serve the broader national interest and has led to calls for politicians to respond less to public opinion.

The reality within the halls of government is quite different. In truth, the use of survey research by politicians has betrayed the founding principles of scientific polling, core democratic norms, and individual liberties to form critical evaluations of their government. The primary traitors are the users of survey research, not the techniques themselves. In reaction to the incentives in a changing political system, political leaders in particular have turned to survey research to alter the public's preferences and evaluations and to redefine the nature of political representation.

The use (or rather misuse) of survey research by presidents and their staffs has important implications. White House use of survey research directly connects to our understanding of presidential power and the institutional development of the presidency, especially its growing public face.[2] There are also, however, significant implications of presidential polling for survey research and its rationale of fostering democracy. This is a primary focus of this chapter.

This chapter outlines the expectations of survey research and how it has been used by the individual with the greatest pubic visibility and administrative capacity in American governance—the president of the United States.

I. Original Purpose of Public Opinion Research: Tool of Broad-Based Democracy

George Gallup, Sr.—one of the early pioneers of scientific survey techniques—mainstreamed polling into a routine feature of press coverage and political life.[3] Dr. Gallup publicly articulated two core purposes of modern polling to foster a science of democracy. The first purpose was to objectively pinpoint the public's policy concerns and preferences, breaking from the ad hoc, imprecise, and often distorted perceptions or depictions that had previously existed: polling would identify the general "will of the people...on all the major issues of the day." Second, polling provided the means for political representation: polling would, Dr. Gallup believed, "bridge the gap between the people and those who are responsible for making decisions."[4]

Dr. Gallup's public case for scientific polling undergirds contemporary survey research by scholars. Measuring and explaining through surveys the characteristics, attitudes, perceptions, and behavior of individuals is one of the primary fields in the social sciences. Publication in leading scholarly journals depends on peer-review evaluations of precision and accuracy in examining public opinion. Survey analysis has also formed the foundation of more than four decades of research on political representation measuring the consistency or congruence of public opinion and government policy.[5]

The attention to public opinion surveys by the press and by scholars raises a fundamental question about how it is used by government officials and political actors: is public opinion research used as a tool of democracy (as Dr. Gallup anticipated) or does it pose a threat to democracy? Gallup's contemporaries did challenge his vision of polling as a threat to America's representative system because it valued individual liberty and deliberation and privileged the opinion of a majority in ways that leveled out differences in cognition, salience, and other factors.[6] These critiques of Gallup have tended to focus, however, on the threat of strengthening the influence of majority preferences rather than on government practice itself and whether government use of survey research actually expanded majoritarian influence. The lingering question remains: how have government officials wielded the survey instrument and to what effect?

A fitting place to start an exploration of polling's contemporary role is by considering how the target population—poll respondents—sizes up polling. The verdict is generally not good: Americans are by and large quite dissatisfied with pollsters and their work. For instance, a July 2006 poll by Harris found that only 34 percent of adults trusted pollsters to tell the truth. This puts pollsters in the basement of public trust with lawyers and stockbrokers; conversely, the proportion trusting doctors, teachers, and professors is more than double.

The potential role of polling in prompting government officials to respond to the general public does not appear to be a source of the public's distrust of polling. When Americans are asked about interests or influences that may exert too much power in shaping government policy, Washington politicians and well-financed special interests lead the list—8 out of 10 or more identify political action committees, big companies, and political lobbyists as exerting too much power. Only 17 percent identify public opinion as overly dominant. Additional research by the National Election Studies and other survey organizations suggests that Americans would like government to listen more and exercise greater responsiveness.[7] The public's support for more government responsiveness contrasts with the skepticism regarding citizen influence expressed by contemporary scholars and generations of political commentators from Alexander Hamilton and Edmund Burke to Walter Lippmann and *Washington Post* columnist David Broder.[8]

The public's low regard for polling may stem from several other factors. There is a widespread misunderstanding of modern survey research that may feed distrust and dissatisfaction. Without an appreciation for probability theory and randomized sampling, individuals may be confused about how generalizations regarding the general population of adults can be drawn from interviewing a small sample of 500 or 1,000 respondents. This confusion may be exacerbated by extensive press coverage of mistaken exit poll results during recent presidential elections or pre-election polls such as those during the 2008 Democratic nomination battle in New Hampshire that were contradicted by the actual vote tally, which was won by Hillary Clinton.

One of the most significant threats to Dr. Gallup's original optimistic vision of a science of democracy is, however, largely unknown to most Americans—the strategic use of survey research by government leaders and political activists. This instrumental use of polling threatens to pervert its core purposes by equipping political leaders to shape existing public opinion and to avoid responsiveness to the public's own policy preferences.

Investigating the institutional and normative implications of this sobering use of survey research requires a different approach to studying polling. In particular, it requires a shift from studying the content of public opinion and the accuracy of surveys to an investigation of how government officials and political activists utilize the survey research they structure and conduct. This directs the analytic focus from the contours of public opinion per se to the strategic motivation and institutional application of the public opinion information that is collected and used. The private polling of U.S. presidents, which is extensively documented in government archives, provides a particularly revealing portal into the strategic use of survey research and its threat to democracy.

II. Polling in the Hands of the Leviathan

One of the most striking changes in the modern presidency has been the establishment of a direct and unmediated relationship with the mass public. Research traces this more public presidency to changing norms of governance and to the individualization of Congress and the interest group community.[9] Presidential appeals over the heads of elites to the mass public appear efficient at reaching large numbers of groups and individuals as well as complementing inside-the-beltway negotiations and bargaining.[10]

As presidents focused on making public appeals, monitoring public opinion took on importance to track their approval and the effectiveness of their appeals as well as to calibrate their words and actions. Monitoring public opinion became enmeshed in the institutional apparatus of the presidency as a functionally differentiated and routine feature of the Executive Office of the President.[11]

The norms and incentives associated with the presidency have propelled a high and sustained level of presidential polling. Figure 8.1 traces the expansion of the White House's public opinion apparatus based on the most basic indicator—the number of its polls contained in White House archives. The Kennedy White House received 15 private polls, which created a floor on which future presidents substantially expanded. Private polling jumped to 110 under Lyndon Johnson, 173 surveys under Richard Nixon, and 204 under Ronald Reagan. Despite George H.W. Bush's reputation as being uninterested in polling, he maintained an extensive survey operation with 73 polls—five times greater than Kennedy's total and comparable to his three predecessors' after factoring in their longer

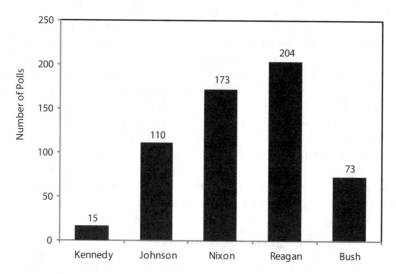

Figure 8.1 Private Presidential Polling

periods in office. (Bush conducted an additional 107 polls during his 1988 election campaign.) We do not have full access to the Clinton archival records, but journalistic accounts and partial records suggest that private polling remained a substantial operation. Today, it continues to be closely integrated into the White House's decision making.

Presidential polling since the Kennedy administration has expanded not only in the number of polls conducted but also in the scope and sophistication of the information collected. Compared to the number of discrete polling results that the Johnson White House assembled, the Nixon administration increased the number of findings by 57 percent, and Reagan and his aides boosted it still more. The increased sophistication of White House polling is partly revealed by the increase in the number of survey questions posed by presidents after Kennedy. Where Kennedy's pollsters relied on open-ended questions that cast a wide net to identify the public's broad concerns and policy views, successive pollsters developed structured survey items that were based on intellectual constructs and specific strategic goals. The survey research and analyses under the Nixon and Reagan administrations were more consistent, pursuing a fairly stable approach in survey after survey as compared to the fluidity in their Democratic predecessors. More telling is that the Republicans' survey questions were more sophisticated in their design, rooted in cutting edge scholarly research. For instance, Nixon's aides borrowed heavily from articles in *Public Opinion Quarterly* and from the expertise of the premier survey research centers such as the University of Michigan. Where Johnson's surveys used an open-ended question to troll for public reactions to the president's personality, Nixon and Reagan used semantic differentials and other constructs to map the president's interpersonal and performance traits, which then fed into discussions of political strategy and plans for going public to promote the president and his policies.[12]

The growing extensiveness, scope, and sophistication of presidential polling represent significant changes in the institutional development of the presidency, but their importance for survey research and its role in American democracy is not well understood. Increased reliance on survey research by the president could, for instance, foster the kind of bridge building between majorities of Americans and government decision making that Dr. Gallup intended. Understanding the role and implication of the widening presence of survey research within the White House requires careful consideration of its use by presidents—an often secretive and deliberately obscure part of American politics.

III. Polling to Reshape Representation

A long line of theorizing predicts that competing candidates in two party systems will converge toward the electorate's median policy preference.[13] Polling by politicians has been considered a microfoundation of median voter theory—a tool to reliably identify the policy preferences of centrist opinion for politicians to respond to.

Research indicates that median voting theory misses, however, an important component of political motivation—namely, the policy goals of politicians and their supporters.[14] In particular, politicians balance electoral goals against what they consider good public policy as well as the intense preferences of party activists and other core supporters who shoulder much of the responsibility for volunteering time, money, and other resources. Since the early 1970s, candidates and officeholders have placed greater weight on policy goals. The enhanced influence of party activists, loyal partisan voters, and single issue advocates, as well as the selective recruitment of candidates with intense political philosophies and the growing importance of campaign contributions, have increased the benefits of pursuing policy goals as well as the costs of compromising them.[15]

Although policy as opposed to electoral goals can pose stark choices, politicians prefer to pursue strategies to balance both. Politicians who are primarily motivated to maximize their vote by consistently responding to the preferences of majorities are constrained by the political need to hold their narrow but core set of supporters. On the other hand, politicians intent on pursuing policy goals search for strategies and tactics to avoid electoral removal of themselves and fellow partisans who are critical for building governing majorities.

The confluence of growing pressure to pursue policy goals while minimizing electoral risks appears to have accelerated interest in survey research and, specifically, the routinization of public opinion analysis within the White House's institutional operations. The growing expertise within the academy and advertising industry, as well as White House experience, boosted the confidence of presidents and their advisers that survey research was a reliable and exacting technique for producing extensive information about public opinion as it existed and as it might be reframed or altered. The development of a public opinion apparatus reduced uncertainty about public opinion and about pinpointing its susceptibility to carefully honed strategies.

Changes in the structure of American politics and the institution of the presidency have propelled successive presidents since Kennedy to use their survey research capacity to avoid a median voter approach in favor of strategies that create the opportunity to promote policy goals while minimizing risks to re-election. Although previous analyses of White House use of survey research have focused on presidential power and the institutional development of the presidency, this chapter focuses on the implications of presidential polling for survey research and its rationale of fostering democracy.

Presidential use of survey research has been investigated using three components. The first is an examination of the White House's strategic calculations and motivations in collecting and using survey research drawing upon archival records, interviews, and secondary sources.

The second component is an exhaustive cataloguing—often the first of its kind—of the extensive private polling that the White House has assembled since the Kennedy administration and that has been stored in presidential libraries and national archives. The third is an intensive content analysis of presidential statements as recorded in the *Public Papers of the Presidents* and the *Weekly Compilation of Presidential Documents*.[16]

Because presidents treat their statements and actions as critical tools for calibrating the public's perceptions of them, these content analyses provide a basis for analyzing some of the impacts of the president's polling. Some studies have also tracked presidential behavior through direct indicators of White House decisions such as Johnson's decisions regarding the number of bombing missions and U.S. troops in Vietnam. Quantitative analyses have been used to study systematically the relationships between monthly measures of the White House's polling results and the president's decisions and statements on policy issues.

Quantitative and qualitative analyses of presidential polling point to three broad White House uses of survey research. In particular, the White House has sought to expand its discretion to pursue policy goals by changing the public's preferences regarding specific policy proposals, by parsing aggregate public opinion, and by shifting the evaluative dimension of presidential performance from policy to non-policy considerations such as personal image.

A. Simulated Representation

While Dr. Gallup and empirical scholars of political representation assume that politicians would respond to existing public opinion, analyses of private presidential polling and decision making document persistent efforts to change the preferences of Americans to support the policy goals embraced by the president and his intense supporters.

Quantitative analyses reveal that Johnson's polling data on the administration's Vietnam policy had no significant positive effect on the president's actions.[17] Indeed, the president defied the public's policy preferences that were reported in his own polls: as the proportion of Americans supporting withdrawal increased, Johnson made decisions to expand bombing sorties in North Vietnam and the levels of U.S. troops committed to the war effort.

Rather than using its survey research to design policy, the Johnson White House relied on its opinion data to fashion public positions that were expected to build support for the president's policy goals (defending South Vietnam and stopping the spread of communism) while minimizing the potential electoral threat.[18] Archival records reveal that Johnson and his aides turned to the White House polling operation to determine how to "handle volatile public opinion" and, in particular, to "change the public mood," and to "marshal[l]... American support for the Administration."[19]

Operationally, the White House used its survey research to identify how to "affect... the tone, the content, and the form of what we say publicly and privately on Vietnam."[20] Testing its framing of policy choices, White House polling consistently explored public reactions toward various policy options: the administration's position of fighting to force a negotiated peace that thwarts the North; the hawk position of "go[ing] all out [to] escalate (short of nuclear weapons) to secure a military victory;" and the dove positions of "reduc[ing] military operations" or "get[ing] out now."[21] White House staff relied on these polling results to fashion Johnson's public statements and to systematically monitor the administration's effectiveness in "persuading people [that] we are making progress [in Vietnam]."[22]

In addition to attempting to increase public support for the administration's Vietnam policy, the White House also used its polling on issue salience and policy preferences to calibrate its public statements in order to divert attention from the unpopular Vietnam War. In particular, the Johnson White House sought to "emphasize, as dramatically as possible, the more hopeful dimensions of America's face today" associated with the Great Society and thereby prevent the "Vietnam War [from] dominat[ing] the headlines and the national mind."[23] Although some aides initially reported to the president that "your agitation [and] your propaganda is finally softening up the opposition" and "reaching the American public in the way [the White House] wants them affected,"[24] Johnson and his senior aides eventually concluded that the depth of public frustration was too deep to be dislodged or reversed.[25] Future administrations would expand White House polling capacities to enhance the effectiveness of their messages and presentations in changing public preferences to support president's policy goals.

Bill Clinton's approach to health care reform followed a similar dynamic. He was inaugurated with a commitment to pursue a middle way approach to pressing national problems including rising health care costs and unmet access to medical care.[26] He and his administration designed a plan for managed competition that melded the intense policy of Democratic activists for universal access with the conservative preference for competition among private health plans. After designing the White House health care plan, Clinton and his senior aides turned to their survey researchers to identify how to sell it. The White House polling was used to identify such key phrases as "Security for All" and the symbol of a health insurance "card" that would provide reliable coverage in an effort to create public support for the Clinton proposal. President Clinton and key administration officials blanketed the country with a communications plan that sought to rally the public behind its novel approach to health reform.

B. *Parsing Aggregate Public Opinion*

Dr. Gallup expected survey research to identify accurately the general public's policy preferences. The presidency is expected to be institutionally hard-wired to focus on the general public: Terry Moe suggests that presidents "addres[s] the needs and aspirations of a national constituency [while]... [legislators] are driven by localism."[27]

Quantitative and qualitative evidence from presidential archives suggests, however, that institutional incentives to pursue distinct policy goals motivate presidents to disaggregate general public opinion in terms of salience and politically important sub-groups. The influence of party activists and other powerful interest groups create incentives for presidents to use survey research to systematically parse public opinion rather than seek out the more amorphous general public. Specifically, presidents have used survey research in two respects in order to calibrate and narrow their behavior and public positions.

The first strategy is to parse public opinion to pinpoint the small number of salient policy issues. The purpose is to strategically allocate scarce resources—the costs of collecting and analyzing survey data and the commitment of the president to policy positions.

Quantitative analyses of Nixon's policy positions and his White House's polling data indicate that the administration disproportionately invested money and the scarce space on survey questionnaires to collecting polling data on the specific issues that were ranked as particularly salient.[28] In addition, Nixon publicly talked more about these salient issues. Conversely, on issues with lower salience, the White House reduced its investment of survey resources in favor of using general ideological data on liberal and conservative attitudes toward government activism. In addition, Nixon avoided comparable levels of public position taking.

In short, the White House capitalized on survey research to parse public opinion in terms of issue salience. Although survey research may have facilitated responsiveness on visible issues, it also equipped the White House to cull a larger number of issues that were developed to follow the policy goals of the president and his supporters.

A second White House strategy was to use survey research to pinpoint and then cater to the intense views of politically important subgroups.[29] Quantitative and qualitative evidence from the Reagan White House points to a consistent pattern of calibrating the president's policy statements to align with the views of critical electoral subgroups. In particular, Reagan's policy positions systematically corresponded with the views of high income earners who favored reducing government spending, lowering taxes, and reforming Social Security to make the program voluntary. He also responded to social conservatives (especially Baptists and Catholics) on issues such as family values and crime and to conservative Republicans on hawkish foreign policy. This illustrates the use of survey research by presidents to decompose aggregate public attitudes in order to pinpoint the commitment of presidential resources to powerful segments of the electorate.

C. Priming Image

Extensive research has examined presidential personality and, especially, its impact on public perceptions and evaluations.[30] A number of studies have analyzed the impact of candidate image on public attitudes and voter choice and the incentives for politicians to construct and maintain an appealing image.[31]

Personality traits are a focus of White House strategizing and survey research. In particular, presidents have used survey research to craft a personal image that appeals to voters on non-policy grounds in order to mitigate the risk that their pursuit of policy goals will alienate important segments of the electorate and expose their allies to electoral defeat.

John Kennedy used selective policy issues for the purpose of constructing and maintaining a public perception of his personality as a vigorous agent of change.[32] Quantitative analyses reveal that Kennedy's polling data on issue salience and the public's policy preferences drove the amount of attention he devoted to particular issues. Of particular significance was the strategy behind this responsiveness. Kennedy and his senior aides calculated that selectively highlighting salient and popular issues would build a "move ahead" image for Kennedy.[33] In other words, they turned to policies that were salient and supported by the public not to "win" their vote by approximating their policy preference (as Downs would predict) as much as to fashion the public's perceptions of Kennedy's personal traits and to broaden his appeal.[34]

Presidents after Kennedy substantially expanded the use of the White House survey research to track public evaluations of the president's personal traits. Figure 8.2 shows that the Johnson, Nixon, and Reagan administrations increased the collection of poll data on personality traits, including perceptions of interpersonal characteristics and performance skills as well as feelings toward the president and other non-policy considerations.

Although Johnson did expand White House polling into non-policy dimensions, there was a notable increase in the scope and, in particular, the sophistication of White House survey research under Nixon. For the first time, the White House commissioned studies that were exclusively devoted to "The Nixon Image." Quantitative analyses found that Nixon systematically responded to negative evaluations of his personality traits by emphasizing bold and aggressive foreign policies. Archival records reveal that Nixon and his senior advisers calculated that decisive foreign policy would bolster his image as competent and strong.[35]

Shifting the focus of public evaluations of the president from his policy positions to his personality offers modern presidents an attractive approach

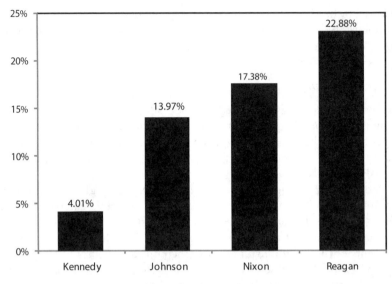

Figure 8.2 Presidential Polling on Non-Policy Dimensions

to seeking policy and electoral goals. Although politicians and presidents have long appreciated the importance of personal appeal, changes in the political system and especially the intensifying pressure of party activists and others have ratcheted-up the incentives for presidents to fashion their public presentations in order to bolster their personal image and thereby minimize the electoral risk for pursuing the policy goals that they and their allies desire.

D. *Presidential Survey Research and the Contemporary White House*

Without access to the official papers of George W. Bush, it would be premature to draw conclusions regarding his administration's strategic use of survey research. Nonetheless, there appear to be signs of a telltale pattern, which might be considered surprising given his strong critical comments in public. He has insisted that "I govern based upon principle and not polls and focus groups." At another point, he explained that "in this White House, we don't poll on something as important as national security."[36]

President Bush's public behavior in light of publicly available polling does seem consistent, however, with past presidential patterns such as using survey research to craft the White House's message. In face of low approval ratings and credibility, President Bush repeatedly justified his continued commitment of U.S. troops in Iraq by insisting that the Commander in Chief deferred to his military officers and, specifically, General David Petracus who commanded U.S. forces in Iraq. Publicly available polls reveal that General Petraeus was considered (according to a Gallup April 2007 poll) "very" or "somewhat reliable" by 80 percent of Americans; only 50 percent rated President Bush as reliable with an equal proportion considering him "not too" or "not at all reliable."[37] According to news reports, Duke political scientist Peter Feaver recommended a similar strategy of message crafting during his two year stint as a White House official; he counseled the White House that publicly emphasizing "victory" would steady public support for Bush's decision to continue U.S. military commitments.[38]

There is also a striking parallel between President Bush's efforts to project an image of a strong and decisive leader and publicly available polling. During the summer of 2007, President Bush met with conservative columnists and conveyed a sense of being "empowered" and possessing great "self-confidence."[39] Meanwhile, available polling indicates that Americans gave President Bush some of his highest ratings for the quality of being "a strong and decisive leader."[40]

Bush's behavior also seemed to fit into the pattern of White House attentiveness to influential subgroups like fellow partisans. President Bush's historically low approval ratings during his second term led commentators to question the remarkable loyalty of Republican members of Congress. Available data may suggest an answer. Although Bush's approval ratings were quite weak among the general public, he enjoyed strong and sustained support from Republicans. A July 2008 CBS survey found that while only 28 percent of Americans favored Bush's handling of his job, 60 percent of Republicans approved of his performance. President Bush's opposition to Democratic proposals to set a timetable for withdrawing all U.S. troops from Iraq displayed a similar split: only 45 percent of the general public backed his opposition to a timetable while 72 percent of Republicans shared the president's opposition to it.[41]

The apparent overlap of President Bush's behavior and publicly available polling data appears consistent with the strategies of previous presidents. Although this correlation may be suggestive, in-depth research in archival records is necessary to draw conclusions. The history of presidential polling is replete with misleading public perceptions: both Richard Nixon and George H.W. Bush were considered to be uninterested in survey research and as having conducted little of it. However, subsequent research in their White House papers revealed substantial survey research and its extensive use by the president and his senior aides.

IV. Implications: Survey Research and Democratic Governance

Three themes emerge from presidential use of survey research since John Kennedy that substantially recast the optimistic expectations of Dr. Gallup and others that public opinion analysis would be a tool of democracy.

First, presidential use of survey research is based on a conceptualization of public opinion as multifaceted. Although Dr. Gallup and empirical scholars of political representation often focus on the public's policy preferences, presidents also define public opinion in terms of personality traits and affective reactions. Evidence of extensive and multidimensional analyses of public opinion challenges current approaches to political representation that concentrate on policy preferences alone. It also challenges a foundational assumption in the application of positive theory to political strategy—namely, that imperfect and limited information impacts political behavior and induces risk aversion.[42]

Second, polling is commonly assumed to shape strategy. For instance, falling approval ratings are expected to affect presidential strategy. Careful analyses of presidential archives reveal, however, that strategy also impacts the White House's decisions about the collection of polling data and use of survey research. Presidential strategies to track, activate, and respond to distinct dimensions and segments of public opinion have guided how the White House has organized, prioritized, and structured its survey research. Strategies to cater to powerful subgroups with intense policy goals while seeking to minimize risks to their electoral goals has motivated the White House to increase its collection and use of survey research on discrete segments of the electorate, non-policy evaluations, and the testing of public messages.

Third, the White House has used survey research to subvert Dr. Gallup's aim of facilitating and expanding government responsiveness to the general public's policy preferences. Instead, presidents and their senior aides have deployed it to shirk substantive representation of the public's policy preferences. For instance, presidents used survey research to pinpoint the small number of highly salient issues in order to identify the far larger pool of issues on which they could exert significant discretion without significant risk of electoral retribution. In addition, presidents have selectively activated personality traits and affective considerations to attempt to advantageously define the terms on which the public evaluates them and to skirt policy-based evaluations by Americans.

The president's use of survey research has not only enabled shirking of the general public's policy preferences but has also facilitated responsiveness to narrow segments of the electorate. Evidence from the Reagan presidency of systematic responsiveness to the preferences of social conservatives, Republican conservatives, and high income earners departs from expectations that survey research would create a science of democracy based on responsiveness to the general public. It is consistent, though, with previous research that finds government policy responsive to higher income groups and to economic interests in domestic and foreign policy.[43]

Presidents have also used survey research to minimize the electoral risk of pursuing policy goals by seeking to change public opinion to support the proposals that they and their key supporters favor. In addition to attempting to shift public evaluation to non-policy considerations like personality traits, survey research has been used by presidents and their aides to pinpoint the words, symbols, and arguments that will resonate with Americans and rally their support for White House proposals. In effect, presidents seek to seize the mantle of responsive democracy by responding to a public opinion that has been primed, framed, and managed to support proposals that majorities of Americans might not otherwise favor.

Research on political behavior has demonstrated that participation in voting and other forms of citizen engagement is heavily skewed to individuals with higher levels of income, education, and social and economic status.[44] Analysis of presidential use of survey research breaks into the black box of how the preferences of these subgroups are processed within government and, in particular, the White House. The irony is that increased polling by presidents appears to coincide with less commitment to responding to the general public's policy preferences. This pattern contradicts common assumptions of pandering politicians and is consistent with a growing body of recent research that detects low and declining government responsiveness to the general public's policy preferences.[45]

Political observers since the Federalist Papers have insisted on insulating presidents from public opinion in order to ensure independence to govern in a way that advances the public's general interest. Analyses of presidential use of survey research demonstrate that presidents may create independence from public opinion in order to pursue narrow, particularistic interests rather than the country's general interest.

Although there is a clear and consistent pattern of administrations using survey research to attempt to shape public opinion and cater to particularistic interests, presidents face significant limits. From Johnson's campaign to mould American attitudes on Vietnam to Clinton's efforts on health care reform and Bush's on the Iraq War, a string of presidents have tried to build strong support and failed. Presidential efforts to shape public attitudes often face countervailing opposition from rival partisans and political actors, who possess their own institutional resources and interests. The media is often drawn to covering the resulting conflict. The effect is that Americans receive multiple and competing messages, which in turn stir uneasiness with presidential direction and magnify attention on real world developments that defy White House expectations. In short, the use of survey research contradicts the expectations that it would be an unambiguous tool for democracy; but nevertheless it may not produce the political dominance that the White House seeks.

Even if presidents fall short of their objectives, presidential use of survey research may contribute to three troubling patterns. First, presidential polling may be a factor in the low and possibly declining responsiveness to public opinion over the past two or three decades. Presidents appear to use survey research to cater their decisions to key subgroups and to avoid politically risky salient issues. Second, sophisticated technology and institutional learning within the White House appears to have fostered confidence that public opinion is malleable. As one Clinton aide put it, the White House can "get away with anything provided you believe in something, you say it over and over again, and you never change."[46] This arrogance may have reinforced legislative partisan polarization and gridlock by feeding the assumption that policy goals may be pursued at minimal risk to electoral goals. For instance, confidence in shaping public opinion contributed to the decisions of Clinton to attempt to fundamentally reform health care delivery and financing and for Bush to propose the restructuring of Social Security, despite narrow electoral wins and deep divisions within their own parties as well as within the opposition party. Third, the commitment of the president's administrative capacity to shaping public thinking and evaluations poses troubling normative questions about democratic government and the autonomy and liberty of citizens to form critical judgments about elected officials free from unwanted government interference. The presidency's institutional apparatus has far exceeded the legitimate role of government to disseminate factual information; it selectively withholds information and strategically manipulates what messages it does distribute for the deliberate purpose of changing public opinion to support its policy goals.

The misuse of survey research for the purposes of elite governance can be checked or at least counteracted. To begin with, the professional associations of academic and commercial survey researchers should take a more aggressive and public role in identifying and criticizing practices aimed at manipulating public opinion and democracy. Organizations like the American Association for Public Opinion Research (AAPOR) are committed to "sound and ethical practice in the conduct of public opinion research and in the use of such research for policy- and decision-making." It has established committees charged with stipulating research standards and identifying professional conduct, which prohibits (among other activities) the use of survey research "not to measure public opinion but to manipulate [public opinion]."[47]

Although AAPOR is committed to rebuking pollsters who violate these standards and code of conduct, its activity as a visible and aggressive public monitor is relatively infrequent and tepid. More active and public guardianship of survey research would contribute to democratic governance and help to counteract the low regard for polling among Americans and many journalists.

In addition, scholars of survey research can play a helpful role in investigating how it is used by presidents and other political actors. Increasing the visibility of political polling may make it costly to utilize survey research in ways that violate democratic norms and citizen liberties.

Moreover, journalists should critically scrutinize how presidents and other political actors use survey research. Too often journalists mistakenly presume that polling by politicians reflects a predisposition to follow public opinion. These journalistic assumptions are welcome by politicians who deliberately obscure their undemocratic uses of survey research to avoid public examination. Indeed, the history of government survey research confirms this fear, and it highlights the value of a watchful press. Investigations of the public opinion research by President Kennedy and the British wartime government produced intense public outcry against what was derided as "snooping" and government excess. The government responses are telling—President Kennedy scaled back his survey work and kept results of what was done in Robert Kennedy's safe in the Justice Department, and the wartime British government similarly reduced its surveillance of the public.[48]

Survey research is a tool. The issue is how it is used. Sustained and intense scrutiny of the often secretive use of survey research by presidents and other government officials is essential for encouraging responsiveness and raising the stakes for its undemocratic uses.

Notes

1. I would like to acknowledge the research assistance of Melanie Burns and the helpful feedback of Bob Shapiro.
2. Samuel Kernell, *Going Public: New Strategies of Presidential Leadership*, 3rd ed. (Washington, DC: Congressional Quarterly Press, 1997); Jeffrey Tulis, *The Rhetorical Presidency* (Princeton, NJ: Princeton University Press, 1987); Lawrence R. Jacobs and Melanie Burns, "The Second Face of the Public Presidency: Presidential Polling and the Shift from Policy to Personality Polling," *Presidential Studies Quarterly* 34 (2004, Fall): 536–56.
3. For fuller discussion of polling history, see Robert M. Eisinger, *The Evolution of Presidential Polling* (Cambridge: Cambridge University Press, 2003); Diane Heath, *Polling to Govern: Public Opinion and Presidential Leadership*, (Stanford, CA: Stanford University Press, 2003); Susan Herbst, *Numbered Voices: How Opinion Polling Has Shaped American Politics* (Chicago: University of Chicago Press, 1993).
4. George Gallup and Saul Rae, *The Pulse of Democracy* (New York: Simon and Schuster, 1940), pp. 14–15.
5. Warren E. Miller and Donald Stokes, "Constituency Influence in Congress," *American Political Science Review* 57 (1963): 45–56; Benjamin I. Page and Robert Y. Shapiro, "Effects of Public Opinion on Policy," *American Political Science Review* 77 (1983): 175–90; Robert S. Erikson, Michael B. MacKuen, and James A. Stimson, *The Macro Polity* (Cambridge: Cambridge University Press, 2002); Larry Bartels, *Unequal Democracy: The Political Economy of the New Gilded Age* (Princeton, NJ: Princeton University Press, 2008); Lawrence Jacobs and Theda Skocpol, *Inequality and American Democracy: What We Know and What We Need To Learn* (New York: Russell Sage Press, 2005).
6. Lindsay Rogers, *The Pollsters: Public Opinion, Politics and Democratic Leadership* (New York: Knopf, 1949); Herbert Blumler, "Public Opinion and Public Opinion Polling," *American Sociological Review* 13 (1948): 542–54.
7. Steven Kull, "Expecting More Say: A study of American public attitudes on

the role of the public in government decisions," Report by Center on Policy Attitudes (1999); "Public Appetite for Government Misjudged," Pew Research Center for the People and the Press (1998, April 17); Lawrence R. Jacobs and Robert Y. Shapiro, *Politicians Don't Pander: Political Manipulation and the Loss of Democratic Responsiveness* (Chicago: University of Chicago Press, 2000).

8. Giovanni Sartori, *The Theory of Democracy Revisited* (New York: Chatham House, 1987); Brandice Canes-Wrone, Michael C. Herron, and Kenneth W. Shotts, "Leadership and Pandering: A Theory of Executive Policymaking," *American Journal of Political Science* 45, no. 3 (2001, July): 532–50.

9. Tulis, *Rhetorical Presidency.*

10. Kernell, *Going Public.*

11. Eisenger, *Evolution of Presidential Polling*; Heith, *Polling to Govern*; Diane Heith, "Staffing the White House Public Opinion Apparatus: 1969–1988," *Public Opinion Quarterly* 62 (1998, Summer): 165–89; Jacobs and Burns, "The Second Face of the Public Presidency."

12. Lawrence R. Jacobs and Melinda Jackson, "Presidential Leadership and the Threat to Popular Sovereignty: Building an appealing image to dodge unpopular policy issues in the Nixon White House," in *Polls, Politics, and the Dilemmas of Democracy,* ed. Matt Streb (Albany, NY: SUNY Press, 2004).

13. Anthony Downs, *An Economic Theory of Democracy* (New York: Harper Row, 1957); Duncan Black, *The Theory of Committees and Elections* (Cambridge: Cambridge University Press, 1958).

14. Richard F. Fenno Jr., *Home Style* (New York: Little Brown, 1978); William T. Bianco; *Trust: Representatives and Constituents* (Ann Arbor: University of Michigan Press, 1994), pp. 36–37.

15. John H. Aldrich, *Why Parties? The Origin and Transformation of Political Parties in America* (Chicago: University of Chicago Press, 1995).

16. *Weekly Compilation of Presidential Documents.* (Washington, D.C.: Government Printing Office, distributor, 1965–); *Public Papers of the Presidents of the United States* (Washington, D.C.: Government Printing Office, distributor, 1965–).

17. Lawrence R. Jacobs and Robert Y. Shapiro, "Lyndon Johnson, Vietnam, and Public Opinion: Rethinking Realists' Theory of Leadership," *Presidential Studies Quarterly* 29 (1999, September): 592–616.

18. Jacobs and Shapiro, "Lyndon Johnson, Vietnam, and Public Opinion."

19. LBJ, Ex FG165, Memo to LBJ from J. Gardner, December 19, 1966; LBJ, Panzer, Box 217, Memo from H. Redmon to B. Moyers, December 17, 1965; Microfilm, Reel 46 (#124), Memo to Bundy, Moyers, Valenti, and Cater, December 14, 1965 (author not indicated); LBJ, Panzer File, Box 186, "A Survey of Political Climate in New York City," March 1965, by Oliver Quayle.

20. Microfilm, Confidential Memo to M.W. Watson from N. Katzenbach, October 27, 1967.

21. The Vietnam question was the following: "Which of the following options below most closely resembles your opinion about U.S. policy in Vietnam? 1) Go all out, escalate (short of nuclear weapons) to secure a military victory; 2) Do as we are. Keep fighting but seek negotiated peace; 3) Stay in Vietnam, but reduce military operations; 4) Get out now, we have no business in Vietnam."

22. Microfilm, Reel 4 (#965), Memo to LBJ from Panzer, November 15, 1967.

23. LBJ, Memo to Cater from E. Duggan, May 31, 1966.
24. Interview with Fred Panzer by LRJ, November 12, 1992; LBJ, Moyers, Box 12, Memo to Moyers from Redmon, August 24, 1966. For instance, a November 1967 poll was commissioned to measure the impact of a several major presidential activities on the public's evaluation of Johnson, and another private poll measured the impact of Johnson's State of the Union address in January 1968. Microfilm, Reel 41, EX PR 16, Memo to LBJ from Panzer regarding Quayle national survey on Nov 20th, November 28, 1967; LBJ, Watson, Box 26, Memo to LBJ from Watson, January 1, 17, 1968 (with Johnson's handwritten comments).
25. LBJ, Moyers, Box 12, Memo to LBJ from Moyers, June 9, 1966; LBJ, Ex PR16, Box 349, Memo to LBJ from Cater, Ben Wattenberg, and Ervin Duggan regarding lunch with Scammon, August 19, 1967; LBJ, Ex PR16, Box 350, Memo to LBJ from Panzer, December 18, 1967; LBJ, Panzer, Box 397, Memo to LBJ from Panzer, February 27, 1968.
26. Jacobs and Shapiro, *Politicians Don't Pander.*
27. Terry Moe, "Presidents, Institutions and Theory," in *Researching the Presidency,* eds. George Edwards, John Kessel, and Bert Rockman (Pittsburgh, PA: University of Pittsburgh Press, 1993), pp. 337-86.
28. James Druckman and Lawrence R. Jacobs, "Lumpers and Splitters: The Public Opinion Information that Politicians Use," *Public Opinion Quarterly* 70 (2006): 453-76.
29. James Druckman and Lawrence R. Jacobs, "Segmented Representation: The Reagan White House and disproportionate responsiveness" (2006) Paper presented at the annual meeting of the American Political Science Association, Philadelphia, PA, August 31.
30. James David Barber, *The Presidential Character: Predicting Performance in the White House* (New York: Prentice Hall, 1992); George Goethals, "Presidential Leadership," *Annual Review of Psychology* 56 (2005): 545–70.
31. Carolyn Funk, "Bringing the Candidate into Models of Candidate Evaluation," *Journal of Politics* 61 (1999): 700–20; Matthew Mendelsohn, "The Media and Interpersonal Communications," *Journal of Politics* 58 (1996): 112–25; Benjamin I. Page, *Choice and Echoes in Presidential Elections* (Chicago: University of Chicago Press, 1978); Samuel L. Popkin, *The Reasoning Voter,* 2nd ed. (Chicago: University of Chicago Press, 1994).
32. Lawrence R. Jacobs and Robert Y. Shapiro, "Issues, Candidate Image and Priming: The Use of Private Polls in Kennedy's 1960 Presidential Campaign," *American Political Science Review* 2, no. 88 (1994, September): 527–40.
33. Louis Harris and Associates, "An Analysis of the Third Kennedy-Nixon Debate," October 19, 1960, box 45, Political, Pre-Administration, JFK/RFK Papers, Kennedy Library; interview with Harris by author, June 17, 1991.
34. Anthony Downs, *An Economic Theory of Democracy* (New York: Harper and Row, 1957).
35. James Druckman, Lawrence Jacobs, and Eric Ostermeier, "Candidate Strategies to Prime Issues and Image," *Journal of Politics* 66 (2004, November): 1205–27.
36. Quoted in Joshua Green, "The Other War Room," *Washington Monthly,* April 2002.
37. Gallup used the following question in its April 23–26, 2007, survey of 1,007 adults nationwide: "Now, thinking about the different sources Americans can turn to for insights on what the situation in Iraq is like. How reliable

a source of accurate information about current conditions in Iraq do you consider each of the following people to be: very reliable, somewhat reliable, not too reliable, or not reliable at all?"

38. Peter Feaver, "Go Negative on the Allies," *New York Times*, June 15, 2004.
39. David Brooks, "Heroes and History" *New York Times*, July 17, 2007.
40. A CNN/ORC survey during December 12–17, 2006, asked the following question: "Thinking about the following characteristics and qualities, please say whether you think it applies or doesn't apply to George W. Bush. How about...?" For the quality of "strong and decisive leader," 48 percent indicated that it applied to Bush and 51 percent indicated that it did not.
41. A Quinnipiac University April 25 to May 1, 2007, poll used the following question wording: "Do you support or oppose Congress setting a time-table for withdrawing all United States troops from Iraq?"
42. Randall Calvert, "The Value of Biased Information: A Rational Choice Model of Political Advice," *Journal of Politics* 47 (May 1985): 530–55.
43. Bartels, *Unequal Democracy*; Martin Gilens, "Inequality and Democratic Responsiveness," *Public Opinion Quarterly* 69, no. 5 (2005): 778–896; Helen Milner, *Interests, Institutions, and Information: Domestic Politics and International Relations* (Princeton, NJ: Princeton University Press, 1997); Robert Keohane, *International Institutions and State Power* (Boulder, CO: Westview Press, 1989); Ronald Rogowski, *Commerce and Coalitions* (Princeton, NJ: Princeton University Press, 1989); Lawrence R. Jacobs and Benjamin I. Page, "Who Influences U.S. Foreign Policy?" *American Political Science Review* 99 (2005, February), pp. 107–24.
44. Sidney Verba, Kay Schlozman, and Henry Brady, *Voice and Equality: Civic Volunteerism in American Politics* (Cambridge, MA: Harvard University Press, 1995).
45. Bartels, *Unequal Democracy*; Gilens, "Inequality and Democratic Responsiveness"; Jacobs and Page, "Who Influences U.S. Foreign Policy?"; Jacobs and Shapiro, *Politicians Don't Pander*.
46. Jacobs and Shapiro, *Politicians Don't Pander*, p. 106.
47. American Association for Public Opinion Research, "AAPOR Code of Professional Ethics & Practice" and "Survey Practices that AAPOR Condemns," downloaded May 12, 2010, http://www.aapor.org.
48. Lawrence R. Jacobs, *The Health of Nations: Public Opinion and the Making of Heath Policy in the U.S. and Britain* (Ithaca, NY: Cornell University Press, 1993).

9 The Political Economy of Mass Media

Implications for Informed Citizenship

Shanto Iyengar and Kyu S. Hahn

Informed citizenship is taken as fundamental to democratic governance. Deliberation, political participation, and holding elected officials accountable for their actions presuppose an electorate capable of expressing informed opinions. In modern democracies, the institution entrusted with delivering relatively costless access to public affairs information is the news media. In recent years, however, as outlined below, significant changes to the regulatory and economic framework within which news organizations function have called into question the media's ability to make good on this civic responsibility.

In this chapter, we focus on two key transformations in the media landscape. First, news organizations the world over are moving in the direction of a profit-driven or market-based model. Second, the revolution in information technology has set off an explosion in the quantity of media choices available to consumers. The net impact of these changes on the news audience is twofold. First, market pressures coupled with enhanced consumer choice have reduced the public's exposure to news programming, thus increasing the number of citizens who are either ignorant or misinformed about current affairs. Second, people who seek out news are increasingly turning to sources that provide a limited perspective on political issues, but one they find agreeable. Thus, the emerging media environment is unlikely to nurture voters' civic potential: on balance, more people will be in a position to tune out the news altogether, while those who tune in are exposed to a narrow range of perspectives on the issues of the day.

Explaining Levels of Information: Demand Versus Supply

Conventional theories of political knowledge posit that attributes of the news consumer (such as educational attainment) are the principal determinants of political knowledge. No matter how knowledge is defined—as textbook-based civic knowledge, the ability to locate the policy positions of political parties, or familiarity with current events and issues—scholars have treated indicators of political involvement or motivation as the key discriminators between the more and less informed.[1] The list of "usual suspects" includes generic interest in politics (e.g., How often do you follow news about government and public affairs?) and the strength of an individual's partisan affiliation (strong partisans are more informed). The argument is that people with stronger political drive regularly pay closer attention to the news and current events.

The demand for political information can also be considered a question of resources. The educated and affluent have more time to keep abreast of the news; for them the opportunity costs of staying informed are lower.[2] Socioeconomic standing also confers stronger material incentives for paying attention to the political world—the more affluent are likely to accrue non-trivial economic benefits through political action, thus making it worthwhile for them to "invest" in the acquisition of information.

In fact, the connection between socio-economic factors and political information is well-documented. For instance, familiarity with topics in the news—across a variety of subjects—was significantly higher among more educated Americans.[3]

Other dispositional or individual-level antecedents of the demand for political information include cultural norms that predispose individuals to become involved in politics. These norms include the sense of political efficacy or competence and civic duty. Efficacy consists of two constituent beliefs, corresponding to internal and external targets. Internal efficacy refers to the individual's self-perception that she is capable of exercising political influence, while external efficacy reflects perceptions of governmental institutions and electoral processes as responsive to public opinion. Efficacy is thus a proxy for the expectation that individuals can intervene successfully in the political process; the efficacious citizen participates because he expects that his actions will make a difference.

Unlike efficacy, the norm of civic duty provides a non-instrumental and more unconditional basis for acquiring political information. The dutiful citizen values political involvement in and of itself no matter what the probability of having an impact and irrespective of the question of anticipated benefits.

A final set of individual-level explanations of political information concern social networks and interpersonal cues.[4] Most forms of political participation are social and people with stronger social ties are more likely to experience pressures to behave in conformity with small group or community norms. Regular church goers and those active in their neighborhood association are not only more likely to encounter meaningful political information through these contacts, but also to consider it important that they keep abreast of political issues and events.

Although it is clearly important to understand the individual-level factors that discriminate between attentive and inattentive citizens, variations in political knowledge can also be considered a byproduct of the political context. Most notably, the sheer amount and frequency of news programming made available on a daily basis is an important conditioning variable that makes it more or less difficult for individuals to acquire information. When news coverage is both substantive in content and delivered regularly, the motivational threshold for becoming informed declines because the less motivated have greater opportunities to encounter the news.[5] Conversely, for people exposed to information-poor environments, or environments where there is an abundance of entertainment-oriented programs, motivational factors become even more important as explanations of information.[6] In these contexts, the acquisition of information becomes more challenging and concentrated among individuals who self-select into the news audience. Thus, the prevailing level of information is necessarily a function of *both* demand and supply side variables. Decreases in the supply of information work to strengthen the importance of motivational factors.

National Media Systems as Information Contexts

Communications scholars have documented systematic variations in the ownership, regulation, and reach of news organizations across the world.[7] The most basic difference is between market-based and public service oriented systems. In market-based systems, all major news organizations are privately owned and subject to minimal government regulation. Public service systems feature governmental ownership and regulatory control over major broadcast news organizations. These properties of national media systems have important implications for the supply and content of news.

In countries with predominantly market-based media systems, news programming tends to be less frequent and more entertainment-centered. However, in countries that actively support public broadcasting and enforce programming requirements on both public and private broadcasters, news content is less "soft" and media users have more frequent opportunities to encounter news programming. Thus, one fundamental difference between market-based and public service oriented media systems concerns the supply of hard news.

Market and public service media systems also differ in the attention devoted to international news. Market-based systems have gradually increased their ratio of domestic to international news as individual news organizations have been forced to scale back on their overseas presence. The major television networks in the United States, for instance, now maintain only a handful of foreign bureaus.[8] Public broadcasting systems, by contrast, have maintained an active presence across the globe.

Finally, and most importantly, market- and public service based systems differ in the availability and timing of news programming. Public service regimes typically deliver multiple daily news broadcasts during the peak hours of the broadcast day. The major television channels in Finland and Denmark, for example, air their main news programs at multiple time slots between 6 p.m. and 10 p.m. Britain's top three television channels broadcast news at 6 p.m., 6:30 p.m., 7 p.m., 10 p.m., and 10:30 p.m. In contrast, market systems offer fewer regularly scheduled newscasts, typically one or two programs per day. The three major American television networks, for instance, transmit their respective national newscasts in the early evening and reserve prime time hours for entertainment programs.

The fact that television news programs in public service systems air more frequently—and are often delivered adjacent to popular entertainment programs such as sporting events—means that *exposure to news is less dependent on individuals' level of interest or motivation*. In effect, the airing of news programs during prime time significantly increases the inadvertent audience for news—individuals who encounter news reports while seeking to be entertained. (We will return to the question of the inadvertent audience in a later section.)

The increased accessibility of news programming, as already noted, has a leveling effect on the distribution of political information. Differences in the level of information between the most and least motivated strata of the public—the so-called knowledge gap—will be narrowed in public service systems because the less motivated find it more difficult to avoid exposure to the news.[9] Conversely, given the reduced opportunities to encounter news programming during prime time, the scope of the knowledge gap will be widened in market systems.

Cross-National Differences in Information

The available evidence on cross-national differences in political knowledge tends to support the prediction that citizens exposed to market-based media will be less informed than their counterparts in public service systems. In the particular case of foreign affairs information, and despite their significant advantage in years of formal education, Americans continue to lag behind citizens of other industrialized democracies. In 1994, for example, citizens of Spain, Italy, Canada, Germany, Britain, and France were generally more likely to provide correct answers to a series of questions tapping knowledge at international affairs. Using the percentage of each national sample unable to provide the correct answer to a single question as the indicator of public ignorance, the level of ignorance was twice as high in the United States: 37 percent of the American sample was classified as ignorant compared with an average of 19 percent for Italy, France, Britain, Germany, and Canada.[10]

Dimock and Popkin have argued that the significantly lower levels of international affairs information in the United States can be attributed to significant cross-national differences in the "communication of knowledge," i.e., the greater prominence of public broadcasting networks in

Europe that devote significant attention to international news.[11] Their conjecture is bolstered by evidence that Europeans who report more extensive use of their country's public television newscasts display greater levels of information about the European Union than those who watch commercial channels.[12]

The most extensive test of the media systems hypothesis comes from a four-nation study covering the United States, Britain, Denmark, and Finland. The countries in this study—all industrialized liberal democracies—represent three distinct locations in the space defined by the market versus public service continuum. Denmark and Finland are closest to a relatively pure public service media model in which stringent programming and regulatory principles still dominate. At the other extreme, the United States exemplifies a pure market-based regime. In between, Britain represents a hybrid media system that combines increasingly deregulated commercial media with strong public service broadcasting.[13]

The authors of the four-nation study coupled a systematic content analysis of television newscasts and newspapers with national surveys designed to measure public awareness of domestic and international news stories, both hard and soft. The results of the content analysis were consistent with the anticipated differences between market-based and public service systems: news reports in the United States and Britain featured substantially more soft than hard news, while Danish and Finnish news coverage was predominantly hard.

The content analysis further revealed significant cross-national differences in the level of international news. As expected, American media were preoccupied with domestic news. The American television networks allocated 20 percent of their newscasts to foreign news (of which nearly half concerned Iraq). In contrast, European public service television channels devoted significantly more attention to international news. As a proportion of programming time, foreign news coverage on the main news channels in Britain and Finland amounted to nearly twice the level in the United States.[14]

The survey responses to the political knowledge questions mirrored the findings of the content analysis. The researchers devised a large battery of questions to measure citizens' awareness of both hard and soft news as well as their familiarity with domestic versus international subject matter. A series of questions tapping awareness of international events and personalities (both hard and soft) were asked in all four countries. This common set included an equal number of relatively easy (international news subjects that received extensive reporting within each country) and difficult (those that received relatively infrequent coverage) questions. For example, the common questions included one asking respondents to identify "Taliban" and the incoming President of France (Sarkozy); more difficult questions included the location of the Tamil Tigers separatist movement and the identity of the former ruler of Serbia.

In the arena of soft news, relatively easy questions focused on highly visible targets such as the video sharing website YouTube and the French footballer Zinedine Zidane. Relatively difficult questions addressed the site of the 2008 summer Olympics and the identity of a professional tennis player (Maria Sharapova).

A different set of survey questions—specific to each country—tapped awareness of domestic news. Most of these questions addressed recognition of public officials and current political controversies. Domestic soft news questions focused primarily on national celebrities, either entertainers or professional athletes. Once again, these items were selected so as to match the difficulty level across countries.

As anticipated, the survey results showed that Americans were especially ignorant about hard news subjects. Overall, the average percent of the American sample that answered the hard news items correctly was 50 percent. This contrasted with 63, 70, and 75 percent in Britain, Denmark, and Finland, respectively. In the case of soft news, the results were as anticipated in one respect, namely, Americans were more likely to answer the soft news questions correctly (the average answering correctly increased from 50 to 63 percent). However, contrary to expectations, the Americans actually trailed the Europeans in the overall level of soft news information.

Turning to international news, the survey results revealed that Americans' knowledge was truly limited. American respondents averaged a 41 percent level of information on international news subjects. In contrast, the comparable averages for British, Finnish, and Danish respondents were 69, 66, and 65 percent, respectively. Clearly, Americans are substantially less familiar with international events than are Europeans.[15]

In general, the cross-national differences in knowledge paralleled the differences in the content of news programming. The U.S. market-based media tend to under produce both hard and international news; Americans are poorly informed about both.

The cross-national study investigated one further difference between market-based and public service media systems, namely, the scope of the knowledge gap on both hard and international news. As discussed earlier, the researchers anticipated that the greater frequency of broadcast news programming in public service systems would increase the probability of chance encounters with news reports. As a result, the knowledge gap between the more and less motivated strata of the citizenry would be enlarged in market systems. The results fully supported these expectations.

As shown in Figure 9.1, a citizen's level of education was a powerful predictor of both international and domestic affairs knowledge in the United States, but proved significantly less consequential in Finland or Denmark. In Scandinavia, where public service requirements continue to be imposed on the broadcast media including commercial broadcasters,

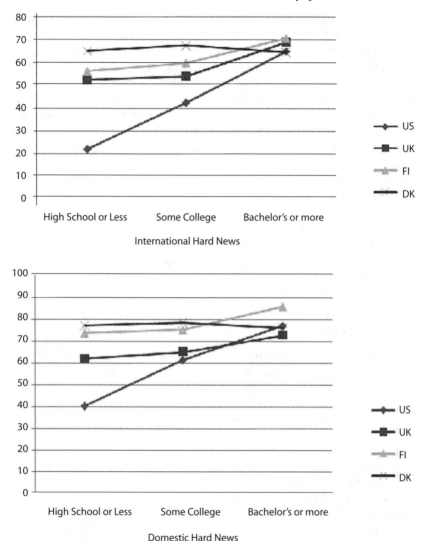

Figure 9.1 Knowledge Gaps Associated with Level of Education. Source: May 2007, four-nation survey of political knowledge (Curran et al., 2008).

the flow of news programming is more extensive and occurs at multiple points during the programming day, making it more likely that relatively apathetic viewers will manage to encounter public affairs information at least on a sporadic basis.

The greater availability of broadcast news is only part of the explanation of the reduced knowledge gap in public service oriented media systems. In these nations, public broadcasters, who have a mandate to serve all sections of society, have been relatively successful in getting disadvantaged groups to join in the national ritual of watching the evening television news. Much higher proportions of the less educated and less affluent watch television news on a regular basis in Finland or Denmark than in the United States.[16] Thus, the knowledge gap between more and less educated citizens may be further reduced in public service oriented systems because public broadcasters make greater attempts to reach all educational levels. By contrast, commercial media prioritize affluent, high spending audiences in order to maximize advertising revenue.

In conclusion, the available cross-national evidence supports the inference that media systems are an important ingredient of the individual citizen's information environment. Public service media deliver more informative news programming and make their news coverage more accessible. Europeans are more familiar than Americans with international news and hard news because their news media are more likely to focus on this subject matter. Americans find questions about hard or international news more challenging because American media focus more extensively on domestic and soft news. The information context affects how much people know about public affairs.

The Effects of New Media

The emergence of new forms of mass communication in the aftermath of the information technology revolution represents a dramatic change in the information context. On the surface, we might expect significant gains in civic information in the era of new media given the exponential increase in the supply of information. After all, citizens interested in the American presidential election have access to thousands of online sources ranging from unknown bloggers to well-established news organizations whose reports and views receive wide circulation through email, viral videos, and other forms of content sharing.

But the availability of more information in the era of new media does not necessarily translate into greater exposure to information. The output of thousands of news sources has created the imminent prospect of information overload; it is humanly impossible to process information on this scale. The immediate question for communication researchers, therefore, concerns consumers' coping strategies; that is, just how do they sort through this vast array of news sources and decide where they get the news?

The question is particularly challenging because the use of newer forms of information is correlated with not only demographic attributes (e.g., age), but also with levels of political motivation. It is well established, for instance, that the young disproportionately avoid conventional news channels and choose instead to congregate in online interactive environments where they are co-producers of messages. Similarly, people who seek out news on the Internet are much more involved in political life than their counterparts who spend their time online shopping for travel bargains or long-lost relatives. Thus, the audience for new media is especially subject to processes of self-selection.

The Fragmentation of the Audience

One of the most striking consequences of the expanded menu of media choices is increased competition for audiences and the erosion of individual news organizations' market share. The more competitive media market has made it less likely that all Americans will be exposed to the same news.

Fifty years ago, Americans depended primarily on television news, and the dominant sources of public affairs information were the daily evening newscasts broadcast by the three major networks. The norms of objective journalism meant that no matter which network voters tuned in to, they encountered the same set of news reports, according balanced attention to parties, candidates, or points of view.[17] In the era of "old media," accordingly, it made little difference where voters obtained their news. The flow of news amounted to an "information commons." Americans of all walks of life and political inclination encountered the same stream of information.

The development of cable television in the 1980s and the explosion of Internet-based media outlets more recently both created a more heterogeneous information environment in which political commentary, talk radio, twenty-four-hour news outlets, and myriad non-political outlets all compete for attention. The rapid diffusion of new media makes available a much wider range of media choices, providing greater variability in the content of available information. This means that stratification and fragmentation of the audience are occurring at the same time. Stratification occurs by level of political involvement: the mainstream media continue to matter for the attentive public, but more and more people are abandoning mainstream news in favor of web-based and more interactive sources of information, most of which provide minimal political content. Thus, on the one hand, the typical citizen (who is relatively uninterested in politics) can avoid news programming altogether by tuning in to ESPN or the Food Network on a continuous basis. On the other hand, the attentive citizen—facing a multiplicity of news sources—is forced to exercise some form of selective exposure to news.

The Demise of the Inadvertent Audience

The premise of this chapter is that some minimal level of exposure to information facilitates the exercise of citizenship. In the first section of the chapter, we argued that the acquisition of information depends on both the availability and supply of news as well as individual-level attentiveness or demand. As outlined below, it is the demand or motivational side of the information function that is most affected by changes in the media landscape.

During the heyday of network news, when the combined audience for the three evening newscasts exceeded 70 million, exposure to political information was less affected by the demand for information because many Americans were exposed to television news as a simple byproduct of their loyalty to the entertainment program that immediately followed the news.[18] These viewers may have been watching television rather than television news. Although precise estimates are not available, it is likely that this inadvertent audience may have accounted for half the total audience for network news.[19]

During the heyday of broadcast news, the massive size of the audience meant that television had a leveling effect on the distribution of information. The evening news reached not only those motivated to tune in, but also people with generally low levels of political interest, thus allowing the latter group to catch up with their more attentive counterparts. But once the networks' hold on the national audience was loosened, first by the advent of cable, then by the profusion of local news programming, and eventually by the Internet, some minimal exposure to news was no longer a given for the great majority of Americans. Between 1968 and 2003, the total audience for network news fell by more than 30 million viewers. The decline in news consumption occurred disproportionately among the less politically engaged segments of the audience, thus making exposure to information more closely correlated with the demand for news programming. Since exposure to news was more contingent on motivational factors, the knowledge gap between the haves and have-nots expanded. Paradoxically, just as technology has made possible a flow of information hitherto unimaginable, the size of the total audience for news has shrunk substantially.

In any given society, the knowledge gap is mainly a reflection of differing levels of demand for information. As noted in the preceding section, demand is contingent on basic cultural norms such as a sense of community identity and civic pride or duty. As these norms have weakened, so too have the psychological incentives for acquiring political information. The principal implication is that under conditions of enhanced consumer choice, the knowledge gap between more and less motivated citizens widens.[20] Thus, part of the explanation for the increased width of the knowledge gap in the United States (as compared with European nations) may be the higher level of media choices on offer.

To reiterate, the increased availability of media channels and sources makes it possible for people who care little about political debates to evade the reach of news programming. As a result, this group is likely to possess very little information about political issues and events, thus increasing the size of the knowledge gap.

Selective Exposure among Information Seekers

The demise of the inadvertent audience is symptomatic of one form of selective exposure —avoidance of political messages among the politically uninvolved members of the audience. But technology and the increasing quantity of news supply also makes it necessary for the politically attentive to exercise some form of choice when seeking information. As outlined below, there are two principal forms of selective exposure mechanisms, reflecting either individuals' partisan predispositions or issue agendas.

Partisan Selectivity

Ever since the development of consistency theories of persuasion and attitude change in the 1950s, communications researchers have hypothesized that a person's exposure to political information will reflect individual partisan leanings. In other words, people will avoid information that they expect will be discrepant or disagreeable and seek out information that is expected to be congruent with their pre-existing attitudes.[21]

In the days of old media, selecting conventional news sources on the basis of partisan preference was relatively difficult given the demise of the partisan press in the nineteenth century. But during campaigns, voters could still gravitate to their preferred candidate, and several studies documented the tendency of partisans to report greater exposure to appeals from the candidate or party they preferred.[22] Early voting researchers deemed this preference for in-party exposure antithetical to the democratic ideal of reasoned choice. As Lazarsfeld, Berelson, and Gaudet put it,

> In recent years there has been a good deal of talk by men of good will about the desirability and necessity of guaranteeing the free exchange of ideas in the market place of public opinion. Such talk has centered upon the problem of keeping free the channels of expression and communication. Now we find that the consumers of ideas, if they have made a decision on the issue, themselves erect high tariff walls against alien notions.[23]

Initially, research on selective exposure to information in the era of mass media yielded equivocal results. In several instances, what seemed to be motivated or deliberate selective exposure turned out to occur on a de facto or byproduct basis instead: for instance, people were more likely to encounter attitude congruent information as a result of their social milieu rather than any active choices to avoid incongruent information.[24]

It is not a coincidence that the increased availability of news sources has been accompanied by increasing political polarization. Over time, polarization appears to have spread to the level of mass public opinion.[25] For instance, Democrats' and Republicans' negative evaluations of a president of the other party have steadily intensified.[26] The presidential approval data reveal a widening chasm between Republicans and Democrats; the percentage of partisans who respond at the extremes ("strong approval" or "strong disapproval") has increased significantly over time. In fact, polarized assessments of presidential performance are higher today than at any other time in recent history, including the months preceding the resignation of President Nixon.

Given the presence of inter-party animus, it is not surprising that media choices increasingly reflect partisan considerations. People who feel strongly about the correctness of their cause or policy preferences are more likely to seek out information they believe is consistent with their preferences. But while as recently as twenty-five years ago these partisans would have been hard-pressed to find overtly partisan sources of information, today the task is relatively simple. In the case of Republicans, all they need to do is tune in to Fox News or *The O'Reilly Factor.* More recently, viewers on the left have found credible news programming on MSNBC.

The more diversified information environment makes it not only more feasible for consumers to seek out news they might find agreeable, but also provides a strong economic incentive for news organizations to cater to their viewers' political preferences.[27] The emergence of Fox News as the leading cable news provider is testimony to the viability of this "niche news" paradigm. Between 2000 and 2004, while Fox News increased the size of its regular audience by some 50 percent, the other cable providers showed no growth.[28]

There is a growing body of evidence suggesting that politically polarized consumers are motivated to exercise greater selectivity in their news choices. In the first place, in keeping with the well-known "hostile media" phenomenon, partisans of either side have become more likely to impute bias to mainstream news sources.[29] Cynical assessments of the media have surged most dramatically among conservatives; according to a Pew Research Center for the People and the Press survey, Republicans are twice as likely as Democrats to rate major news outlets (such as the three network newscasts, the weekly news magazines, National Public Radio (NPR), and the Public Broadcasting Service (PBS)) as biased.[30] In the aftermath of the *New York Times'* front-page story on Senator McCain's alleged affair with a lobbyist, the McCain campaign was able to use this "liberal attack" as a significant fund-raising appeal.[31] Given their perceptions of hostile bias in the mainstream media environment, partisans of both sides have begun to explore alternative sources of news. During the 2000 and 2004 campaigns, Republicans were more frequent users of talk radio, while Democrats avoided talk radio and tuned in to late night entertainment television.[32]

Experimental studies of news consumption further confirm the tendency of partisans to self-select into distinct audiences. In one online study administered on a national sample, the researchers manipulated the source of news stories in five different subject matter areas ranging from national politics and the Iraq War to vacation destinations and sports.[33] Depending on the condition to which participants were assigned, the very same news headline was attributed either to Fox News, NPR, CNN, or the BBC. Participants were asked which of the four different headlines they would prefer to read, if any. The results were unequivocal: Republicans and conservatives were much more likely to select news stories from Fox, while Democrats and liberals avoided Fox in favor of NPR and CNN. What was especially striking about the pattern of results was that the selection applied not only to hard news (i.e., national politics, the war in Iraq, healthcare), but also to soft news stories about travel and sports. The polarization of the news audience extends even to nonpolitical subject matter. The partisan homogenization of the Fox audience is also confirmed in a Pew national survey reported in Bennett and Manheim.[34]

There is reason to think that the interaction between increasingly individualized reality construction and proliferating personal media platforms has accelerated in just the last few years. For example, the news selection study reported earlier revealed strong evidence of partisan polarization in news selection, yet seven years earlier, in a similar study of exposure to campaign rhetoric, the researchers could detect only modest traces of partisan selectivity.[35] In this study, the investigators compiled a large selection of campaign speeches by the two major presidential candidates (Al Gore and George W. Bush) along with a full set of the candidates' television advertisements. This material was assembled on an interactive, multi-media CD and distributed to a representative sample of registered voters with Internet access a few weeks before the election. Participants were informed that they were free to use the CD as they saw fit and that their usage would be recorded on their computer. Following the election, they were provided instructions for downloading and transmitting the data to the market research firm from which they received the CD.

The CD tracking data in this study showed only modest traces of a preference for information from the in-party candidate. Republicans and conservatives were significantly more likely to seek out information from the Bush campaign, but liberals and Democrats showed no preference for Gore over Bush speeches or advertisements. These findings suggest either that the intensity of partisan identity is higher among Republicans, or that selective exposure has become habitual among Republicans because they were provided earlier opportunities than Democrats (with the launch of the Fox Network in 1986) to engage in biased information seeking. The news selection study, conducted in 2007, suggests that Democrats are now keeping pace; in 2000, very few Democrats in the CD study showed an aversion to speeches from Governor Bush, but by 2007 hardly any Democrats selected Fox News as a preferred news source.

Issue Salience as a Basis for Selective Exposure

People may respond to the problem of information overload by paying particular attention to issues they most care about while ignoring others. Given that citizens' vote choices are based, at least in part, on their perceived agreement-disagreement with the candidates on salient issues, it is likely that they will seek out information that reveals the candidates' attitudes on those same issues. Thus, members of an issue public will be especially motivated to encounter information on "their" issue.

Price and Zaller tested the issue salience-based exposure hypothesis, although only indirectly.[36] They examined whether people whose characteristics suggested they might belong to a particular issue public were more able to recall recent news on the issue. They found support for the issue public hypothesis in about half of their tests. In another related investigation, Iyengar found that recall of news reports about social security and racial discrimination increased significantly among older and minority viewers, respectively.[37] This study found other evidence consistent with the issue public hypothesis as well: African Americans, for instance, though less informed than whites on typical "civics knowledge" questions, proved more informed on matters pertaining to race and civil rights.[38] Burns, Schlozman, and Verba (2000) reported parallel findings on gender and information about women's issues: women knew more than men.[39]

The most direct evidence concerning the effects of issue salience on information-seeking behavior is provided by the CD study described earlier. The authors tested the issue public hypothesis by examining whether CD users with higher levels of concern for particular issues also paid more attention to the candidates' positions on those issues. In terms of their design, the key outcome measure was amount of CD usage: did issue public members register more page visits for issues of interest? The findings supported the hypothesis in multiple policy domains including healthcare, education, and abortion. In terms of CD usage, members of issue publics registered between 38 percent and 80 percent more usage than non-members.[40]

In summary, a media environment featuring an abundance of consumer choice implies first that we will witness increasing inequality in the acquisition of political information. The haves will find it easier to keep abreast of political events, and the have-nots will find it easier to ignore political discussion altogether. Second, the increased availability of information implies an important degree of selective exposure to political information. Among the relatively attentive stratum, partisans will gravitate to information from favored sources, while ignoring sources or arguments from the opposing side. Information seekers also limit their attention span to issues that affect them most directly. Meanwhile, the large ranks of inadvertent citizens remain disconnected from the political world, frustrating those who attempt to communicate with them, fueling the costs of political communication, while diminishing the effects.

General Implications

The emerging changes in the American news environment are likely to exacerbate inequalities in the distribution of information. The less informed—who are most in need of exposure to news—will fall further behind their more-informed counterparts. And even though the presence of new media makes it possible for the more attentive segments of the citizenry to expand the breadth of news sources they encounter, the tendency of individuals to rely on familiar and comforting sources means, at least in a normative sense, that citizens are less able to deliberate over questions of public policy.

From the perspective of ownership, the changing composition of the news audience is promising. As this audience increasingly polarizes over questions of politics and ideology, rational media owners stand to gain market share by injecting more rather than less political bias into the news.[41] The emergence of Fox News as the cable ratings leader suggests that in a competitive market, politically slanted news programming meets demand and allows a new organization to create a distinct niche for itself.

The Fox experience is likely to result in other news sources following suit. Recent theoretical work in economics, for instance, shows that under competition and diversity of opinion, daily newspapers will provide content that is more biased: "Competition forces newspapers to cater to the prejudices of their readers, and greater competition typically results in more aggressive catering to such prejudices as competitors strive to divide the market."[42] In the world of cable television, the significant increase in the ratings enjoyed by MSNBC is especially revealing. The network's fastest-growing evening program is *Countdown with Keith Olbermann*. This program, which has frequently won the daily ratings contest with Fox, conveys an unabashedly anti-conservative perspective. The network now plans to "to showcase its nighttime lineup as a welcome haven for viewers of a similar mind."[43] When the audience is polarized, "news with an edge" makes for market success.

The evidence concerning the effects of partisan bias on news consumption and production is generally consistent with the argument that technology narrows rather than widens the news audience's political horizons. Over time, avoidance of disagreeable information may become habitual so that users turn to their preferred sources automatically no matter what the subject matter. By relying on biased but favored providers, consumers will be able to "wall themselves off from topics and opinions that they would prefer to avoid."[44] The end result will be a less informed and more polarized electorate, with the political communication game aimed, paradoxically, at those who have largely tuned out.

The increasingly self-selected composition of audiences has important consequences for those who study media effects. Survey researchers, who rely on self-reported measures of news exposure, will find it increasingly difficult to treat exposure as a potential cause of political beliefs or attitudes. Those who say they read a particular newspaper or watch a network newscast are likely to differ systematically in their political attitudes, and it will be imperative that survey-based analyses disentangle the reciprocal effects of media exposure and political attitudes or behaviors.

Self-selection also has consequences for experimental research. Actual exposure to political messages in the real world is no longer analogous to random assignment. As we have noted, news and public affairs information can easily be avoided by choice, meaning that exposure is limited to the politically engaged strata. Thus, as Hovland pointed out, manipulational control actually weakens the ability to generalize to the real world where exposure to politics is typically voluntary.[45] Accordingly, it is important that experimental researchers use designs that combine manipulation with self-selection of exposure.

In substantive terms, we anticipate that the fragmentation of the national audience reduces the likelihood of attitude change in response to particular patterns of news. The persuasion and framing paradigms require some observable level of attitude change in response to a media stimulus. As media audiences devolve into smaller, like-minded subsets of the electorate, it becomes less likely that media messages will do anything other than reinforce prior predispositions. Most media users will rarely find themselves in the path of attitude-discrepant information.

The increasing level of political polarization will further bring into question findings of significant media-induced persuasion effects. Findings suggesting that audiences have shifted their position in response to some message will be suspect because discrete media audiences tend to self-select for preference congruence. Further, those who choose to watch the news will be more resistant to any messages that prove discrepant; thus, we would expect to observe reinforcement effects *even when voters encounter one-sided news at odds with their partisan priors.* For example, after the revelations in the news media that the Bush administration's pre-war intelligence claims were ill-founded, the percentage of Republicans giving an affirmative response when asked whether the United States had found weapons of mass destruction (WMD) in Iraq remained essentially unchanged, while at the same time the percentage of Democrats giving a "no WMD" response increased by about 30 percentage points.[46] In short, the Republicans remained unaffected by a tidal wave of discrepant information.

The increasing level of selective exposure based on partisan preference thus presages a new era of minimal consequences, at least insofar as persuasive effects are concerned. But other forms of media influence, such as indexing, agenda-setting or priming may continue to be important. Put differently, selective exposure is more likely to erode the influence of the tone or valence of news messages (vis-à-vis elected officials or policy positions), but may not similarly undermine media effects that are based on the sheer volume of news.

The stratification of the news audience based on level of political involvement, however, conveys a very different set of implications. The fact that significant numbers of Americans are chronically unexposed to news programming means that this segment of the electorate knows little about the course of current issues or events. On those infrequent instances when they can be reached by political messages, therefore, they are easily persuadable.[47] When political events reach the stage of national crises and news about these events achieves a decibel level that is sufficiently deafening even for those preoccupied with entertainment, the impact of the news on these individuals' attitudes will be immediate and dramatic. In the case of the events preceding the U.S. invasion of Iraq, for instance, many Americans came to believe the Bush administration's claims about the rationale for the invasion, since that was the only account provided by news organizations.[48] In short, during periods of high-profile and one-sided news coverage of particular issues, the inattentive audience can be manipulated by the sources that shape the news.

In summary, the changing shape of the American media universe has made it increasingly unlikely that the views of the attentive strata of the audience will be subject to any media influence. But as increasing numbers of Americans fall outside the reach of the news, they become both less informed about current affairs and more susceptible to the persuasive appeals of political elites.

Notes

1. For a discussion of alternative definitions of political knowledge, see Michael Schudson, *The Good Citizen: A History of American Civic Life* (New York: Free Press, 1998).
2. See Steven J. Rosenstone and John Mark Hansen, *Mobilization, Participation, and Democracy in America* (New York: Longman, 1993).
3. Vincent Price and John R. Zaller, "Who Gets the News?: Alternative Measures of News Reception and Their Implications for Research," *Public Opinion Quarterly* 57 (1993): 133–64.
4. Robert Putnam, *Bowling Alone: The Collapse and Revival of American Community* (New York: Simon and Schuster, 2000); Diana C. Mutz, *Hearing the Other Side: Deliberative versus Participatory Democracy* (Cambridge: Cambridge University Press, 2006).
5. For a pioneering analysis of the joint effects of individual-level and contextual factors on knowledge, see Jennifer Jerit, Jason Barabas, and Toby Bolsen, "Citizens, Knowledge, and the Information Environment," *American Journal of Political Science* 50 (2006): 266–82.
6. Markus Prior, "Any Good News in Soft News? The Impact of Soft News Preference on Political Knowledge," *Political Communication* 20 (2003): 149–71; Markus Prior, "News v. Entertainment: How Increasing Media

Choice Widens Gaps in Political Knowledge and Turnout," *American Journal of Political Science* 49, no. 3 (2005): 594–609.

7. See for instance Daniel C. Hallin and Paolo Mancini, *Comparing Media Systems: Three Models of Media and Politics (Communication, Society and Politics)* (Cambridge: Cambridge University Press, 2004); and Jay Blumer and Michael Gurevitch, *The Crisis of Public Communication (Communication and Society)* (New York: Routledge, 1995).

8. See Claude Moisy, *The Foreign News Flow in the Information* Age (Cambridge, MA: Harvard University Press, 1996); Pippa Norris, "The Restless Spotlight: Network News Framing of the Post Cold-War World," *Political Communication* 12, no. 4 (1996): 357–70; Shanto Iyengar and Jennifer McGrady, *Media Politics: A Citizen's Guide* (New York: Norton, 2007).

9. Most research on the attentiveness-based knowledge gap has been conducted by researchers in mass communication; see Phillip J. Tichenor, George A. Donohue, and Clarice N. Olien, "Mass Media Flow and Differential Growth in Knowledge," *The Public Opinion Quarterly* 34 (1970): 159–70; B.K. Genova and B. Greenberg, "Interests in News and the Knowledge Gap," *The Public Opinion Quarterly* 43 (1979): 79–91;Cecile Gaziano, "The Knowledge Gap: An Analytical Review of Media Effects," *Communication Research* 10 (1983): 447–85; Nojin Kwak, "Revisiting the Knowledge Gap Hypothesis: Education, Motivation, and Media Use," *Communication Research* 26 (1999): 385–413; William P. Eveland and Dietram A. Scheufele, "Connecting News Media Use with Gaps in Knowledge and Participation," *Political Communication* 17 (2000): 215–37. Although the standard knowledge gap is typically defined in terms of socioeconomic status (e.g., education), there is also evidence of differential acquisition of information in relation to gender. See Jeffrey J. Mondak and Mary R. Anderson, "The Knowledge Gap: A Reexamination of Gender-Based Differences in Political Knowledge," *Journal of Politics* 66 (2004). 492–512.

10. Andrew Kohut, Robert C. Toth, and Carol Bowman, "Mixed Message about Free Press on both Sides of the Atlantic," Times Mirror Center for the People and the Press news release, March 16, 1994.

11. Samuel L. Popkin and Michael A. Dimock, "Knowledge, Trust and International Reasoning," in *Elements of Reason: Cognition, Choice, and the Bounds of Rationality*, eds. Arthur Lupia, Mathew D. McCubbins, and Samuel L. Popkin (Cambridge: Cambridge University Press, 1997), p. 223.

12. Christina Holtz-Bacha and Pippa Norris, "To Entertain, Inform, and Educate: Still the Role of Public Television in the 1990s?"*Political Communication* 18, no. 2 (2001): 123–40.

13. For a more detailed description of the four media systems, see James Curran, Shanto Iyengar, Anker Lund, and Inka Salovaara-Moring, "Media Systems, Public Knowledge and Democracy: A Comparative Study," *European Journal of Communication* 24 (2008): 5–26.

14. See Curran et al., "Media Systerms, Public Knowledge, and Democracy."

15. Indeed, the American-European gap was truly striking in some topics: for example, 62 percent of Americans were unable to identify the Kyoto Accords as a treaty on climate change, compared with a mere 20 percent in Finland and Denmark, and 39 percent in Britain.

16. See Curran et al., "Media Systems, Public Knowledge, and Democracy."

17. Michael J. Robinson and Margaret A. Sheehan, *Over the Wire and on TV: CBS and UPI in Campaign '80* (New York: Basic Books, 1983).

18. Michael J. Robinson, "Public Affairs Television and Growth of Political Malaise: The Case of the 'Selling of the Pentagon'," *American Political Sci-*

ence Review 70 (1976): 409–32; Markus Prior, *Post-Broadcast Democracy* (Cambridge: Cambridge University Press, 2007).

19. In Robinson's words, "Public Affairs Television and the Growth of Political Malaise," p. 426, the inadvertent audience consists of those who "fall into the news" as opposed to the more attentive audience that "watches for the news."

20. See Prior, "Any Good News in Soft News?"; Markus Prior, "News v. Entertainment: How Increasing Media Choice Widens Gaps in Political Knowledge and Turnout," *American Journal of Political Science* 49, no. 3 (2005): 594–609; for a contrary view, see Matthew Baum, *Soft News Goes to War: Public Opinion and Foreign Policy in the New Media Age* (Princeton, NJ: Princeton University Press, 2003).

21. See for instance Diana C. Mutz, *Hearing the Other Side: Deliberative versus Participatory Democracy* (Cambridge: Cambridge University Press, 2006).

22. Paul F. Lazarsfeld, Bernard R. Berelson, and Hazel Gaudet, *The People's Choice* (New York: Columbia University Press, 1948); Wilbur Schramm and Richard F. Carter, "Effectiveness of a Political Television," *Public Opinion Quarterly* 23 (1959); David O. Sears and Jonathon L. Freedman, "Selective Exposure to Information: A Critical Review," *Public Opinion Quarterly* 31 (1967): 194–213.

23. See Lazarsfeld et al., *The People's Choice*, p. 89

24. See Sears and Freedman, "Selective Exposure to Information."

25. See Alan I. Abramowitz, and Kyle L. Saunders, "Exploring the Bases of Partisanship in the American Electorate: Social Identity vs. Ideology," *Political Research Quarterly* 59 (2006): 175–87; Gary C. Jacobson, "Party Polarization in National Politics: The Electoral Connection," in Jon R. Bond and Richard Fleisher, eds. *Polarized Politics* (Washington, DC: CQ Press, 2000); Gary C. Jacobson, *A Divider, Not a Uniter: George W. Bush and the American People* (Upper Saddle River, NJ: Pearson, 2006); for a dissenting view, see Morris P. Fiorina, Samuel J. Abrams, and Jeremy C. Pope, *Culture Wars? The Myth of a Polarized America* (Upper Saddle River, NJ: Pearson Longman, 2005).

26. Jacobson, *A Divider, Not a Uniter*; Abramowitz and Saunders, "Exploring the Bases of Partisanship in the American Electorate."

27. Sendhil Mullainathan and Andrei Shleifer, "The Market for News," *American Economic Review* 95 (2005): 1031–53.

28. Pew Research Center for the People and Press, "Online News Audience Larger, More Diverse: News Audience Increasingly Polarized" (2004).

29. Robert P. Vallone, Lee Ross, and Mark R. Lepper, "The Hostile Media Phenomenon: Biased Perception and Perceptions of Media Bias in Coverage of the 'Beirut Massacre'," *Journal of Personality and Social Psychology* 49 (1985): 577–85; Albert C. Gunther, Cindy T. Christen, Janice L. Liebhart, and Stella Shih-Yun Chia, "Congenial Public, Contrary Press, and Biased Estimates of the Climate of Opinion," *Public Opinion Quarterly* 65 (2001): 295–320; Ted J. Smith III, S. Robert Lichter, and Louis Harris, *What the People Want from the Press* (Washington, DC: Center for Media and Public Affairs, 1997).

30. Pew Center, "Online News Audience Larger, More Diverse."

31. Im Runtenberg "Cable's War Coverage Suggests a New 'Fox Effect' on Television Journalism, *New York Times*, April 2, 2003, B9.

32. Micahel J. Pfau, Brian Houston, and Shane M. Semmler, *Mediating the Vote: The Changing Media Landscape in U.S. Presidential Campaigns* (Lanham, MD: Rowman and Littlefield, 2007).

33. Shanto Iyengar and Kyu Hahn, "Red Media, Blue Media: Evidence of

Ideological Polarization in Media Use," *Journal of Communication* 59 (2009): 19–39.

34. W. Lance Bennett and Jarol B. Manheim, "The One-step Flow of Communication," *Annals of the American Academy of Political and Social Science* 608, no. 1 (2006): 213–32.

35. Shanto Iyengar, Kyu Hahn, Jon A. Krosnick, and John Walker. "Selective Exposure to Campaign Communication: The Role of Anticipated Agreement and Issue Public Membership," *Journal of Politics* 70 (2008): 186–200.

36. Price and Zaller, "Who Gets the News?"

37. Shanto Iyengar, "Shortcuts to Political Knowledge: Selective Attention and the Accessibility Bias," in John A. Ferejohn and James H. Kuklinski, eds. *Information and the Democratic Process.* (Champaign: University of Illinois Press, 1990).

38. Iyengar, "Shortcuts to Political Knowledge?"

39. Nancy Burns, Kay L. Schlozman, and Sidney Verba, "What if Politics Weren't a Man's Game? Gender, Citizen Participation, and the Lessons of Politics," unpublished manuscript (2000).

40. Iyengar et al., "Selective Exposure to Campaign Communication."

41. Matthew Gentzkow and Jesse M. Shapiro, "Media Bias and Reputation," *Journal of Political Economy* 114 (2006): 280–316.

42. Mullainathan and Schleifer, "The Market for News," 18.

43. Jacques Steinberg, "Cable Channel Nods to Ratings and Leans Left," *New York Times* (November, 6, 2007) p. A1. More recently, the network attempted to extend this model of partisan style reporting to the Democratic and Republican nominating conventions. MSNBC coverage was anchored by Chris Matthews and Keith Olbermann, both of whom are commentators rather than "objective" reporters. The more interpretive coverage provided by the MSNBC anchors clashed with the more mainstream norms of the NBC correspondents (such as Tom Brokaw) leading to periods of tension and disagreement during the convention coverage, and to ratings that were disappointing to the network. Tom Brokaw went so far as to publicly distance himself from the views of Olbermann and Matthews [Brian Stelter, "MSNBC Takes Incendiary Hosts from Anchor Seat," *New York Times* (September 7, 2008) p. C1.]. In the aftermath of the controversy, NBC announced that their debate coverage would be anchored by David Gregory—a reporter from the news division—rather than Matthews or Olbermann.

44. Cass R. Sunstein, *Republic.com* (Princeton, NJ: Princeton University Press, 2001), pp. 201–02.

45. Carl I. Hovland, *Communication and Persuasion: Psychological Studies of Opinion Change* (New Haven, CT: Yale University Press, 1959).

46. Steven Kull, Clay Ramsay, and Evan Lewis, "Misperceptions, the Media, and the Iraq War," *Political Science Quarterly* 118 (2003): 569–98.

47. See John Zaller, *The Nature and Origin of Mass Opinion* (Cambridge: Cambridge University Press, 1992), for a discussion of persuadability.

48. W. Lance Bennett, Regina G. Lawrence, and Steven Livingston, *When the Press Fails* (Chicago: University of Chicago Press, 2007).

10 Exploiting the Clueless

Heresthetic, Overload, and Rational Ignorance*

Andrew Sabl

This chapter is about a particular kind of political manipulation, the kind that makes use of what William Riker called "heresthetic."[1] This word, invented by Riker and derived from the Greek for "to choose," refers to the art of strategically setting up, to one's own advantage, the alternatives among which others get to choose. The basic idea is that even when one's choice among alternatives is completely free, the content of those alternatives is determined. The party that determines it is usually a designated leader or agenda setter—not the individual chooser, much less the outsider who later judges that choice, usually in ignorance of who framed the alternatives and why.

Riker's examples range across all kinds of domains, from academic politics to a vote on nerve gas, but two will serve as quick illustrations. In the first, a flying club is meeting to choose which planes to buy (for its affluent members to have available to rent). The club president knows he wants a slightly different composition of planes than the average club member—in particular, he has a family and wants some six-seater planes rather than smaller ones. With the advice of an economist, he manages to structure the agenda through a series of binary alternatives (What kind of aircraft should be the primary fleet? How many planes do we want? Do we want a mixed fleet?") so as to virtually guarantee his favored outcome. In subsequent experiments with students assigned the same preferences as the flying club members, professors aiming at four *different* outcomes were able, through structuring the agenda, to achieve the desired outcome three out of four times. The point is that none of the questions is ridiculous and no votes are coerced are bribed—yet the power to frame and order the questions at will lets the person with that power get almost any outcome desired.[2] This is the politics of a private club; in politics, not just the outcome but voters' judgment of a choice can be crucial. Riker's portrayal of the Lincoln-Douglas debates highlights this. Douglas sought a coalition of southern and northwestern (we would now say midwestern) voters. But by demanding at Freeport that Douglas respond to the Dred Scott decision, popular among the former but not the latter, Lincoln rendered this coalition impossible.[3] Again, Lincoln let Douglas answer any way he chose. It was the fact of having to make the choice, not the outcome chosen, that presented Douglas with an insoluble dilemma.[4]

My question is why this counts as manipulation at all—though Riker called it precisely "political manipulation"—and why, if at all, it should worry us. In theory, after all, political actors can equally try their hand at heresthetic, and Riker hoped they would. It seems odd to call manipulative a situation in which all know how the game is played and have equal opportunities to compete. The answer will have to do with what Anthony Downs called "rational ignorance": the fact that, for most voters, the time and effort needed to make reasoned political choices costs more than one voter's likely effect on the outcome is worth.[5] In practice, though not necessarily in theory, sophisticated forms of heresthetic systematically take advantage of rational ignorance. They exploit the clueless—and exploit the fact that when it comes to political strategy it would be insane for most people not to remain clueless.

So heresthetic is ethically and politically worrying for empirical rather than analytic reasons, because of how it works rather than how it is defined. The powerful can systematically use heresthetic to obscure their own actions and to avoid accountability in such a way that outsiders will find it difficult to understand. Some examples, especially from Jacob Hacker and Paul Pierson's *Off Center*, will illustrate the point. I will close by suggesting what might be done about the problem. I am not optimistic. I argue that Riker's heresthetic is worse than it seems, harder to combat than we might think, and more dangerous than we appreciate.

I. Heresthetic: No Victim, No Crime?

People don't normally write books portraying themselves as evil. But Riker's book *The Art of Political Manipulation*[6] seems to do just that. It not only fails to condemn its subject, but commends heresthetic as an unheralded liberal art, worthy of being universally appreciated and widely taught.

Why do we usually have moral worries about manipulation, and why doesn't Riker? The worry can be described in various ways. In psychiatry, manipulation involves using people for one's own gratification when they are unwilling or at least reluctant: a habit hard to reconcile with equal relationships and perhaps with democratic ones. The manipulator sadistically likes getting people to do what they don't want to; a healthy personality does the opposite.[7] Manipulation is on this view a *failure of compassion*. In ethics, manipulation is said by Patricia Greenspan to involve trading on the victim's ignorance of, or lack of attention to, a choice situation. In so doing, the manipulator leaves victims with the impression that they have more agency in the situation than they in fact do. Manipulation is to this extent a failure of *respect*.[8] In politics, manipulation, on Robert Goodin's view, is said to involve deception and getting victims to do something they "would not otherwise have done...contrary to their putative will."[9] Goodin's main concern is, not surprisingly, political: he worries a little about the deception as such but more about the "distributive bias" whereby some forms of manipulation are systematically easier for the powerful than the powerless to use.[10] Manipulation is a failure of *political equality*.

Riker's kind of manipulation might seem to avoid these worries. For manipulation, as he defines it, *does not operate on persons*. Riker consistently and explicitly speaks of manipulating impersonal entities—institutions, agendas, selections, choices, "profile[s] of preferences," (indirectly) outcomes, most generally "the world"—rather than human beings' desires, wills, impulses, or goals.[11] The three basic forms of heresthetic—agenda control, strategic voting, and the deliberate introduction of new issues to disrupt existing coalitions—indeed operate, and must operate, on overall situations. For Riker, following mainstream microeconomics, assumes that individual preferences are "given" or fixed as a matter of fact, and (it seems) rightly immune to pressure and moral judgment as a matter of value.[12]

Riker explicitly disavows the elements of deception or concealment that are often said to make manipulation ethically dangerous. He not only delights in revealing how manipulation can be practiced but claims that instruction in the techniques of manipulation is a *moral* imperative. To ensure equality, strategic knowledge must be public and universal.[13] So one might say: if we are manipulating only the circumstances of choice (not the wills behind choice) and if we openly reveal our intention to do so, we need not harm, use, fool, or disrespect anyone. Elections, committee votes, and so on will be "manipulative" in the sense that the word is used to describe a set of Tinker Toys, with just as much morally neutral praise for able performance due in both cases. Perhaps less fancifully, whatever one thinks of the military, nobody blames generals for "manipulating," on a map, markers that represent soldiers. (Nor is it at all the case that generals who do this lack concern for soldiers' lives. Careful strategy represents maximal respect for those lives: the worst general gets the most soldiers killed for nothing.) None of the reasons just mentioned for criticizing manipulation apply to Riker's kind directly. Riker's political strategists take pride in their skill but no sadistic pleasure in using others. His examples would work just as well, and give just as much pleasure, if the actors were faceless collectives, or well-liked colleagues, or, as in his more abstract work, anonymous mathematical variables.

This is necessary. Given that heresthetic consists in bringing about the collective decisions one likes without changing anyone's individual preferences, individual agency is not affected—so the sadist could take no pleasure in overcoming it. The contrast with Greenspan's worries about deceiving people about their degree of agency is particularly clear. Riker's manipulators do the opposite of giving persons exaggerated views of their own agency. On the contrary, Riker's strategists, and Riker himself, believe and openly avow that isolated individuals have *no* control over collective decisions and choice circumstances: bleak, but hardly deceptive.[14] Finally, as noted, Riker's project is in principle devoted to reducing distributive bias; he aims to spread knowledge of strategic tricks universally and equally.

On the last point, however, Riker's moral intentions far exceed his analytic rigor (a claim unlikely to have been made about Riker until now). He misses the ways in which strategic knowledge is systematically different from other kinds of knowledge in ways that make it harder to universalize—and, if universalized, hard for those outside the circles of power to use. Though heresthetic manipulation and ethically problematic manipulations of choice situations are *analytically* distinct, they often coincide in practice.

To anticipate the argument, actual manipulation of choices requires three things: (1) knowledge of heresthetic technique, (2) control over the agenda, and (3) political knowledge of two kinds: (a) what agents' likely preferences are, and (b) how in detail various heresthetic strategies can turn those preferences into desired outcomes. Riker is obsessed with equalizing (1). Some critics of power have stressed (2), the ability of the powerful systematically to keep issues off the agenda;[15] others (3a), the ability of those with great political research resources to use polling and other techniques in ways their democratic opponents cannot match.[16] But here I would like to stress (3b). Many in theory can know *that* their choices might be manipulated through heresthetic, but most must in any given case remain ignorant of *how* this is operating, or has already operated. And the resulting asymmetry in power is great.

II. Goodin's Overload

To see why this is so, we may examine one of Goodin's techniques of political manipulation—one that he thinks relatively innocuous because it lacks distributive bias. Goodin calls this technique "overload," and notes that it operates in a mode directly opposite to those forms of manipulation that rely on secrecy.

> In the place of secrecy this strategy recommends maximal disclosure; and in the place of lies this strategy recommends full and accurate reporting. The opportunity it sees for manipulation lies not at the level of fudging facts but rather at the level of interpreting them. Once you have overloaded people with information, all of it both pertinent and accurate, they will be desperate for a scheme for integrating and making sense of it. Politicians can then step in with an interpretive framework which caters to their own policy preferences.[17]

Goodin suggests that national security issues provide the most opportunity for this kind of manipulation. He does not elaborate, but perhaps means that interpretive frames are easier to sell when the subject at hand lies outside the audience's experience.

Having set forth this strategy, Goodin gives two reasons for not being very worried about it. First, its distributive bias is small. When huge amounts of data are dumped on the public, all sorts of parties can and do propose simple frames for making sense of it.[18] Second, the manipulators often end up fooling themselves, believing their own biased frames. The second reason seems not to imply Goodin's conclusion. A cohesive group of people that comes to believe its own frames can, at least in the short term, become *stronger* as a result, more capable than before of dominating others whose viewpoints are more varied and weaker.[19] The first reason seems more to the point. But in certain very important cases it is not valid.

III. Heresthetic Overload

Such cases are those involving what I shall call "heresthetic overload." As with regular overload, heresthetic overload occurs when a team of actors deliberately provides, or at least encourages, the release of colossal amounts of information, followed by a biased frame put out to make sense of it—a frame that serves the purpose of the team, not the audience. But in the case of heresthetic overload, the information involved concerns not the substance of a public issue but the processes of decision making that politicians have deliberately set up in considering the issue. These processes are designed to obscure that their positions on the issue are unpopular. Regular overload involves biased frames about policy; heresthetic overload involves biased frames about how politicians are manipulating the available choices about policy. It is no accident that this is complicated, a sort of meta-overload that is hard to summarize, let alone to portray. That is why it works and why it is so dangerous. Since heresthetic is harder to understand than, say, whether people are dying in a war, overload strategies concerning heresthetic are systematically easier to get away with.[20] This claim might be hard to justify analytically but it is, fortunately, easy to illustrate in practice. Jacob Hacker and Paul Pierson's book *Off Center*, I will claim, does precisely that.

Hacker and Pierson ask why a thin Republican majority in the presidential vote and in Congress was able from 2000 to 2006 to push through very conservative policies, much more conservative than the median voter prefers, "and why the normal mechanisms of democratic accountability have not been able to bring them back."[21] That book is often convincing on the particulars but lacks a simple summarizing thesis. The missing thesis, I submit, is that accountability has been frustrated by heresthetic overload.

Hacker and Pierson argue that a cohesive Republican strategy has formed "rhetoric and policies to make it difficult for even the well informed to know what is going on."[22] This doesn't mean that it is harder than it used to be for people to get information about policy. (Though Hacker and Pierson do not take up the question, the Internet presumably makes it easier.[23]) What is hard for the well-informed to know is what administrative and congressional leaders "are up to"[24]: what they are doing *procedurally*, what, in terms of policy substance, the decisions that they have made and the fights they have staged amount to. What Hacker and Pierson call "backlash insurance," which insulates party conservatives against moderates who disagree with their policy choices, involves the power "to decide which issues get debated and which alternatives get considered": more specifically,

> agenda control and policy design—the choice and framing of issues and alternatives, and the construction of policies so that ordinary voters have difficulty correctly understanding policy effects or attributing responsibility for them.[25]

This is precisely heresthetic power, the power not to win over votes on a statically defined issue but to choose, dynamically, what will be voted on.

Without claiming to do full justice to Hacker and Pierson's examples, the headings below capture several of the instances of heresthetic manipulation that they chronicle, while fleshing them out theoretically in ways that may promote further argument.[26]

First, leaders can control the agenda. This is one of Riker's central techniques of heresthetic and the most self-explanatory. Hacker and Pierson point out that controlling the agenda means influencing not only which issues come up for formal discussion and voting, but which get attention—a crucial point from the perspective of accountability. For example, a majority of the public and a majority of both senators and members of the House of Representatives supported censuring Bill Clinton rather than impeaching them. Most people, including most political junkies (as well as this author), probably did not know that before reading Hacker and Pierson. The reason we did not know it is that House Majority Whip Tom DeLay made sure that censure never came up for a vote. This not only let him win the vote on impeachment, but directly affected how we think about the whole issue. The idea that censure might have been a more appropriate way than impeachment of holding the president accountable for perjury hardly entered the public conversation: by design.[27]

Second, leaders can "run from daylight." Administrative agencies, Hacker and Pierson note, regularly make crucial regulatory decisions in procedurally complicated ways that the media rarely report and that (again) even well-informed voters are rarely able to parse.[28] One might add, though Hacker and Pierson do not place this instance under this category, that the use—or abuse—of conference committees to undo compromises struck in the House or Senate is likewise impenetrable to most voters. Moderates can claim credit for watering down extreme proposals, knowing that voters will not notice conference committees distilling the water back out later.[29]

Third, leaders can exploit short time horizons. Hacker and Pierson note that the 2001 tax cuts were designed in ways that made no sense as policy but excellent sense from the perspective of avoiding political accountability and structuring future agendas. The biggest cuts for the middle class kicked in right away; those for the rich, in future years. The tax cuts were set to expire in 2011, keeping estimates of their costs down while ensuring a politically terrifying time for anyone who would let those costs stay at the estimated level by allowing what would by then scan as a big tax increase.[30] Hacker and Pierson do not refer here to "time horizons" (though Pierson uses the concept extensively in other work), but doing so would illuminate the stakes. Behavioral economics shows how irrational we are in the face of changes in how decisions are framed.[31] Heresthetic overload relies on choosing so many frames at once, and frames that are so complicated, that the exploitation of our psychological weaknesses can be neither noticed nor fought.

Crucially, *none of these techniques requires secrecy or concealment.* Administrative regulations are published; conference reports are readily available; the future-year provisions of the tax cuts were right there in the bill and reported at the time. Heresthetic overload depends on the true facts on these matters being technically public but practically incomprehensible. One last example from the book: "When a reporter skeptically inquired as to whether the bill just passed [in 2003] was 'smoke and mirrors' designed to make a large tax cut appear smaller, Senator George Allen of Virginia said, 'I hope so.' All the senators laughed." Hacker and Pierson stop there. But we might ask why Allen felt free to declare his intentions so openly. It was because he knew that this was the kind of *strategic* issue that ordinary voters cannot understand and will probably not even hear about. Hacker and Pierson report the incident based on a story on National Public Radio (NPR). This is itself an elite medium; the show on which this somewhat complicated story appeared (*Weekend Edition*) is surely followed by very few voters indeed. Besides NPR, the only other source that covered the comment was the even more elite, and insider-conservative, *Washington Times*.[32]

Heresthetic as such may be morally neutral, immune to the normative concerns often leveled at manipulation. But heresthetic overload is a different matter. Normal heresthetic may lack victims, but heresthetic overload has plenty. Politicians who use it are trying to frustrate the practices of accountability that would otherwise be available to particular sorts of constituents—those who are both moderate and not the kind of extreme junkie who follows procedural issues. They are relying on both these constituents' static ignorance of political processes and on their inability to keep up with deliberately rapid changes in those processes.[33] They are practicing not just simplification but "tailored disinformation," using their expertise in what people know to hide behind what they do not know.[34] Some political figures are characteristically praised for their talent at explaining complex public issues to lay voters. Surely some blame is due for doing the opposite, for deliberately obscuring what one is doing and why. The issue at stake is whether knowledge of what people can and cannot understand should be used as a reason to inform people or, on the contrary, to exploit them and even increase their ignorance.

Hacker and Pierson's story portrays heresthetic overload—more or less equivalent to their "backlash insurance"—as a new strategy and one uniquely exploited by Republicans. One may doubt this. Some of the reasons why this might be the case have been overcome by technology.[35] Some (like a simple dislike of party discipline) seem to be the Democratic Party's own fault and not that of the system. Some—like the claim that backlash insurance makes a "permanent majority" of Republicans likely[36]—seem simply falsified by the 2006 and 2008 elections.[37] While one can argue that Republican leaders brought virtuoso talent to the art of heresthetic overload, they certainly did not invent it. Expert chroniclers of congressional rules have observed both parties using rules for just this purpose, with increasing sophistication—and impenetrability—in recent years.[38] But the larger value of heresthetic overload does not depend on its specific partisan predictions. Even if heresthetic overload has been used in the past, and even if it is not invincible in particular cases, it is worth noting precisely on the basis of its being a persistent, systematic temptation, usable by both parties and potentially dangerous even when other factors might momentarily overwhelm it.

IV. Distributive Bias

In other words, heresthetic overload has what normal overload lacks: distributive bias. My reasons for thinking this seem strong (though for now unproven). First, the kind of activists and opposition figures who might be willing and able to provide alternative frames to cut through substantive overload may simply not understand heresthetic overload. The precise purposes to which agendas have been finessed or policies tweaked to improve their political frame will sometimes be secret to all but the agents directly involved. They will almost certainly be difficult for "outsider" activists or public intellectuals to dissect without paying obsessive attention.[39] Even citizens who are very conscientious about informing themselves about issues may be rationally ignorant of heresthetic maneuvers. Conversely, those who are political junkies to the degree required to follow heresthetic processes closely will frequently be self-styled insiders who revel in the fact that they, and not the average citizen, understand the game. (How many local school board members, or Ph.D.s in American History or Health Economics, know that the conference committee process was fundamentally changed under Republican leadership of both houses, or the precise ways in which the budget assumptions of the 2001 tax cuts were misleading?) Thus heresthetic overload brings the overload strategy of manipulation, which Goodin thinks only mildly worrying, closer to what he calls the "coordination" strategy—the concerted shaping of which issues are talked about and how—which he thinks very worrying indeed. Heresthetic overload gives a concerted set of centrally located elites systematic advantages in the political game, even when they fail at Goodin's coordination—which we might distinguish as *substantive* coordination. Heresthetic overload does not distort discussion of the issues, but weakens the relationship between that discussion and political outcomes.

Heresthetic manipulation is also systematically different from the "traceability" problems well known to students of American politics. Legislation is complex, and it is difficult for those with views on an issue to know the details of what a particular legislator did on either side of it. This has long favored well-informed and well-organized interests over the diffuse public.[40] But procedure again raises very different problems than substance. Douglas Arnold notes that legislators casting votes fear not what the public will spontaneously know about the vote but what a challenger or activist could *tell* the public about it, putting resources behind the telling. But while challengers might be able to showcase an unpopular vote or even a reputation for incompetence or inaction, one can hardly imagine a candidate attacking a senator for doing an end-run around conference committees, or for being one of fifty-seven legislators to vote yes on an amendment enshrining strange sunset provisions in the tax laws.[41]

The troubling fact is that knowledge of political maneuvering is inherently an insiders' game even when, or if, knowledge of substantive issues is not.

V. Suggestions

Political theorists disappoint if we do not tell other people what to do. Following Dennis Thompson, who in turn followed Dewey and others, I will separate my dogmatic and moralistic claims into two categories: constructive suggestions that would take effort but might happen soon, and reconstructive suggestions that are not so immediately practical.[42]

On the constructive side, we can imagine making things better by changing some political and journalistic norms.

First, we should reformalize political debate and make it more elitist. The press should demand that party leaders designate spokespersons on crucial issues; the party leaders should conspire with, threaten, bribe, and cajole their members to stick with the bargain. Legislators who stake out innovative and idiosyncratic positions on legislative strategy are the greatest enablers of heresthetic overload; they have both an interest in covering up procedural shiftiness and the collective ability to do so easily, simply by telling different stories (hence overload). Designated spokespeople would give someone the power to say "this alleged compromise was no compromise. The president got all the tax cuts he wanted, and the so-called moderates, whatever they might say, went along with a swindle." The opposition could of course deny this, but that is a fair fight without distributive bias.[43] It might seem that the press would have to cooperate for this to work. Not so, as long as politicians not chosen as spokespeople were induced to remain silent and deprive press outlets of competitive content. (The networks all cover the State of the Union rather than other news because there is a norm of every national politician attending it: they cannot compete by offering other good political news.) Given the likelihood of American politicians remaining silent or deferring to party leaders, perhaps this is reconstructive after all.

Second, the media could *cover the details of legislation—in a particular way.* This might seem a misguided "civic" suggestion, and opposed to the above claim that there are limits to the amount of strategy people find interesting. But the kind of coverage relevant here can be made much more exciting than coverage of policy details, which are indeed mind-numbing to most citizens. "GOP conservatives maneuver to win huge tax cut, mostly for wealthy: moderates complain, but cave" is not a story impossible for moderately attentive voters to grasp, even if only a few are interested in the procedural details.

Heresthetic overload is in fact a refreshingly direct and personal act: an identifiable agent with hidden motives really is behind the curtain manipulating the outcome. Exposing such things potentially allows for the excitement of a thriller—especially since there is an automatic hero, an actor whose purposes are both popular and shunted aside and who can be counted on to be angry about it. (It seems likely, by the way, that media coverage can do this more effectively than 30-second spots by challengers or activist groups: the stories involved can be simplified by good journalists, but there are limits.) If, as I claim, heresthetic overload is more of a danger to democracy than the regular kind, the remedy is precisely personalized, dramatic political reporting—not of a horse race but of a demolition derby.[44] Heresthetic manipulation is very vulnerable to a personalized, moralized method of political reporting—and less vulnerable to the systematic observations of political scientists.

Reconstructive solutions would require altering some very durable structures of status—in the press, Congress, and the political theory discipline.

First, we could give congressional reporters higher status than presidential ones, not because Congress matters more in principle—though a strong case for that can be made—but because the job is harder. The president, as chief executive, takes a great many decisions on his (someday her) own authority; the mere words of the president or his spokesperson have some inherent drama. Both choices and words are easy to report. Covering Congress, however, requires discovering and then making comprehensible the meaning of a series of intricate maneuvers. It requires telling a story about *collective* action. The hallmark of such action is that individuals don't make choices—rather, they adopt strategies whose fulfillment relies on how effective they are in predicting and molding others' behavior.[45] I have claimed that telling this story can involve the excitement of a thriller; it also can require the combined qualities of a detective and a detective novelist.

Second, we could institute question time for party leaders in the House and Senate, with a view to provoking the drama, exaggeration, and personal attacks that would smoke out heresthetic overload. (Hacker and Pierson propose instituting question time for the president,[46] but their own story suggests that it makes more sense for congressional leaders, for Congress is where most of the heresthetic action is.) Even to consider this would require upending strong cultural norms of our executive-centered political culture in favor of the more Whiggish notion that power comes from law, and law from lawmaking.

Third, and perhaps most unrealistic of all, political theorists should pay attention to the details of legislative maneuvers and institutional design, restoring a part of our vocation that past giants from Plato and Aristotle to Hume, Madison, Condorcet, and Mill thought to be of central importance. The institutional and ideological barriers to this happening are very high, probably insurmountable. Our whole training teaches us to regard principles, ideas, and opinions as the driving forces of politics. Put less charitably, theorists are just as likely as anyone else, perhaps more so, to rely on ideological shortcuts rather than engaging in the painstaking work of exploring political decisions in their institutional context. But this is unspeakably useless when the action is in the details of legislative and informational maneuvering, when the whole game is to conceal the fact that one is pursuing the principles one is.

This brings up a final thought. The debate over so-called deliberative democracy often turns on the question of how much knowledge ordinary people can ever have, and how much they should be expected to have. Those who take different sides in the debate disagree as to whether democratic legitimacy depends centrally on the quality of opinions as well as their quantity (the number of people who hold them), and what it would mean for quality to improve. But if heresthetic overload plays the role argued here, both sides of the debate are missing the point. The problem is not what the median voter knows about issues but what he knows about who is doing what about them. Heresthetic overload is insidious because it tries to undercut the link between voters' wishes and representatives' actions, while leaving the average voter completely unaware that this is happening.[47] Whether substantive opinions are informed or uninformed literally does not matter.

The matter is not just factual but normative. The fixing of a conference committee report or the fiddling of a budget projection are not the kind of political issues ordinary citizens should *have* to care about. Again, strategic ignorance is fundamentally different from issue ignorance. Proposals for overcoming the latter or counteracting its effects, to the extent that they are possible and desirable, do not help us with the former. If this is right, both sides of the deliberative democracy debate are missing the real action—and, since our missing it is part of the plan, both of us are in danger of falling for manipulation ourselves.

Notes

* I would like to thank for their comments and suggestions the editors of this book and the audience members at the "Manipulating Democracy" conference at Loyola Marymount University and the Political Ethics working group at the 2008 Annual Meeting of the American Political Science Association. Rose McDermott's comments were especially valuable.

1. William H. Riker, *The Art of Political Manipulation* (New Haven, CT: Yale University Press, 1986): ix and passim.

2. Riker, *Art of Political Manipulation*, chapter 3.

3. Riker, *Art of Political Manipulation*, chapter 1. (Douglas' doctrine was that antislavery territories could de facto annul the Dred Scott decision by refusing cooperation with it on the ground. This was a popular answer in Illinois, where Douglas beat out Lincoln for the Senate, but not in the South.)

4. Riker adds to his account of manipulation a skeptical theory of interest aggregation. Following Kenneth Arrow and others, he claims there is no such thing as a group will or preference, for any outcome can, through a properly structured series of choices, end up preferred to any other. (William H. Riker, *Liberalism Against Populism* [Long Grove, IL: Waveland Press, 1982]); Gerry Mackie, *Democracy Defended* (Cambridge: Cambridge University Press, 2003) has powerfully objected to this strong claim, asserting that this so-called "cycling" has never been observed in practice, that all Riker's examples of it (including Lincoln at Freeport) distort the evidence, and that ideological consistency tends to rule out cycling in practice. But the relevance of heresthetic as a technical skill and ethical concern does *not* in fact require a belief in cycling or extreme skepticism about the idea of group preferences, as long as *some* significant outcomes, in substantively

important cases, can be affected by structuring agendas. The point here is one of political ethics, not democratic theory or social choice.

5. The phrase is associated, in political science at any rate, with Anthony Downs, *An Economic Theory of Democracy* (New York: Harper & Row, 1957), chapter 13, who, while not employing the exact phrase, defends as crucial to understanding democracy the phenomenon that the phrase summarizes. I would stress that the examples discussed in this paper can be explained by rational ignorance even granting non-instrumental reasons for pursuing knowledge, even political knowledge. Procedural tricks seem unlikely to become popular hobbies (objects of non-instrumental interest). Many follow baseball for pleasure, independent of expected payoffs. A substantial number follow campaigns for the same reason. Few spontaneously follow the House Rules Committee.

6. Riker, *The Art of Political Manipulation*.

7. Harvey R. St. Clair, "Manipulation," *Comprehensive Psychiatry* 7, no. 4 (August 1966): 248–58. St. Clair ends with Lincoln's claim that his "idea of democracy" is that "as I would not be a slave, so I would not be a master" (p. 258). This suggests, though St. Clair provides no argument, that manipulation is a fundamental threat to a society based on of equal political and social status (though why the category here should be manipulation and not overt power is less clear).

8. Patricia Greenspan, "The Problem with Manipulation," *American Philosophical Quarterly* 40, no. 2 (April 2003): 155–64; pp. 156, 158.

9. Robert E. Goodin, *Manipulatory Politics* (New Haven, CT: Yale University Press, 1980), p. 13. Goodin's use of "putative" wills—since he wants to preserve the government's legitimate authority to do things that are good for people without their knowing it—raises all sorts of issues that do not seem relevant here.

10. Goodin, *Manipulatory Politics*, p. 35.

11. Riker, *Art of Political Manipulation*, pp. ix, xi, 142; cf., *Liberalism Against Populism*, e.g., pp. 25, 137, 172. (Riker does have a phrase for coercive domination that keeps individuals from voting as they choose: "crude manipulation" or "physical control." Riker finds this distasteful and does not advocate it: *Liberalism Against Populism*, p. 173).

12. This seems clearest in Riker, *Liberalism Against Populism*, p. 197. In social choice theory, as in mainstream microeconomics, preferences or desires can even be considered sacrosanct to a *greater* degree than in Kantian or other forms of ethics. Judging others' preferences can be labeled as a great vice, "egomorphism," "structuring one's perception of others like one's perception of oneself" (*Art of Political Manipulation*, p. 60). Bernard Mandeville, who probably coined *de gustibus non est disputandum*, famously endorsed cunning institutional design but also criticized, with apparently sincere outrage, judgmentalism towards others' desires: Bernard Mandeville, *The Fable of the Bees*, ed. F.B. Kaye, Vol. 1 (Indianapolis, IN: Liberty Fund, 1988 [1732]).

13. Riker, *Art of Political Manipulation*, p. 32 (citing eminent logician Charles Dodgson); Riker, *Liberalism Against Populism*, p. 252.

14. Riker is also co-author of a famous—not secret—article arguing that individual voters lack instrumentally (as opposed to value- or expressive-) rational reasons for voting. William H. Riker and Peter C. Ordeshook, "A Theory of the Calculus of Voting," *American Political Science Review*, 62, no. 1 (March 1968): 25–42.

15. Peter Bachrach and Morton S. Baratz, "Decisions and Nondecisions: An analytical framework," *American Political Science Review* 57, no. 3

(September 1963): 632–42; and the discussion in Steven Lukes, *Power: A radical view*, 2d ed. (New York: Palgrave Macmillan, 2005), pp. 20–37.

16. Lawrence R. Jacobs and Robert Y. Shapiro, *Politicians Don't Pander: Political Manipulation and the Loss of Democratic Responsiveness* (Chicago: University of Chicago Press, 2000).

17. Goodin, *Manipulatory Politics*, section 2.5, p. 59. Benjamin Ginsberg, "Autonomy and Duplicity: Reply to DeCanio," *Critical Review* 19, no. 1 (2007): 165–80, makes a similar argument.

18. Goodin also points out that the powerful often fall victim to overload, as the executive branch depended on national security elites to make sense of excessive information about Vietnam.

19. There may be an implicit zero-sum assumption here: something that frustrates one's own putative will cannot at the same time frustrate that of one's opponents. Yet there is no reason to suppose this. A disaster like the continuation of the Vietnam War certainly manipulated the war's actual and potential opponents—but hardly served the purposes of the Johnson administration either. That false or stupid beliefs can work to the disadvantage of both sides of a political struggle—that ignorance results in deadweight losses—is in fact a central theme of Enlightenment polemics.

20. Goodin's "overload" examples, which make particular reference to the Vietnam War, may be unintentionally stacked to minimize the danger of overload. As one scholar who thinks framing strategies very powerful has admitted to me, the one fact that is very hard to frame positively is a body bag. (Personal conversation with Franklin D. Gilliam, Jr.) For an argument that the relative number of war casualties in each district explains Republican losses in 2006 extremely well, see Scott Sigmund Gartner and Gary M. Segura, "All Politics are Still Local: The Iraq War and the 2006 Midterm Elections," *PS: Political Science and Politics* 41, no. 1 (January 2008): 95–100.

21. Jacob S. Hacker and Paul Pierson, *Off Center: The Republican Revolution and the Erosion of American Democracy* (New Haven, CT: Yale University Press, 2005) p. 3.

22. Hacker and Pierson, *Off Center*, p. 8.

23. Though still not easy, the average voter is clearly ignorant of the overwhelming majority of policy decisions and even of the existence of the agencies that control them. See Samuel DeCanio, "Mass Opinion and American Political Development," *Critical Review* 18, nos. 1–3 (2006): 143–55. DeCanio's analysis suffers from a failure to define the "state autonomy" that he believes is the result of voter ignorance. He seems, oddly, to assume that ordinary voters are supposed to serve as a direct check on administrative agencies, and that the finding that they cannot do so should therefore cause great worries.

24. Hacker and Pierson, *Off Center*, p. 17.

25. Hacker and Pierson, *Off Center*, pp. 11, 12.

26. See Hacker and Pierson, *Off Center*, pp. 70–71.

27. Hacker and Pierson, *Off Center*, pp. 72–75.

28. Hacker and Pierson, *Off Center*, pp. 94–100.

29. Hacker and Pierson, *Off Center*, pp. 90–91, pp. 154–5.

30. Hacker and Pierson, *Off Center*, pp. 58ff. Hacker and Pierson also note something similar about the Alternative Minimum Tax: if it kicked in as the tax cuts "promised," it would limit the cost of the tax cuts around now—but Republicans predicted that there would be immense pressure not to let the opaque AMT operate in this way. And so it proved: the AMT was recently "fixed" at the cost of big increases in the deficit.

31. The seminal article is Amos Tversky, "Features of Similarity," *Psychological Review* 84, no. 4 (July 1977): 327–52.
32. Hacker and Pierson, *Off Center*, pp. 66, citing Steve Inskeep, "Tax Bill Congress Passed This Week," *National Public Radio—Weekend Edition*, 24 May 2003, http://www.npr.org/templates/story/story.php?storyId=1273727. A Lexis-Nexis "News, All sources" search (7 February 2008) revealed the only other mention as Stephen Dinan, "Cheney Vote Breaks Tie as Tax Cut Passes; Benefits Due by Summer," *Washington Times*, May 24, 2003, p. A1.
33. The Bush aide who derided opponents as "the reality-based community" was not, as often thought, defending fabrication or fantasy but rather asserting that the administration's opponents could not keep up with rapid shifts and new actions that were constantly "creating new realities." Ron Suskind, "Faith, Certainty, and the Presidency of George W. Bush," *New York Times Magazine*, October 17, 2004.
34. "Tailored disinformation": Hacker and Pierson, p. 166. Compare p. 17: "We are not arguing that political elites are ignoring public opinion. In fact, they have never paid more attention to it or had greater capacity to chart its every ripple. Yet they are using their knowledge of public opinion not to respond to the public's wishes and concerns but to blunt the tools that citizens use to hold them to account."
35. I am thinking here especially about the role of the website Talking Points Memo (http://www.talkingpointsmemo.com/) in derailing Social Security privatization in 2004–05. (The project began with a post on December 22, 2004: http://www.talkingpointsmemo.com/archives/149731.php, accessed August 31, 2009.) By demanding that Democratic candidates state early and unequivocally their position on reductions in guaranteed benefits, and soliciting local news information from the weblog's readers to aid in doing so, the site's organizer made it impossible for wavering Democrats to defect to the Republican position and provide bipartisan cover—as they had in the case of tax cuts and prescription drug coverage for reasons Hacker and Pierson regard as inevitable.
36. Hacker and Pierson, *Off Center*, p. 15.
37. And some things in the book have little to do with its main thesis: for instance, the (true) assertion that the structure of the Senate guarantees that many Democratic senators come from states where Republican presidents win, and are loath to cross the latter. Very late in the drafting of this chapter, I became aware that *Off-Center* has been re-issued with a new afterword discussing the 2008 election. I have not had a chance to consult this edition.
38. R. Douglas Arnold, *The Logic of Congressional Action* (New Haven, CT: Yale University Press, 1990), pp. 99–118; Barbara Sinclair, *Unorthodox Lawmaking: New Legislative Processes in the U.S. Congress*, 3d ed. (Washington, DC: CQ Press, 2007), pp. 32, 34, 66, 146, 181, 204, 250, 263. The normative conclusion varies. Both Arnold and Sinclair in places defend such practices as enabling "difficult" (i.e., unpopular) votes or smoothing the passage of legislation (but see Arnold, p. 272 and Sinclair, pp. 285–87).
39. One piece of anecdotal evidence: during the nomination fight over Robert Bork, the former head of the Southern California ACLU—one of the country's foremost experts on the substance of civil liberties—called me, a college student intern, into her office to ask me what a filibuster was. This example is extreme, but less extreme levels of ignorance make heresthetic overload very possible.
40. See Arnold, *Logic of Congressional Action*, p. 47 and passim.

41. In 2008, both George W. Bush and John McCain, without apparent reper-
cussions, claimed credit for supporting a GI Bill for former service members
that they had virulently and explicitly opposed. See http://thinkprogress.
org/2008/06/30/bush-mccain-credit-gi/, posted June 30, 2008, accessed
August 31, 2008; http://www.thecarpetbaggerreport.com/archives/16597.
html#more-16597; posted August 18, 2008; accessed August 18, 2008.
Arnold, *Logic of Congressional Action*, p. 272n5, gives two and only two
examples in which procedural rules were explained and made politically
salient by those who opposed the outcomes that they enabled. One involved
a speech by Ronald Reagan calling for a closed rule on a tax bill. The other
involved a *Wall Street Journal* editorial on a matter that lacked broad public
salience. Standard political reporting does not regard making these matters
vivid as part of its job.

42. See Dennis F. Thompson, *The Democratic Citizen* (Cambridge: Cambridge
University Press, 1970).

43. Hacker and Pierson, *Off Center*, p. 219, advocate something similar and
give the analogy of responses to States of the Union. But while they propose
a formalized opposition, their analysis suggests the need specifically for a
unique formalized opposition, so that marginal figures, while free to speak,
do not distract from the attention given to a party leadership who would
gain the chance to highlight deceptive maneuvers.

44. Here I differ with Hacker and Pierson, *Off Center*, pp. 177–78, who bemoan
a shift "away from political substance and toward political theater." Moral-
izing and personalizing the issue is tremendously useful and we need more
of this. Except to political scientists, it is not very exciting to hear that policy
outcomes are not what the median voter (the mythical person at the center
of the political spectrum) would favor. The much more gripping story line
is "somebody is trying to hide the truth about what's happening." Better
on this and many other questions surrounding proper press responses to
rational ignorance is Michael Schudson, *Why Democracies Need an Unlov-
able Press* (Cambridge: Polity Press, 2008).

45. "In social contexts I do not choose an outcome; I choose a strategy." Russell Hardin, *David Hume: Moral and Political Theorist* (Oxford: Oxford
University Press, 2007), p. 171.

46. Hacker and Pierson, *Off Center*, p. 219.

47. As such, heresthetic overload should neither comfort nor be practiced by
constitutional conservatives who hold that representatives should often
flout constituents' wishes out of superior expertise or wisdom. A Burkean
explains why he or she cannot follow constituents' wishes, and is proud
of the intelligence required to do so (as in a Burke or Mill parliamentary
speech). A heresthetic overloader exerts all his energies towards avoiding
having to explain anything, indeed towards obscuring what the legislative
vote means in the first place.

Index